MW00980572

The Three Secrets of Wise Decision Making

Barry F. Anderson

Single Reef Press
Portland, Oregon

Single Reef Press
PO Box 1954
Portland, OR 97207-1954

ISBN 0-9722177-0-3

TABLE OF CONTENTS

PREFACE

As the world has become more complex and information more abundant, decisions have become more difficult; as the pace of change and the range of choice have increased, decisions have to be made more often. Yet, most of us still make decisions with no more knowledge about decision processes than our ancestors had in a simpler age, hundreds of years ago.

Thanks to mathematicians, economists, psychologists, and decision analysts, we now know a good deal about decision making. We know something about what constitute good decision processes, and we know that good decision processes tend to lead to good outcomes. For example, those who employ good decision processes tend to get higher grades and earn higher salaries (Larrick, Nisbett, & Morgan, 1993); and, when decision makers' judgments are incorporated into decision models, the models tend to outperform the decision makers, themselves (Dawes, 1979, 1989).

One study (Herek, Janis, & Huth, 1987) evaluated major decisions made by the United States government over several years. For each decision, independent ratings were made of (a) the quality of the decision process and (b) the extent to which U. S. objectives were met. The correlation between these two measures was a whopping +.63! (This is better than the correlation between the heights of parents and the heights of their children.) This indicates that, even at the level of governmental decisions, where so many things can go wrong, good decision processes are strongly related to good decision outcomes.

We also know that good decision processes can be learned, and we know something about how to teach them. For example, economics professors and students, who have formal training in decision making, are more likely than others to decide rationally, even when the decisions are not closely related to the content of economics courses (Larrick, Morgan, & Nisbett, 1990). (See also Whimby & Whimby, 1975).

Yet we are not communicating what we know as effectively as we might. At the college level, courses in decision psychology are typically focussed on the presentation of research findings and theoretical explanations of these findings, providing, essentially, declarative, or factual, knowledge. Instruction in good decision-making practice is ancillary, at best, and actual practice in decision-making skills, rare in such courses. While courses of this kind are necessary, they aren't sufficient. Only the exceptional student can pass from declarative knowledge to procedural, or performance, knowledge without help.

We need another kind of course, both for the students who take the courses that focus on declarative knowledge and for those who don't. Such a course should provide for

v

stimulus learning: how to recognize a decision situation, how to recognize irrationality, how to recognize uncreative thought, how to recognize information overload, and how to recognize bad decision logic. Such a course should also teach appropriate responses for these situations, along with their underlying logic. Finally, such a course should provide students abundant practice in applying abstract principles to concrete cases.

Personal decisions, both the students' own and those of their fellow students, are the most convenient and relevant, but organizational and societal decisions are also appropriate, especially when current. If we are to maximize the benefits of research in decision making, we must take more seriously the teaching of the procedural aspects of decision making to those who will raise children, hold jobs, vote, and engage in other behaviors that affect their quality of life and that of those about them. Courses in personal decision making fill this important gap—and they are interesting and fun, both to teach and to take. A course that can't be based entirely on lecture notes but must evolve in response to decision problems in the students' lives is a continuing adventure for both professor and student.

The *Three Secrets of Wise Decision Making* covers the Courage to be Rational, Creativity, and Balanced Judgment—the "Three Secrets". All academically respectable treatments of decision making recognize the problem of limited information-processing capacity and consider ways in which decision makers can deal with complexity in a judicious manner, by means of heuristics and decomposition algorithms. An increasing number are also coming to recognize limited creativity as a problem and to provide some help with it. Few, however, even recognize irrationality as a problem. Yet the courage to be rational is an absolute prerequisite for sound decision making. If the decision maker is seeking only to justify a favored alternative, the other aids to decision making may only make it easier to proceed in the wrong direction! *The Three Secrets* appears to be unique in providing a balanced treatment of all three aspects of decision making.

The Three Secrets is organized around the Decision Ladder, a structured array of techniques to suit a variety of decision problems and a variety of decision makers. The Ladder extends from largely intuitive approaches, at the bottom, to highly analytic tree/table decision diagrams at the top. The key rung on the Ladder is the decision table and its variants: fact tables, plusses-and-minuses value tables, and 1-to-10 value tables. It is recommended that the reader start at the bottom of the Decision Ladder when beginning work on any decision problem and work up only so far as necessary. This keeps the process of decision making from becoming more complicated than would be appropriate for either the decision problem or the decision maker.

The biologist Thomas Huxley said that all nature is like an art museum, but for most of us most of the paintings are facing the wall. Interesting decision problems surround us all nearly every day. Yet we fail to recognize many as decision problems, and those we do recognize we seldom see very deeply into. As you read this book, all that should change. As you turn this page, you'll be drawing back the curtain on a new window to the world. I hope you find it as exciting as many of us do.

I'd like to thank Michael Johnson, Heidi Stardig, and Linda Newton-Curtis, who provided substantial help with both the Personal Decision Making course and the book, and Gretchen Oosterhout, Benson Schaeffer, Charles Schwenk, John Settle, and Jerry Guthrie, who provided help with the book, and I'd also like to thank all of these people, in addition, for the many valuable conversations we've had that have, in a less direct way, enhanced the quality of the book. As you read *The Three Secrets*, you may hear one voice, but as I read it I hear their and others' helpful voices. Finally, I'd like to thank Winky Wheeler (http://whimsicalplanet.com), whose art livens up the book and helps the reader keep track of the concepts of courage, creativity, and balanced judgment.

BFA

The unassisted hand and the understanding left to itself possess but little power. Effects are produced by the means of instruments and helps, which the understanding requires no less than the hand....

Sir Francis Bacon,
Novum Organum, 1620
First Book, Aphorism 2

"If we take the [concept] of cultural evolution seriously, we might look for the disappearance of decision analysts. There is a precedent. At one time, professional scribes wrote for those who could not. Later, professional arithmeticians served the needs of merchants deficient in arithmetical skills. Both professions have disappeared."

von Winterfeldt, D. & Edwards, W.,
Decision Analysis and Behavioral Research,
1986, p. 544. (Reprinted with the permission of Cambridge University Press.)

Chapter 1. DECISIONS, DECISIONS, DECISIONS

All decisions involve alternatives and values, and all decision processes involve problem structuring and evaluation. Yet there are many kinds of decisions. Most are easy, but many are both hard and important to get right. Decisions become hard when there are many values to think about at once and tradeoffs have to be made or when there are many possible futures to think about at once and uncertainty has to be weighed. Tools are available for problem structuring and evaluation that address both kinds of difficulty.

"You said that I'd have to *earn* my cup of coffee, that you had a big decision to make."

Mike: "We've been thinking about this decision for quite a while now and talking to friends, but we're still not comfortable about it."

Leah: "Mike gets out of medical school this June, and we have to decide on a residency."

Mike: "The choice is between Ob/Gyn and EM—with a definite preference for Ob/Gyn. But we're still unsure."

"EM?"

Mike: "Emergency medicine."

"Any other alternatives that are attractive to you?"

Mike: "No. These two are well above any others, and I'm sure that I could get a residency in either area."

"What is it that attracts you to Ob/Gyn?"

Mike: "Well, I like the work. I just love it."

Leah: "Also, with Ob/Gyn, Mike could do his residency right here. We already know the people here and get along wonderfully with them."

"So you'd have to go elsewhere for an EM residency, and that wouldn't be so good. What is it that you find attractive about EM?"

Mike: "The work load, 50 hours a week, compared to about 80 hours a week for Ob/Gyn. EM would leave me a lot more time for the family we'll soon be having."

"Any other values involved?"

Leah: "Those are the big ones."

"Income? Location?"

Mike: "No. We've got the big ones."

"Well, let's take the two alternatives and the three values and diagram your decision on this napkin.

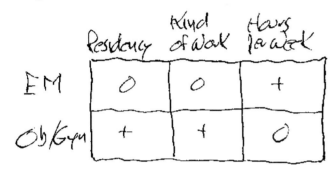

"This is a *decision table*. The EM row represents the choice of a career in emergency medicine. The cell where the EM row and the Residency column intersect represents the quality of the experience you anticipate for a residency in EM; the cell just to the right of that, in the Kind of Work column represents the quality of the work experience you anticipate for a career in EM; and the last cell to the right, in the Hours per Week column, represents the weekly commitment that you anticipate a career in EM would require, taking away time from your family. Similarly, the Ob/Gyn row represents the choice of a career in obstetrics & gynecology, and the cells in that row represent the future you anticipate for an ob/gyn residency and career. Plusses represent good outcomes, and zeroes represent outcomes that are just o.k."

"At some point, we may be putting numbers in this table, so let's consider for a moment the relative importance of Residency, Kind of Work, and Hours per Week. One consideration that's usually relevant to importance is duration of impact. How long does a residency last?"

Mike: "Three or four years."

"And your career lasts, say, forty years?"

Mike: "About."

"Then, to the extent that the annual impacts are the same, Kind of Work and Hours Per Week should be about 10 times as important as Residency, since they last about 10 times as long?"

Mike: "Wow! From that perspective, residency really isn't important at all. I think we'd best just leave it out of the analysis."

Leah: "Heavens, yes! We'd been thinking primarily about the near term. Out of sight, out of mind. This table certainly helps brings everything into relationship!"

Mike: "I feel a little silly. Residency had seemed such an important part of the decision! We'd talked about it so much!"

"So your table now looks like this?"

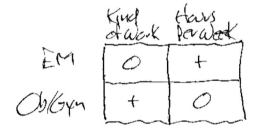

Leah: "That looks better."

"Now, what about the relative importance of Kind of Work and Hours per Week? The impact of Kind of Work will last about 40 years, and whatever relationship you establish with your kids will last longer than that. But what about the *annual* impact of Kind of Work and Hours per Week?"

Mike: "Hours per Week is *much* more important. The kids are the most important thing in this decision."

Leah: "The kids are 90% of the decision. Mike could be a real father if he had to work only 50 hours a week. Eighty hours a week would leave little time for family life. That difference would affect us for the rest of our lives."

Mike: "I can see right now, without going any further, that EM is the right choice."

Leah: "Yes! Once again, it looks as though out of sight was out of mind. We'd been attaching all the importance to Mike and me and little, if any, to the kids that haven't come along yet."

Mike: "It all seems so clear now, whereas before things seemed just as clearly to favor Ob/Gyn. It's easy to see now that that was a false clarity. We can't thank you enough!"

"You should thank yourselves, too. Few people in your position would have had the sensitivity to realize that there was something wrong with the way they were looking at the problem, and fewer still would have had the imagination to try to improve on their decision processes by coming to someone like me."

Leah: "Could we ask you one more favor?"

"Sure. For a refill."

Leah: "Tell us a little more about 'decision analysis'. It sounds interesting."

No two decisions are quite alike, yet all have certain features in common. Since all decisions involve choice, all decisions have alternatives. Since we choose alternatives we believe to be good and reject ones we believe to be bad, all decisions involve values. Since our knowledge of the world is uncertain, all decisions involve some uncertainty regarding the consequences that will follow implementation of any alternative. In all decisions, it's important to distinguish between facts and values, that is, beliefs about what is or will be true and preferences as to what we would or wouldn't like to be true.

Not only do all decisions involve alternatives, values, and uncertainty, but the process of decision making has certain constant features. Decision making consists of two phases: problem structuring and evaluation. *Problem structuring* involves the identification of alternatives, values that distinguish the alternatives from one another, and uncertain events that can affect the values associated with a particular alternative. *Evaluation* is a matter of weighing the relative desirability of various outcomes and the likely impacts of various uncertain events in deciding which alternative is, on balance, preferable.

Decision problems are like other problems in that there is a difference between where the problem solver is and where the problem solver wants to be and yet he or she doesn't know how to get from one place to the other (Anderson, 1980). Decision problems are thus like other problems in requiring creative thinking about ways to get from where we are to where we want to be. Work in the problem structuring phase of a decision problem is much like work on any other problem.

What distinguishes decision problems from other problems is the difficulty of determining whether a solution is satisfactory. In classic problems of the puzzle variety, there is at first no solution, and then there is a solution that is obviously satisfactory, often accompanied by an "Aha!" experience. The following problem is typical in this respect.

> *A man got a flat tire while driving on the edge of town and got out to change it. As he removed the lug nuts from the wheel, he placed them carefully in the hubcap, which lay on the side of the road like a bowl. Suddenly, he knocked over the hub cap and saw all five nuts fall, irretrievably, through the storm drain grating. What to do?*

The solution was to borrow one lug nut from each of the other three wheels. When we find such a clearly satisfactory alternative, where there previously had been little hope of finding any at all, we don't feel inclined to look for additional alternatives. We simply put on the wheel and drive off to the nearest service facility.

Decision problems are unlike problems of this sort in that more than one solution is available, and there are either a number of criteria against which to evaluate these solutions, or a number of possible futures in which to evaluate them, or both. It's this complexity that necessitates an extended evaluation phase in decision problems.

Despite the facts that all decisions involve alternatives, values, and uncertainty and that all decision processes involve problem structuring and evaluation, decisions differ in important ways. Most obviously, decisions differ enormously in difficulty. Most, in fact, are trivial. You're going through a buffet line and see four pieces of a cake that you'd like. They differ only in size. You take the largest. You drive into a parking lot. It's raining. There are two parking spaces, one right by the entrance and one about fifty feet away. You pull into the one right by the entrance.

Even important decisions can be quite easy. You've decided to invest $25,000 into a Standard & Poor's 500 index fund. You know of two brokers that offer such funds. The only difference is that one charges a fee of .5%, and the other charges a fee of .2%. You go with the one that charges .2%. You're considering two kinds of surgery for cancer. The probability of a cure is the same in both cases. The only difference is that one is less likely to result in serious side effects. You choose the one that's less likely to result in serious side effects.

Some decisions, like the medical specialty decision, are more difficult and would be helped by sitting down over a cup of coffee and drawing a decision table on a napkin. A few decisions—one every year or so—are sufficiently difficult and important to warrant a more thorough analysis—a few days of research, quantification of values, and perhaps the use of a computer. For most decisions that people consider difficult, though, some hard thought over a cup of coffee can make a big difference—if you know how to make good use of the time.

As noted, decisions become more difficult when multiple factors are involved. Difficult decisions are of two kinds: multiattribute decisions and risky decisions.

Multiattribute decisions involve tradeoffs. Difficulties arise when one alternative is best in terms of some values, while another alternative is best in terms of others. The classic example of a multiattribute decision is purchasing a car. Cars differ with respect to many value attributes, among them cost, safety, reliability, aesthetics, and comfort. The cheapest car isn't likely to be the safest or the most reliable. The medical residency alternatives differed with respect to the residency, itself, kind of work in the specialty, and hours per week required in the specialty. In decisions of this sort, tradeoffs are involved.

Risky decisions involve uncertainty. Difficulties arise when one alternative would be best in one future, while another alternative would be best in another. The classic example of a risky decision problem is deciding whether or not to take an umbrella. The difficulty is that, if it rains, it will be better to have taken the umbrella, but, if it doesn't rain, it will be better to have left it at home. Investment decisions are of this kind. If the market goes up, it will be better to have invested in it; if it goes down, it will be better not to have. Tradeoffs are involved here, also, but in risky decisions the tradeoffs are across futures rather than values.

Difficult decisions require hard thought, yet thinking is the most fragile of cognitive abilities (Anderson, 1975). Many of humankind's greatest disasters have been the result of thinking gone awry. Wars surely fall in this category, as do current environmental and population disasters. Good thinking requires supplementing intuition with analysis, and analysis is not a gift of evolution but a human achievement. Because good thinking is so important and so difficult, we rightly hold in high regard those who become proficient at it. The best we call "wise". The goal of this book is to help all of us choose more wisely.

The *Oxford English Dictionary* defines "wisdom" as:

> ...*Capacity of judging rightly in matters relating to life and conduct; soundness of judgment in the choice of means and ends....* (OED, 1933, pp. 191-192).

The position taken in this book is that wisdom requires the courage to be rational, creativity, and balanced judgment. (See Sternberg, 1990; Baltes & Smith, 1990.)

These three secrets are defined and discussed in the next chapter. As will become clear, we are often diverted from *rationality* by our need to think well of ourselves, getting entangled in a quagmire of defensiveness; we are often held back from *creativity* by our reliance on habit, trapped in the familiar and the comfortable; and we are often blocked from balanced *judgment* by our limited capacity to think about more than one thing at a time, unable to see the inadequacy of our own oversimplifications.

Fortunately, there are correctives for these failings, and that's what this book is about. *Hope, distancing,* and *process orientation* can enable us to move from defensiveness to rationality; *stimulus variation and force fit* can get us out of ruts and onto creative paths; and *external memory, priming, heuristics,* and *decomposition* can give us the capacity required for balanced judgment. The next chapter will provide an overview of the ways in which these correctives can aid cognition; then the rest of the book will present in detail various tools for implementing the correctives—tools such as *decision tables, creative conversation, checklists,* and *decision trees.*

A word of warning before we start: To those not experienced in their use, some of the cognitive aids described in this book may seem artificial. They may *seem* like academic games that are irrelevant to real problems or, at best, that approach them in a very indirect or superficial way. For example, plusses and minuses or numbers may seem incapable of representing in any useful way the complex and profound emotions that are often involved in important decisions.

e. e. cummings (1959, p. 29) expressed a disdain for numbers eloquently, referring to:

> *Some one-eyed sonofabitch who invented an instrument to measure spring with.*

And Walt Whitman (1892/1963, p. 269) expressed a similar view, though in a more constructive way:

> *You must not know too much,*
> *or be too precise or*
> *scientific about birds, and*
> *trees, and flowers, and watercraft.*
>
> *A certain free margin, and even*
> *vagueness—perhaps ignorance,*
> *credulity—helps your enjoyment*
> *of these things.*

As appropriate as Whitman's stance may be for opening oneself up to the richness of life *between* decisions, it's not appropriate for decision making, itself. It's understanding, not enjoyment, that is the mark of sound decision making.

While plusses and minuses and numbers are no match for the *experiences* they represent, they can, if used properly, be far superior to other *representations* of these experiences as vehicles for certain phases in a high-quality decision process. And it is high-quality decisions that are likely to leave us the most free to enjoy birds, trees, flowers, and watercraft.

Another objection to decision analysis is that it places too much weight on quantifiable aspects of decision problems. This objection reveals an incomplete understanding of decision analysis. One of the great strengths of decision analysis, as we'll see, is its ability to quantify what's commonly considered "unquantifiable" and thus put it on an even playing field with the quantifiable. Decision analysis is the champion of the "unquantifiable".

Another word of warning: Cognitive aids usually *add* to the work to be done. While they should always improve quality, they won't always reduce effort. Their justification, like that of a trial over a lynching, is, not an easier solution, but a better one. No claim is made here that wise decisions are easily achieved. The claim is vigorously made, however, that the benefits of wise decision making vastly outweigh the costs.

At the very end of the last chapter, I list and introduce briefly a number of other books on decision making that I suggest for your further reading. Why not just skip this book, then, and start with one of them? If your primary interest is in understanding the field of decision making, including its history, findings, and current controversies, you *should* start with one of them. If your interest is in the psychology of decision making, for example, I'd suggest that you start with the Hastie & Dawes book or the Plous book, and, if your interest is in an overview of decision analysis, I'd suggest that you start with the Clemen book. If, however, your primary interest is in applying these areas of knowledge to improving your decisions, then I believe that you've already made the best start by beginning with this book.

The following checklist provides a preview of the major points that will be made in the remainder of this book, in the form of a decision checklist.

- Make sure you're approaching the problem rationally.

- Make a list of values.

- Make a list of alternatives.

- Make a decision table.

- Try to create a win-win alternative.

- Try to create an "uncertainty proof" alternative.

- If your decision isn't clear by this point, compute total value, and select the alternative with the highest total value.

A more complete version of this checklist, which is a summary of the entire book, appears on the inside front cover. It can help in a number of ways.

- Right now, it can help you see what's coming.

- As you read the book, miniature copies of the checklist will appear at major headings to help you keep track of where you are in the checklist, and, on the inside back cover, an index to the key words in the checklist can help you find your way around the book.

- Once you've gotten into the book, you might want to make a reduced copy of the version on the inside front cover, plasticize it, and carry it in your wallet or purse to help you remember and apply what you've learned.

Chapter 2. COURAGE, CREATIVITY, & BALANCE

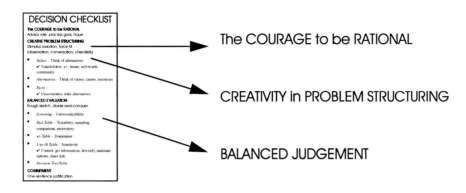

The COURAGE to be RATIONAL

CREATIVITY in PROBLEM STRUCTURING

BALANCED JUDGEMENT

The three secrets of wise decision making are courage, creativity, and balance in the management of complexity. The courage to be rational faces up to complexity in order to get the problem solved; creativity adds to complexity in order to achieve a more complete understanding of the problem; and balanced judgment evaluates complexity in an even-handed manner in order to reduce it to a choice of the single best alternative.

The warning signs of a need for greater courage are emotionality and resistance in response to challenging information. The paths toward greater courage are hope that a rational process will lead to the best outcome, appropriate emotional distance from the decision outcomes, and process orientation.

The warning signs of a need for greater creativity are coming up with no more ideas or coming up with the same ideas over and over again. The paths toward greater creativity are stimulus variation to vary ideas and force fit to turn the resulting new ideas into truly creative ones.

The warning signs of a need for more balanced judgment are a feeling of information overload, simplistic thinking, and vacillation. The paths toward more balanced judgment are external memory and priming as supplements to working memory and educated guesses and analysis into subproblems to simplify the problem in ways that eliminate the unimportant and retain the important.

At various points in the book, our guide below will summarize key concepts, wearing a thinking cap that will make clear which of the Three Secrets is involved.

- The Courage to be Rational

- Creativity

- Balanced Judgement

Curiously, the Three Secrets seem to be secrets to different people. Balanced judgment seems to be a secret to decision makers without formal training, since they so often try to evaluate decisions "in their heads" without formal analysis. Courage seems to be a secret to decision scientists, since they rarely mention it. And, while both decision makers and decision scientists recognize the importance of creativity, neither offers much in the way of suggestions for promoting it.

Rationality is a matter of direction in thought. Rational decision making begins with fact and value premises and proceeds from there to a logical conclusion as to which alternative is to be preferred. Creativity is a matter of richness of thought. Creative decision making considers broad ranges of alternatives, bases for evaluating those alternatives, and events that might affect their value. Judgment is a matter of balance in thought. Judicious decision making weighs the various fact and value considerations in proportion to their importance.

Instances of insufficient courage to pursue a rational course are all too common, for example, stubborn resistance in parents, bosses, and political leaders to evidence of weaknesses in a course of action they've advocated. Failures in creativity are also common, as indicated by the frequency with which we learn about better alternatives after we have already committed to a decision. Failures in judgment are also common, for example, failures of young people to attach proper importance to planning for their working years, failures of adults to attach proper importance to planning for retirement, and failures of society to attach proper importance to planning for the next generation.

Why are we so often less than wise? What inclines us to decide irrationally? What keeps us from being more creative? What accounts for biased judgment? Finally and most importantly, how can we correct each of these deficiencies? This chapter begins to answer these questions.

Motivational concepts, specifically *cognitive conflict,* will play a key role in our attempt to understand courage, creativity, and balance. High-conflict decisions are "hot" decisions; low-conflict decisions are "cold" ones, and the various decision tools can be seen as either increasing or decreasing cognitive conflict. It's level of cognitive conflict that distinguishes rational decision making ("warm") from both disinterest ("cold"), on the one hand, and panic ("hot"), on the other. Also, within rational decision making, creative thinking increases cognitive conflict, and judgment decreases it. In the end, we'll have to add the concept of hope to that of cognitive conflict in order to distinguish rational decision making from decision avoidance. However, cognitive conflict is the best place to start.

Cognitive Conflict

Cognitive conflict (or "cognitive dissonance", Festinger, 1957) is related to both (a) the amount of uncertainty about the consequences of various alternatives and (b) the importance of those consequences (Berlyne, 1965, Ch. 9). For example, a path out of a forest that branches into three paths should result in more uncertainty, and hence greater cognitive conflict, than a path that branches into two paths. And either amount of uncertainty should result in greater cognitive conflict if we're trying to escape a forest fire than if we're going for an afternoon walk. The relationships among cognitive conflict, importance, and uncertainty can be expressed in the following equation:

Cognitive Conflict = Importance x Uncertainty

If importance is zero (we don't care where we're going), no amount of uncertainty will produce cognitive conflict, and if uncertainty is zero (there's only a single path with no branch), no amount of importance will produce cognitive conflict (terror, perhaps, but not cognitive conflict).

As cognitive conflict increases, emotional arousal increases; and as arousal increases, attention narrows (Easterbrook, 1959). At low levels of conflict, attention is broadly diffused and quickly turns to other matters. We aren't sufficiently interested in the decision problem and easily get distracted. At moderate levels, attention is properly concentrated on the task, and we're most open to problem-relevant information. We're interested, engaged, or challenged. At high levels, we develop tunnel vision to the point where we're likely to ignore important considerations. We're too highly motivated and experience panic. It's moderate levels of conflict that are most conducive to good decision making.

We work best on decision problems that stimulate "warm" interest. If we feel "cold" about a decision, we aren't likely to give it enough thought; and, if it's a "hot" decision, we're likely to try to get it resolved too quickly. The Importance-x-Uncertainty equation is useful to keep in mind, for it can make us more sensitive to the factors that determine level of conflict and also suggest ways to increase or decrease it—ways to turn the "heat" up and ways to turn it down.

If uncertainty is too low, we can "turn the heat up" and become more focused on the decision problem by spending some time thinking about what may be wrong with what we're doing, that is, risks associated with the current course of action and risks associated with alternative courses of action. A famous story involving Alfred P. Sloan, Chairman of the Board of General Motors during its "Golden Age", illustrates the valuable role that cognitive conflict can play in successful decision making (Drucker, 1974, p. 472).

At one point in a meeting of General Motors' Board of Directors, Sloan is reported to have said, "Gentlemen, I take it we are all in complete agreement on the decision here."

Everyone around the table nodded assent.

"Then," continued Sloan, "I propose we postpone further discussion of this matter until our next meeting to give ourselves time to develop disagreement and perhaps gain some understanding of what the decision is all about."

The cognitive conflict encouraged by Sloan indeed led to deeper thought—and ultimately to rejection of his proposal! If Sloan hadn't placed such positive value on disagreement, the Board would probably have gone on to make a decision they'd later have regretted. For thinking about risks associated with the current course of action, stimulus variation, discussed in the section on Creativity, can help. In particular, imagining that your decision has had an unfortunate outcome can help you think of deficiencies (Jones, Yurak, & Frisch, 1997).

So, if uncertainty is too low, we can "turn the heat up" by adding alternatives through creative thinking, as well as increasing uncertainty about existing alternatives by thinking about what's wrong with preferred alternatives and what's good about non-preferred alternatives.

If it's importance that's too low, we can "turn the heat up" and become emotionally more engaged in the problem by imagining that the solution is due tomorrow, rather than next month, that the responsibility for the solution is entirely ours, rather than partly someone else's, or that the consequences will occur to us directly, rather than to someone else.

If uncertainty is, on the other hand, too high, we can "turn the heat down" and become less narrowly focused on some portions of the decision problem to the exclusion of others by using external memory, heuristics, or decomposition to reduce complexity. These methods are all discussed in the section on Judgment.

If it's importance that's too high, we can "turn the heat down" by distancing ourselves emotionally from the problem in a variety of ways. We can prepare to accept the worst that could happen. Or we can imagine that the problem is someone else's and that we're giving advice to them. Even though the decision is really yours, ask yourself, "How would I advise someone else making this decision?" Just as it's easier to see irrationality in others than in ourselves, it's easier to be rational about someone else's decisions than our own. Discussing the problem with someone else is yet another way to achieve distancing.

If the heightened importance is a consequence of time pressure, we can relax artificial deadlines we've set for ourselves, find ways to relax genuine deadlines that are externally imposed, find extra time between now and the deadline, or place less importance on the immediate deadline and more on long-term deadlines. One trick for distancing yourself from a problem is to regard it as "practice" for a more important problem you'll have to deal with later. This focuses attention more on long-term benefits and less on short-term consequences and takes some of the pressure off, enabling you to perform better and increasing the chances that you'll achieve both the short-term and the long-term benefits. A good way to relax inappropriate self-generated time pressure is to pour yourself a cup of coffee before sitting down to work on a decision problem. Not only is a more relaxed approach to time likely to improve the quality of your decision, but it can also, paradoxically, reduce the time required—the opposite of "Haste makes waste."

Process orientation is a particularly important way to reduce both importance and uncertainty. Process orientation is redirecting attention from the outcomes of the decision to the decision process, itself. For example, if you focus too much on how much you might gain or lose, you could put off making an investment decision longer than you should. If you worry too much about how the other person might react, you could put off dealing with an interpersonal problem too long. If, instead, you ask yourself whether you've given adequate thought to the values involved and the courses of action open to you, whether you've checked information sources adequately and sought the perspectives of others, and whether you've put this information together systematically, you'll soon realize that you're ready to make a sound decision and will be more likely to act on it in a timely fashion.

Process orientation is holding yourself responsible more for making a good decision than for achieving a good outcome. The idea is to place greater importance on being rational, fair, and a good decision maker than on being "right" about the outcome.

To the extent that we evaluate ourselves on the basis of the process we're engaged in, we both reduce importance and shift it to events over which we have greater control and about which there need be less uncertainty. By reducing both importance and uncertainty, process orientation enables us to tolerate greater complexity in working on a decision problem and achieve higher quality solutions. Process orientation seems to be important in the personalities of creative people (MacKinnon, 1962). The comfort creative thinkers experience with complexity was well described by Eric Fromm (though in the gender-biased language of his time), "Thinking man is necessarily uncertain." It was described in an even more positive way by Tennyson in his poem "Ulysses":

> *Yet all experience is an arch where-thro'*
> *Gleams that untravell'd world, whose margin fades*
> *Forever and forever when I move.*

Hold yourself responsible for being rational and fair and making good decisions, and good outcomes will be more likely to follow.

The next three graphs summarize what has been said to this point about cognitive conflict and decision making. They show how various levels of cognitive conflict are related to the problem identification, problem structuring, and evaluation phases of decision making. In each graph, conflict is represented on the vertical axis, and time, on the horizontal axis. The two dotted lines on each graph represent the range of cognitive conflict that stimulates interest in the decision maker. Above this range, the decision maker's response is panic, and, below this range, it is boredom. Rational decision making occurs within the range that stimulates interest.

The way to read the first graph, for example, is to see that conflict is moderate (3.0) during the problem identification phase, increases (to 6.0) during the problem structuring phase, and declines (to 1.0) during the evaluation phase. Because the initial level of conflict is above the lower dotted line, it's not so low as to create boredom (as in the second graph), and, because it's below the upper dotted line, it's not so high as to create panic (as in the third graph). The decision problem thus generates interest and is responded to with appropriate problem structuring and evaluation.

In addition to an optimal level of cognitive conflict, the courage to be rational requires *hope*. The fourth graph shows how hope fits into the overall picture. The hand that says "Stop!" represents emotional resistance to thinking about this decision problem, resistance that stems from the absence of hope that such thinking would do any good.

The final graph, on the next page, summarizes methods for enhancing courage, creativity, and balance. The hand that says "Go!" represents emotional openness to thinking about this decision problem brought about by the presence of hope that such thinking will lead to the best outcome. "EM" refers to external memory, discussed later.

INTEREST

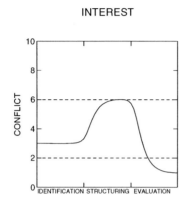

Interest. An intermediate level of conflict generates interest. This is followed by creative thought during problem structuring, which increases conflict, and judgment during evaluation, which decreases it. At the end, a single alternative has been chosen, conflict has been brought below the range of interest, and the decision maker's attention turns to other matters.

BOREDOM

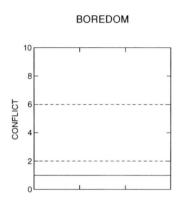

Boredom. The level of conflict is never great enough to generate interest and stimulate thought, so there's no problem solving activity. For example, the teenager who plans on being a rock star is not interested in even talking about other career possibilities.

PANIC

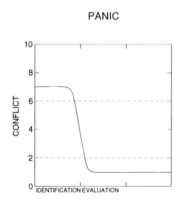

Panic. The level of conflict is so great that it produces discomfort. As a consequence, there's a desperate attempt to reduce this discomfort. There's no problem structuring but simply hasty evaluation to reduce intolerable conflict. For example, a person fleeing a burning building takes foolish things and leaves important ones behind and may persist in trying to escape by a blocked route.

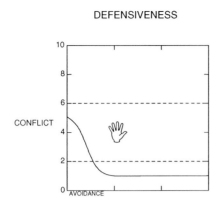

DEFENSIVENESS

Defensiveness. Even though the level of conflict may not be unacceptably high, unbiased problem solving does not occur, because personal threat closes off options; and defense mechanisms, in a distortion of evaluation, reduce conflict to the point where the problem is not seen as interesting. Because the problem is not solved, however, it may reappear from time to time, reawakening conflict and reactivating the defense mechanisms. For example, a person never interprets correctly others' responses to his abrasive behavior and thus never corrects the behavior.

Methods for increasing hope, summarized to the right of the forward-pointing finger in the diagram, are discussed in the next section of this chapter, on the Courage to be Rational. Methods for increasing complexity and cognitive conflict, summarized next to the upward-pointing arrow, are discussed in the section after that, on Creativity. And methods for decreasing complexity and cognitive conflict, summarized next to the downward-point arrow, are discussed in the final section of this chapter, on Judgment.

With an understanding of conflict motivation and its importance, we now look more closely at each of the three secrets of wise decision making.

MAINTAINING RATIONALITY

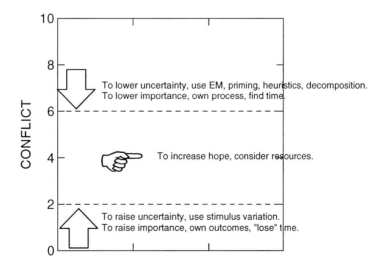

To lower uncertainty, use EM, priming, heuristics, decomposition.
To lower importance, own process, find time.

To increase hope, consider resources.

To raise uncertainty, use stimulus variation.
To raise importance, own outcomes, "lose" time.

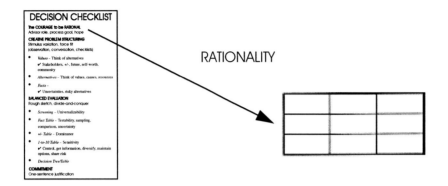

RATIONALITY

Secret One: The Courage to be Rational

"When people are required to make major decisions, defensive avoidance is probably the most pervasive defective pattern as well as the most difficult to prevent or correct."

Janis & Mann, 1982, p. 61

So far, we've been talking about reactions to different levels of conflict motivation—and ways to turn either "cold" boredom or "hot" panic to "warm" interest. However, neither boredom nor panic is irrational, because neither involves active avoidance. The difference between rationality and irrationality appears to be more than a difference in conflict motivation.

Recognizing Lack of Rationality

While, in rational choice, cognitive conflict is reduced by processes of reasoning, in decision avoidance, it's reduced by processes of rationalization. We ordinarily think of the beliefs that reduce uncertainty as serving a representative function (Katz, 1960). Let's call these beliefs representational beliefs. They can be thought of as the mental equivalent of a

20

photograph or a tape recording, representing reality in a relatively unbiased fashion. For example, right now I experience little uncertainty about where my car is. I believe that it's in the garage. Beliefs of this kind enable us to select courses of action that are adaptive. If I want to go somewhere in my car, I'll go out to the garage. We're interested in representational beliefs being accurate. If my car isn't in the garage, I want to know that, and I want to know it soon. We value accuracy in representing such beliefs, since they're able to serve their representative function only if correct.

The cognitive conflict we experience when representational beliefs are challenged serves as a stimulus for unbiased problem solving that improves the accuracy of these beliefs and leads to better decision making. Falsification of such beliefs requires changes that we have some hope of being able to make, and so we tend to respond to such falsification rationally. If you tell me that my car isn't in the garage, I have some hope that I can do something about the situation, and so I perceive the message as helpful. I don't get angry with you. I don't need to put off looking in the garage. I don't need to seek out like-minded people to discuss reasons for believing that my car is, indeed, in the garage. I go out and check to see whether my representation corresponds to the reality it's assumed to represent.

Not all beliefs are representational beliefs, however, as similar as they may appear on the surface. Some are self-enhancing beliefs, functioning primarily to reduce cognitive conflict in a way that enables us to feel good about ourselves (Katz, 1960). The belief that our country is the best country in the world, the belief that "I'm O.K., you're O.K.", various philosophical and religious beliefs, and various political beliefs aren't beliefs that people are eager to put to the test. Our feeling is that we know that they're right, that there's no point in putting them to the test, or even that it'd be wrong to put them to any test. The fact that people are reluctant to put some beliefs to a test suggests that they, curiously, don't really believe these "beliefs", themselves! After all, what harm could come from testing a correct belief and showing others that you're right?

The following experience concerning a televised town hall discussion on beliefs in the supernatural provides a good illustration.

> *At the end of the program, one of the believers said, "The trouble with you skeptics is you're so negative!"*
>
> *I replied, "I'll make a positive offer. None of us has said that any of your claims is false; all that we've said is that you haven't given us enough evidence to justify rational belief in them. If any of you has a phenomenon you'd like to be able to convince others of, give me a call at the University,*

and I'll be happy to help by designing a demonstration that should get the serious attention of skeptics."

Immediately after we went off the air, a number of believers crowded around me to take me up on my offer, and, over the next several days, believers who'd been watching the show called me at the University, some ten in all. In every case, the pattern was the same: As soon as it became clear that the procedure I outlined allowed not only for the possibility of confirming their beliefs but also equally, in an unbiased manner, for the possibility of disconfirming those beliefs, they abruptly lost interest. Not one followed through on my suggestions. All, apparently, were simply looking for facts to support beliefs they'd already become committed to—and, apparently, weren't very confident in!

A delightfully transparent example is that of a child who believed that he had a magic ring that would grant any wish when he rubbed it. He never tried it, however, because, if it didn't work, he knew he could no longer believe that he had a magic ring! Irrational beliefs are about "magic rings"—beliefs we want to keep, whether correct or not.

"Magic rings" take many forms. Today, confronted by the increasing scarcity of water and arable land, the alarming loss of species, and a human population that doubles every 40 years and seems to be becoming more violent, many turn from the complex solutions that science requires to simplistic solutions based on wishful thinking—fad cures, astrology, cults, hate groups or simply the belief that "technology" will magically solve our problems. In the long run, these head-in-the-sand "solutions" can lead only to greater problems, for ourselves and our children.

Let's be clear that it isn't the statement of the belief that's rational or irrational, and it's not even its truth or falsity. The statement, "I'm smart enough to get into med school", could be rational or irrational, true or false. It's rational if the person who makes it is willing to define it clearly and put it to a test, and it's rational whether or not it eventually passes that test. A belief is rational if it's accepted or rejected on the basis of the degree to which it conforms to observation. A belief is not rational if it's accepted or rejected on the basis of the degree to which it conforms to the believer's self-concept, lifestyle, or feelings. Although belief in the paranormal, for example, needn't be irrational, for many the primary function of these beliefs is to provide them with friends, topics of conversation, and activities that enrich their lives. Falsification is the great threat that it is because it could change all this. How can I say that I don't believe in space aliens and continue to belong to the Close Encounters Club? The value of "magic rings" is not in granting wishes but in making us feel good about ourselves.

Irrational thought may respond to cognitive conflict in either of two ways (Janis & Mann, 1977). It may reduce the perception of importance in the importance-by-uncertainty equation by shifting the responsibility onto someone else or procrastinating, which is, in effect shifting the responsibility onto one's future self. It may also reduce the perception of uncertainty by bolstering, conducting a biased search for information that supports the belief and avoidance of information that challenges it. Whether it's importance or uncertainty that's reduced in these ways, reality is distorted and cognitive conflict is reduced prematurely, taking away the stimulus to the continued thought that could lead to genuine problem solving and sound decision making.

Shifting responsibility ranges from the "Now look what you made me do!" of the child to blaming everything on "the government" to the Nazi's claim that he was just "following orders." (See Milgram, 1974.) In shifting responsibility, we reduce importance by disowning the decision. Failure can't affect our image of ourselves if the failure isn't ours.

Procrastination shifts responsibility from the present self to the future self. A fellow, who knows better, said that he'd quit smoking as soon as he got his Ph. D. Then he said that he'd quit as soon as he got tenure. Now, though he has both his Ph. D. and tenure, he's still smoking! What makes procrastination work is our profound tendency to discount the future. As anticipated events recede into the future, they seem to diminish in importance. This is particularly true for negative events (Brown, 1948; Wright, 1974; Wright & Weitz, 1977).

We don't ordinarily shift responsibility or procrastinate when representational beliefs are involved. If someone tells me that my car isn't in the garage, I'm not going to say, "The Police Department should be doing something about it" and then do nothing myself (shifting responsibility); and I'm not going to say, "I'll do something about it as soon as I get a chance" (procrastinate). I'll do something myself and now, because I have some hope that it will make a difference.

Whereas shifting responsibility and procrastination reduce importance, bolstering reduces perceived uncertainty by biased thinking that's directed toward strengthening whatever alternative we're committed to ("sweet lemon" thinking) or weakening other alternatives ("sour grapes" thinking). We can accomplish this by devoting more thought to either the positive features of the alternative we're committed to or the negative features of competing alternatives (Montgomery, 1983). Fortunately, with practice, we can learn to catch ourselves when we do this.

One warning sign of bolstering is an excess of reasons pointing in the same direction. The weaker the belief, the more reasons it seems that people feel they need to support it. "Methinks the lady doth protest too much." This is not the case for representational beliefs. I have only two reasons for believing that my car is in my garage: I put it there every night that I'm home, and I remember having put it there tonight. If someone casts doubt on the validity of that belief, I'm not going to try to come up with additional reasons.

A special form of bolstering is seeking social support for one's beliefs. When we're insecure, we tend to seek the support of peers or authority figures. This isn't true for representational beliefs. If someone tells me that my car isn't in my garage, I'm not going to seek out like-minded people and discuss reasons why the car must be in the garage.

Any of these defense mechanisms can easily be confused with rational responses to conflict. After all, not everything is our responsibility; not all of the decisions we're responsible for need to be made immediately; and many of the decisions we make involve little uncertainty that they were the right decisions. In fact, similar appearing mechanisms were suggested earlier for achieving an optimal level of cognitive conflict. The critical difference is between

- Rigid beliefs erected to block out cognitive conflict, so that we won't have to engage in serious decision making (cognitive "red lights") and

- Hypothetical stances we experiment with to reduce cognitive conflict just enough so that we can engage in serious decision making (cognitive "green lights").

To use another metaphor, it's like the difference between using a key to lock a door and using the same key to unlock it. The difference is in the purpose, not the tools.

The best overall test for irrationality is the response to challenging information. "There's no sense in talking about it any more!" "I've been through all that, and it's just not worth our spending any more time on!" "Don't be silly!" "I don't want to talk about it!" "We don't do things that way around here!" "I can see right now that that won't work!" "I don't want any experiments!" "There's really no other alternative!" "I find this whole discussion upsetting!" People who make statements like these are clearly not making any effort to come up with new ideas—nor are they encouraging others to do so.

The person thinking rationally will respond with interest to challenging information, whereas the person thinking irrationally will respond with emotion and resistance.

A critical test of the courage to be rational, then, is a willingness to put our beliefs or values to a test—in the language of scientists to maintain testability or falsifiability (Anderson, 1971). The statement that I have $20 in my pocket is testable; the statement that I have "enough" money in my pocket is not. The first tells you something about the world and can provide the basis for a sound decision. The second may tell you something about me, but it tells you little about how much money is in my pocket. Rational beliefs are open to falsification; irrational beliefs aren't. People with "magic rings" are reluctant to leave open any way in which their belief in them can be put at risk.

A famous illustration of non-falsifiability involves the reaction of an end-of-the-world cult to the failure of their prophecy (Festinger, Riecken, & Schachter, 1956). The members of the cult had sold all their worldly belongings and had gathered in the home of the leader to await the end of the world, which was predicted for midnight. These beliefs seemed to be eminently testable. The world would either end at midnight, or it wouldn't. If it did, their belief system would be confirmed; if it didn't, their belief system would be disconfirmed.

Tension mounted as midnight approached—and continued as the clock ticked beyond midnight, then well beyond midnight. Finally, the leader finally broke the silence. "Our faith has saved the world!" she proclaimed. The cult then set out—with their faith strengthened by the failure of their prediction—to seek new converts (the defense mechanism of seeking social support for beliefs). The belief that the world would end at midnight was testable, but their belief system was not!

Some warning signs of insufficient courage to be rational are:

(a) shifting responsibility,
(b) procrastinating,
(c) seeking social support for beliefs,
(d) avoiding falsifiability,
(e) actively seeking ideas that strengthen your position or avoiding those that weaken it,
(f) reacting with excessive emotionality when challenged.

A good way to test for the courage to be rational when you're making a decision is to ask yourself the following question:

Would I be willing to commit to and actually follow through on whichever of the alternatives the analysis indicates is the best?

If you find yourself balking when applying this test to any alternative, there may be an important "hidden" value that you haven't yet taken into account. Often such hidden values relate to how we feel about ourselves, and often they're values that we'd prefer not to think about. Sometimes hidden values are relevant to our decision and should be taken into account, and sometimes they're irrelevant and should be ignored. The only way to tell is to identify them and think about them.

We turn now to a pattern of irrational decision making that's sufficiently important to warrant separate treatment.

Escalating Commitment. We've all had the experience of having made a decision that's now going badly and of being inclined to invest even more into the failing effort in order to turn the bad decision into a good one. We call this "throwing good money after bad" or "escalating commitment" (Staw, 1976; Staw & Ross, 1987). The United States' conduct of the Vietnam War seems to fit this pattern well. If we'd known how badly the Vietnam War was going to turn out, we'd never have gotten into it, in the first place; yet, once we were in, failure led us to invest increasingly more lives and dollars. Up to a point, at least, the clearer it became that the investment was a bad one, the more we invested. This is precisely what's meant by the term "escalating commitment". The principal cause of increased commitment in such cases appears to be an unwillingness to admit to ourselves or others that the initial decision was a bad one.

This pattern is also called the "sunk costs effect." Rationally, the costs that have already been incurred are irrelevant to the decision, since they're the same no matter what we decide to do next. They're "spilt milk" or "water over the dam". Irrationally, however, they reflect on our competence as decision makers—and that's why we try so hard to justify them, by turning the bad decision into a good one.

The second-highest-bidder auction provides a dramatic demonstration of escalating commitment (Shubik, 1971). A dollar bill is auctioned off to the highest bidder, but, unlike other auctions, this auction requires that both the highest bidder and the second-highest bidder pay their bids. Usually, in such auctions, the highest bidder and the second-highest bidder each wind up paying more than a dollar, and yet only one of them gets this much in return. How can people be so irrational?

Both bidders were probably drawn into the auction thinking that they'd stop before they reached a dollar. We've all had the experience of having gotten ourselves into a bad situation as a result of a poor initial decision. The question here is, What do we do now? Even when the bids have gone beyond a dollar, the second-highest bidder hopes, for example, by bidding 5 cents higher, to get the dollar and thereby cut losses by 95 cents. The feeling is, "I've invested too much to stop now!"

One corrective for escalating commitment is to reduce cognitive conflict by reducing importance. You can do this by setting limits on commitment in advance, while you're still distanced from the decision, and informing others, who are even more distanced, of that commitment. Or you can discuss the decision to continue with persons who have no investment in the alternative (Bazerman, 1994). In competitive situations, another corrective is to view the decision from the other party's perspective; if it looks equally attractive from the other perspective, something has got to be wrong (Shubik, 1971).

Hope

So how can we avoid irrationality? As we've seen, rational decision making requires (a) an optimal level of cognitive conflict and (b) hope. Cognitive conflict is motivational; hope is directional. They are the sails and compass of the ship of the intellect. If cognitive conflict is too low, like an under-canvassed ship you'll make little progress. If cognitive conflict is too high, like a ship under a heavy press of sail you'll be in danger of failure. If there's little hope of reaching an acceptable destination, you'll sail around the harbor and never get anywhere.

We've already considered cognitive conflict and ways to reduce high conflict. Those techniques, from distancing to decomposition, remain relevant and are important in maintaining rationality. To these, we now add ways to increase hope realistically.

What "hope" means here is the belief that a rational, unbiased approach to decision making is likely to result in the best outcome (Janis & Mann, 1977). Such a belief is justified to the extent that we have good problem-solving skills, we have adequate resources, and similar problems have yielded to rational approaches in the past. Reading this book should increase your problem-solving skills, and having this book (or, at least, the checklist on the inside front cover) available for ready reference can add to your resources for solution possibilities. For example, knowing how to break difficult problems down into simpler sub-problems should quite realistically increase your confidence that you can solve difficult problems rationally. Developing relations with others with whom you can discuss important problems can add another resource. Finally, practice, especially on simpler problems or analogous problems that are emotionally less threatening, can strengthen your skills and enable you to accumulate successful experience in dealing rationally with difficult problems.

To resist irrationality:

- Reduce importance

- Reduce uncertainty

- Increase hope

(There seems to be a form of procrastination that isn't a form of defensive avoidance, at all, since challenging information doesn't lead to emotion and resistance. In such cases, the remedy is to increase conflict by increasing importance and uncertainty.)

The above suggestions come close to describing the behavior of expert decision makers (Shanteau, 1988). Those who are recognized within their professions as expert decision makers go about making decisions in ways that appear to be consistent with the following attitudes.[1]

> - We don't have to make decisions by ourselves.
> - We don't have to be right on the first try.
> - We don't have to be exactly right, even in the end.
> - We don't have to be able to think about everything at once.
> - We can learn from our mistakes.

Expert decision makers seldom work in isolation. They work with a group or, at least, obtain feedback from others. Expert decision makers don't expect to get everything right at first, but are willing to make adjustments, realizing that making corrections is more important than being consistent. Expert decision makers are more concerned about being "in the ball park" and avoiding large mistakes and less concerned about being exactly right. Expert decision makers almost always use some form of decomposition (discussed in the section on Balanced Judgment). Expert decision makers learn from their mistakes, rather than rationalize or defend them. (Shanteau, 1988). All these attitudes should give expert decision makers greater hope.

Hope seems to be important in the personalities of creative people (MacKinnon, 1962). Creative people tend to be highly self-confident. The independence of judgment that characterizes creative people seems to be well described in the opening lines of Rudyard Kipling's poem "If":

> *If you can keep your head when all about you*
> *Are losing theirs and blaming it on you;*
> *If you can trust yourself when all men doubt you,*
> *Yet make allowance for their doubting too....*

---

1.   Reprinted with permission of Elsevier Science from Shanteau, J. (1988). Psychological characteristics and strategies of expert decision makers. *Acta Psychologica*, **68**, 203-215.

Openness in decision making, commitment in decision implementation. Benjamin Franklin said that we should keep our eyes open before marriage and half closed afterwards. Our behavior is generally in agreement with this principle in that we're less likely to entertain irrational positive illusions when making important decisions but more likely to do so once the decision has been made and we're carrying out the plan we've decided upon (Taylor & Gollwitzer, 1995). We remain uncommitted until we've evaluated the alternatives, but then, once we've chosen an alternative, we commit to that alternative. This seems appropriate. After all, once we've engaged in a thorough, rational process of decision making, there comes a point when we should have little hope of doing better—we've already done the best we can. The time has come no longer to be "sicklied o'er by the pale cast of thought" but to act! This is the time when optimism is appropriate; it's a time when you want a clear vision of success. It's the time to "Go for it!", to "Just do it!".

> We are most likely to be successful if we are uncommitted during decision making and committed afterwards.

Of course, we must always maintain some openness to the possibility that the decision should be re-evaluated. Conditions may have changed, or we may have overlooked something important, in the first place. A good practice is to evaluate progress toward your goals at regular intervals.

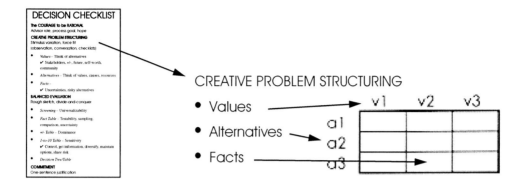

CREATIVE PROBLEM STRUCTURING
- Values
- Alternatives
- Facts

	v1	v2	v3
a1			
a2			
a3			

Secret Two: Creativity

"...It is no failure to fall short of realizing all that we might dream. The failure is to fall short of dreaming all that we might realize."

Dee W. Hock, President
VISA
Bionomics Annual Conference, 1994

Wise decision making requires creativity, in addition to the courage to be rational. When Solomon was confronted by two women each of whom claimed the same infant as her own, he suggested that the infant be cut in half and divided between them! The real mother objected, saying that she'd rather give up her baby to the other women than have it killed. Solomon then knew who the real mother was and gave her the baby.

Creative thinking, it's widely agreed, is the generation of ideas that (a) are new and (b) satisfy some standards of value. To say that half of 8 is 4 satisfies the standards of correct arithmetic but is not new and is, therefore, not creative. To say that half of 8 is 100, though new, satisfies no standards and is, therefore, also not creative. However, to say that half of

8 is 0 (when cut horizontally!) or 3 (when cut vertically!) is both new and satisfies some external standards and is thus, in some small measure at least, creative.

Decision problems are structured in terms of alternatives, values, and events, and it's important that we think creatively enough to have considered all important alternatives, taken account of all important values, and anticipated all important events. If not, our decision will be less likely to result in a good outcome.

Recognizing Lack of Creativity

Why is it so hard to think creatively? Frequently, on learning the solution to a problem, we ask ourselves, "Why didn't I think of that?" We actually knew enough to solve the problem, but somehow we never made use of the information we had.

Two forces tend to close our minds to new ideas. One we've already had a look at, fear of new ideas. The other, and the focus of this section, is inability to come up with new ideas. Even when we're doing our honest best to come up with creative ideas, it can be difficult to do so. If we can learn to sense when we're unable to come up with new ideas and know what to do about the problem, we should become more creative.

There are two indications that we're having difficulty coming up with new ideas, despite genuine effort: coming up with no more ideas or coming up with the same ideas over and over again.

There are two warning signs of inability to come up with ideas:

• Coming up with no more ideas or

• Coming up with the same ideas over and over again.

The remedy for inability to come up with new ideas is stimulus variation. The openness of creative thinkers to experience is a general openness to stimuli, and even the most creative thinkers seem to benefit from specific stimulus variation techniques. Indeed, virtually all of the stimulus variation techniques that we'll consider were originally developed by recognized creative thinkers to enhance their own already exceptional abilities.

Automatic Processes

The time has come for a "one-minute course in cognitive psychology". If we take a moment to distinguish between automatic and controlled cognitive processes (Shiffrin & Schneider, 1977; Shiffrin, 1988), the discussion of both creativity and balanced judgment in the rest of this chapter will make better sense.

To get a feel for the difference between controlled and automatic processes, consider the two lists below:

List A	
Left	
	Right
	Right
Left	
	Right
Left	

List B	
	Left
Right	
	Right
Left	
Right	
	Left

Starting with List A, try to report aloud the position (left or right) of each word. Ignore the meaning (left or right) of each word. List A is easy, because controlled processes, which are attempting to carry out the instructions to report the position of each word, and automatic processes, which tend to read each word aloud, select the same responses. All the "rights" are on the right, and all the "lefts" are on the left.

List B is more difficult, because controlled and automatic processes are in conflict. Now, you can't perform the task correctly by simply reading the words. Some decisions are like this, where our "better self" tells us to do one thing, but our habitual self inclines us to do otherwise. Even in the many cases that are not this clear cut, controlled and automatic processes have different roles to play in decision making, and it's worth learning how to get the best out of each.

Controlled processes. The most dramatic limitation of the human intellect is the limited capacity of working, or active, memory. Working memory is the "desk top", or "workbench", where we do our thinking. It's where controlled, or effortful, processing takes place. It's where, with some effort, we hang onto a telephone number that we've just looked up. Working memory is to be contrasted with long-term memory, where our own telephone number and others that we use frequently reside effortlessly. For items to be retained in working memory, they have to be attended to frequently, so that they stay active. If we're interrupted on the way from the telephone book to the telephone, we're

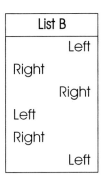

likely to forget the number we've just looked up and are holding in working memory—though not our own number, which resides securely in long-term memory.

Our capacity for controlled processing is quite limited. The longest string of unrelated numbers the average person can hold in working memory is about seven, the so-called "magical number seven", and the longest string of unrelated words the average person can hold in working memory is around five, a "mental handful". One credible line of thought even has it that the number of truly independent thoughts we can entertain at one time is actually closer to three (Broadbent, 1975)!

Automatic processes. A quite remarkable design feature has the effect of greatly expanding the capacity of working memory. This is thinking in terms of patterns, or what cognitive psychologists call "chunks", laid down in long-term memory (Miller, 1956). For example, the following number is much longer than the magical number seven, yet it's quite easy to regenerate on the basis of what's held in working memory:

1234567891011121314151617181920

The reason is obvious: it involves a well-learned pattern.

Patterns laid down in long-term memory provide working memory with a shorthand for thinking about the complex problems that reality throws at us. We could easily hold the following three chunks in working memory: "letters", "digits", "months", and then, on some later occasion, translate them into 26 letters + 10 digits + 12 months = 48 items! Chunks provide our intellect with seven-league boots, enabling us, for example, to summarize a three-hour movie in a single sentence: "Schindler began by using Jewish prisoners as cheap labor to save money but, in the end, spent all the money he had to save what had become 'his' Jews."

Yet chunking isn't without its costs. Since chunking is based on associative patterns in long-term memory, thinking in chunks inclines us to think in familiar directions and disinclines us to think creatively. Because perspectives are based on automatic processes, they are difficult for an individual to change. Associative paths tend to take us back over the same old ideas, "like a broken record".

Another mechanism, in addition to associations, tends to keep our thoughts going around in circles and returning to familiar ideas instead of moving on to creative ones. This is priming (Posner, 1978; Ghiselin, 1952; Szekely, 1945; Maier, 1931; Silviera, 1971). Priming is an effect that's intermediate in duration between the long-term memory of associations (lasting indefinitely) and the short-term memory of attention (lasting only seconds). Once ideas have been activated in working memory, they tend to remain in a ready, or primed, state for a few days, so that our thoughts come back to them more readily. This is the basis for the old trick that goes: If "folk" is spelled "f-o-l-k", and the president's name "Polk" is spelled "P-o-l-k", how do you spell the name for the white of an egg?

These two mechanisms, associations among ideas and priming of individual ideas, working together as they do, can create an intellectual box that it's difficult to see our way out of. Often, when we've lost something, we first look in all the places that it can reasonably be and then, unable to think of others, revisit the places we've just tried!

As an example, consider the following problem:

> *A father and his son were driving a sports car down a mountain road on a lovely autumn day, when suddenly the car spun off the road and crashed. The father was killed immediately, but the son was still alive, though seriously injured. He was flown by helicopter to the best hospital in town, where the hospital's top surgeon, summoned by cellular phone from a hunting trip, was already waiting. On seeing the injured man, the neurosurgeon said, "I can't operate on this boy! He's my son!"*

How can this be?

This sentence is here to give you a chance to stop reading and work on the problem if you wish to. If you're ready for the answer, here it is: The surgeon is the boy's mother! Working against the problem solver is the stereotypical associative connection between being a surgeon and being male. Also working against the problem solver is the fact that maleness was primed by the words "father", "son", "his", "he", "hunting trip", and "man". Associations and priming have created a box of maleness from which it's difficult to escape. (The fact that even women's rights activists have difficulty with this problem suggests that the difficulty is not motivational but cognitive.)

Priming and associations are generally helpful. They wouldn't have been likely to have evolved otherwise. They free attention to deal with novel problems. As Pascal said, "Habit is the hands and feet of the mind." One of the things that distinguishes good problem solvers from poor problem solvers, however, is the ability to realize quickly when familiar approaches are not getting them anywhere. Expert problem solvers are more ready to abandon the old path, and start searching for new ones (Shanteau, 1988). Good problem solvers and decision makers are not bound by a single pattern but are able to move from pattern to pattern.

To be good decision makers, we must be able to explore different perspectives.

Stimulus Variation

How do we get off "automatic pilot", break out of associative boxes, and enlarge our view of reality? In the association lie both the problem and the solution. Depending on how we use them, associations can keep us from new ideas or lead us to them. So long as the stimulus situation stays the same, associations will tend to keep us in the box. However, if we change the stimulus situation, this same mechanism can get us out of the box (Stein, 1974, 1975; Keller & Ho, 1988; Pitz, 1983). The basic principle is: To change ideas, change stimuli. If we keep stimuli changing, we'll keep our thoughts moving. This simple principle is the basis for a variety of techniques for suggesting new perspectives and stimulating creative thought.

To change ideas, change stimuli.

The techniques of stimulus variation have been referred to, collectively, as a technology of foolishness (March, 1972). Ordinarily, we think about problems in reasonable ways, using the patterns and perspectives that have served us well in the past, being "sensible" and "intelligent" and "adult". And, ordinarily, this leads quickly to solutions. However, occasionally we come up against a problem that fails to yield to reason. Even for decisions where the best thing to do is what we'd immediately consider reasonable, it can still be worthwhile to look beyond the "reasonable" possibilities to make sure we haven't overlooked a better way.

Why would Columbus sail west to go east? Why would foresters allow forest fires to burn in order to preserve the health of the forests? Why would a masseur intensify pain in order to get rid of it? Why would an expert in jui jitsu accept the force of an opponent's blow, rather than oppose it? What initially seems counter to reason is often what's later seen as creative.

The difficulty in coming up with creative solutions is that the answer may be in a place we aren't accustomed to looking and wouldn't think it worthwhile to look. Before the germ theory of disease and the adoption of aseptic procedures, it was difficult for medical researchers to conceive of the possibility that the cause for childbed fever might be the enemies of disease—themselves, the physicians—who carried germs to the mothers on unwashed hands (Leeper, 1951). Today, it's difficult to see the love we feel for innocent, bright-eyed, smiling babies as a major cause, by way of overpopulation, for some of humanity's greatest ills—starvation, disease, and violence.

When "reasonableness" fails us, the key is not in places where we might reasonably have placed it; reasonable attempts to bring childbed fever under control had failed; building more homes and increasing the efficiency of food production haven't solved our housing or food supply problems—we've no choice but to take the path of "foolishness". (In reading this sentence, it's important, or course, to understand that "reasonableness" isn't always reasonable and "foolishness" isn't always foolish.) It's precisely because association isn't a rational process that it can lead where reason can't and can thus get us out of the box. In this chapter, we'll see how positive affect, observation, creative conversation, taking breaks, and checklists can do this. In later chapters, we'll have a look at stimulus-variation methods more specific to thinking creatively about values, alternatives, and uncertainty, though the ones considered here always apply. In the end, of course, reason must be employed to evaluate where stimulus variation has gotten us, but that's a topic for the last section of this chapter, on Balanced Judgment.

Force Fit

Stimulus-variation techniques simply activate a portion of long-term memory that wouldn't likely be activated by rational processes searching "intelligently". As a consequence, they generally don't produce creative ideas; they usually produce foolish ones. What's required to get from the foolish ideas to creative ones is force fit (Gordon, 1961). Force fit is simply an attempt to turn a foolish idea into a workable solution. Force fit treats foolish ideas as stepping stones to creative ideas, first, looking at the problem from the fresh perspective provided by the foolish idea and then searching for a connection between this idea and the problem criteria.

It takes force fit to get from foolish ideas to creative ones.

I often use what I call the "World's Worst Creative Thinking Technique" to demonstrate the power of force fit. First, I ask each member of the audience to write down a word. What makes this the World's Worst Creative Thinking Technique (and distinguishes it from the techniques to be described later in this section) is that the words the audience writes down can bear no efficient relationship to the problem I'm about to pose, since no one in the audience yet knows what that problem is. Finally, I pose a problem, call upon members of the audience for their words, and, by means of force fit, the audience and I use each word to come up with potential solutions to the problem. It's surprising how well this technique works, considering that all that it has going for it is the basic mechanism of stimulus variation and force fit, without any attention to efficiency.

As an example that's pretty close to the World's Worst Creative Thinking Technique, consider a person using a checklist in trying to come up with an idea for a way to mount a compass. The compass had to be mounted in the cockpit of a small sailboat in such a way that it could be easily removed when not needed and stowed out of the way. Looking through The Last Whole Earth Catalogue, he came across a picture of a fish net. A fish net is certainly foolish as an idea for a way of mounting a compass—but it can be forced into a better one. With the fish net and the problem criteria as stimuli, he searched associatively for some idea that would connect the two and came up with a fishing reel. A fishing reel wouldn't work either, but the device that attaches a reel to a fishing rod by means of a bar and rings could be adapted for attaching the compass to the centerboard trunk.

Not satisfied with this, however, he continued. He next came across a picture of an ax. An ax, also, is foolish as a solution to this problem; you can't mount a compass with an ax. However, force fit led from the ax to the idea of a pocket knife, which is like an ax. Something like a pocket knife, with the blade on the compass and the receiving part on the centerboard trunk could work.

He then thought of inverting this arrangement, with the centerboard trunk as the "blade" and something on the compass to receive it. This line of thought led to a very satisfactory solution: mount the compass on a four-inch length of one-and-one-half inch rubber hose by means of two stainless steel bolts, then slit the bottom of the hose lengthwise, so that it would snap over the centerboard trunk. This arrangement was easy to make, easy to use, rustproof, and non-magnetic. And it cost only seventy five cents!

Creative ideas virtually always come in the guise of fools. For this reason, it's essential, during creative thinking, to respond to new ideas in a constructive way (even if these ideas have come from a person with whom we're in disagreement!) Our first inclination should be to try to see what's good in ideas and make them better. Negative criticism is inappropriate at this point. Negative criticism merely stops thought; it tends to mire us down in defensive avoidance and offers no solution. Negative criticism is appropriate later, when we're evaluating alternatives. However, while we're still structuring the problem, it's essential to keep our thinking open and constructive, trying to force fit foolish ideas into problem solutions.

The advice to force fit is quite different from the frequently given advice to suspend judgment during the idea-production phase of problem solving. If our problem-solving sailor had simply suspended judgment—positive evaluation as well as negative evaluation—he'd have added the ideas of a fish net and an ax to his list of possible solutions! Suspending judgment leaves us with the original foolish ideas and fails to take us to any creative ones. What our problem solver did, instead, was look for what was good in these ideas. This requires an evaluative judgment. To suspend judgment, we have to forget about the problem criteria, to forget about what we're trying to do. To force fit, however, we have to keep the problem criteria in mind (Gordon, 1961, 1971; Jungermann, von Ulardt, & Hausmann, 1983).

The best statement of the relationship between suspending judgment and force fitting requires distinguishing among three phases in the overall process.

- In coming up with a foolish "stepping stone", no evaluation should be employed. This is stimulus variation in the problem-structuring phase of decision making.

- In moving from the stepping stone to a potential solution, positive evaluation only should be employed. This is force fit in the problem-structuring phase of decision making.

- In evaluating potential solutions in order to determine whether any is satisfactory, both positive and negative evaluation should be employed. This is the evaluative phase of decision making.

The time has come to see how to put stimulus variation to work and look at some specific techniques. First, however, some general points should be made.

- There's no point in using creative thinking techniques as long as we're coming up with ideas. We should wait until we're coming up with no more ideas or are coming up with the same ideas over and over again.

- Force fit must be applied to get from the "foolish" stepping stones produced by these techniques to ideas that might be truly creative.

- The techniques will work most efficiently on decision problems if applied first to values and then to alternatives and events, and if applied to big-picture considerations, rather than details.

- It isn't necessary to use all of the techniques that will be discussed. Start with those that appeal to you most, and try the others later when and if time becomes available.

Here, I discuss five widely applicable techniques for stimulus variation: observation, creative conversation, breaks, checklists, and mood. In later chapters, we'll consider additional stimulus-variation techniques more specifically adapted to thinking of values, alternatives, and events. Even in cases where the more specific techniques are applicable, however, these general techniques are always applicable.

Mood

We begin with an important internal stimulus, mood. People who are in a good mood tend to come up with more ideas and with ideas that have more "reach", in that they go beyond narrowly defined bounds (Isen, 1997; Isen, Daubman, & Nowicki, 1987; Isen, Means, Patrick, & Nowicki, 1982). This may be because we're more often in a positive mood, so positive moods become associated with more ideas than negative moods. So try to put yourself in a good mood when you're working on your decision problem, or put off working on your decision problem until you're in a good mood. Being in a good mood should be congruent with feeling hope and not feeling time pressure. This is the playful attitude that creatives frequently refer to.

Observation

The most fundamental implementation of stimulus variation is thoughtful, or mindful (Langer, 1989), observation of the world about us, especially parts of the world relevant to our decision problem. Nietzsche said, "Don't think. Look!"

Thus, the artist looks at patterns in nature and at works by other artists to get ideas. The writer observes people and reads and, furthermore, attempts to write about subjects he or she has had personal experience with. The scientist pays close attention to data and is very often forced to new ideas by the data, themselves. A technique for getting management trainees to think creatively about management is to have them tour industries looking for problems. Getting the facts straight is a good way to get ideas for solving a problem, and, if you're stuck on a problem, a good thing to do is to go over the facts once again.

One study (Getzels & Csikszentmihalyi, 1976) presented art students with objects they might include in a still life and then observed their behavior. The principal finding was that those who explored these objects the most thoroughly and took the longest to decide on a composition and treatment produced the best paintings and had the most successful careers as artists. The best artists were more likely to walk around the table on which the objects had been placed, to pick them up and handle them—even to bite on them!

Dale Chihuly, the world-renown Seattle glass blower, traveled to Finland, Ireland, and Mexico, looking for stimulation for his project "Chihuly over Venice" (Chihuly, 1997). As he flew to Finland to work with their top glass blowers, he had no idea what he was going to do, so open was he to the influence of the stimuli he'd encounter. Yet he'd no intention of simply copying Finnish glass. He expected to force fit Finnish ideas to his style and his themes. The high point of the trip began when he moved outside the studio and started setting his glass objects up along a nearby river. He hung them from trees, stuck them in the ground, and even threw some that would float in the water—then rowed around among them. The result was the creation of some forms that were both strikingly new and yet consistent with his style.

Another study (Szekely, 1950) showed that manipulation of an object results in a deeper understanding of the physics of the object, with the result that the object can be used more creatively in solving new problems. We often get to the point where we can repeatedly solve a mechanical puzzle without "knowing" how we do it and then have to watch ourselves to "learn" the solution.

Careful observation and careful attempts to establish and understand the facts, as unpretentious as they may sound, may very well be the best sources of ideas.

Creative Conversation

In conversation, new internal stimuli are created when we speak, and new external stimuli are experienced when others speak. As one example of the way in which putting our thoughts into words can activate new internal stimuli, consider the case of a medical researcher who'd worked on and off for eight years trying to determine why injection of the enzyme papain causes "wilting" of the ears in rabbits (Barber & Fox, 1958). He finally found the answer while lecturing on the problem. In attempting to explain the problem to students, he had to consider more closely an hypothesis that he'd rejected at the outset on the basis of assumptions that would have been clear to anyone working in the area, but not to the students. In demonstrating an experiment that he'd never thought necessary, he found that the rejected hypothesis was, in fact, the correct one! Similarly, how many times do we answer our own question before we finish asking it? And how often do we find flaws in our thinking only when we try to explain it to someone else?

Writing can be as effective as talking in changing internal stimuli. Both involve efforts to put our thoughts in a form that can be communicated convincingly to others and thus can generate internal stimuli that we wouldn't generate when thinking "for ourselves".

When we go to write our thoughts down, we usually find omissions and errors that lead us to re-write—and re-write!

In addition to our producing new internal stimuli when we engage in creative conversation, other people may provide new external stimuli. For instance, a boat owner had been trying for over an hour to repair his diesel auxiliary, while his guest waited in the cockpit, unable to help because of the small size of the engine compartment. Finally, the guest said, "What exactly is the problem? Maybe I can make a suggestion." The owner described the problem; the guest made a suggestion; and, within minutes, the owner had solved the problem! The guest felt pretty smug, but as it turned out, his solution was not the correct one. He hadn't even understood the situation correctly. The importance of his idea was in providing the owner with a different way of looking at the problem, which led quickly to a genuine solution.

As this example suggests, a person need not be knowledgeable or creative to say something that will stimulate creative ideas in others, especially in creative others. An old Chinese proverb has it that, "A wise man learns more from a fool than a fool learns from a wise man." Because people coming from different experiences are inclined to chunk the world in different ways, people with different experiences and perspectives have the potential for thinking more adequately about the problem together than any one could alone.

The fact that talking with others provides stimulus variation in two distinct ways, producing new internal stimuli and providing exposure to new external stimuli, should make it an especially effective way to come up with creative ideas. Talking with others is more efficient, of course, when the conversation is about the problem and is especially efficient, as we'll see later, when it's about big picture concerns and goals or sub-goals.

> Talk with others about your decision problem.

For creative conversation to work, it's, as always, important to apply force fit. In part, this means thinking constructively about what we hear ourselves saying in an attempt to turn it into something even better. In part, it means thinking constructively in a similar way about what the other person is saying. (If we do manage to turn what the other person says into something of value, we shouldn't forget that allowing him or her at least to share in the credit for the idea can encourage a sense of control over the process and, with it, a greater openness to future ideas. This is especially important when working with others on a joint decision or trying to settle a conflict.)

Different people not only may bring different perspectives that can stimulate creative thought in conversation, they also, of course, bring different information and expertise that can help complete the fact picture. Both contributions can be of value. At the highest levels of science, technology, business, and government, the best thinking is most often done by problem-solving teams. This is one of the true values of diversity. Instead of being thought of as the red light of trouble, differences are usually better thought of as the green light of opportunity, the opportunity to get from minds in conflict to minds in concert or, better, to the smoothly functioning "super mind" of an effective problem-solving team. The Wright brothers understood this well and placed a high value on the vigorous arguments they frequently had with one another.

There are three specific variations on talking with others that are broadly applicable: the Devil's Advocate, the giant fighter's stratagem, and networking.

The Devil's Advocate. A Devil's Advocate is a person whose express role is to provide arguments against the prevailing direction of the group. This practice was first formalized by the Roman Catholic Church as part of its canonization process. When the Roman Catholic Church is deciding whether a person should be recognized as a saint, it appoints a person, the Devil's Advocate, to present the case against canonization. The practice of assigning a person or group of persons specifically to argue against the prevailing opinion has been found by a number of organizations to be a valuable one and has been recommended as a corrective for groupthink (Janis, 1972). (Groupthink is the tendency for members of a cohesive group to regard their perspectives as representative of the best thought on the matter and to resist discrepant views.)

The value of a Devil's Advocate is dramatically illustrated in Arthur Schlesinger's account (1965, pp. 803-4) of the meeting of President Kennedy's Executive Committee on the first day of the Cuban missile crisis. Initially, most of the members thought that the best alternative would be an air strike to destroy the missile sites. Then Attorney General Robert Kennedy urged them to seek additional alternatives. As it happened, the alternative that was finally chosen, a naval blockade, was one of those generated in response to his suggestion.

The value of having a Devil's Advocate seems to have been demonstrated by the Catholic Church in a negative way, as well. The current pope abandoned the practice, and the number of persons admitted to sainthood has skyrocketed.

The Devil's Advocate principle also underlies our adversarial system of justice, in which specific persons are assigned to represent the plaintiff or prosecution and specific other persons are assigned to represent the defendant. The Devil's Advocate principle seems to work best when the Devil's Advocate merely questions the assumptions on which the dominant alternative is based and refrains from actually becoming an advocate for a competing alternative (Schwenk, 1990; Schwenk & Cosier, 1980).

The giant fighter's stratagem. A children's story tells of a boy who found himself having to defeat two giants. He accomplished this seemingly impossible task by arranging for the giants to fight, and defeat, each other. The elegant feature of the giant fighter's stratagem is that it uses intelligence to redirect the superior force of others to one's own advantage. In applying this stratagem to decision making, we use the knowledge and thought of experts to help us structure our decision problem.

Let's say that we're trying to decide on a car. Car A appears, on balance, to be the best; however, Car B also has some very attractive features. We go to the person who's selling Car B, give our reasons for preferring Car A, and ask him or her to talk us out of our preference. If the person selling Car B manages to do so and to convince us that Car B is preferable to Car A, we then go to the person who is selling Car A and repeat the process. It's amazing how often this stratagem can, in the end, get the person selling the inferior product to admit that, at least for our purposes, the competitor's product is superior. This admission, alone, can give us a great deal of confidence in our decision.

Networking. When you seek information relevant to your problem from anyone, there's one question you should always consider asking: Who else would you suggest I talk with?

Ask, "Who else would you suggest I talk with?" and, "Who would be likely to disagree?"

Exploring a network of contacts can greatly expand the range of stimulus variation in creative conversation.

Breaks

According to one view, taking a break achieves stimulus variation by simply allowing time for internal and external stimuli to vary on their own (Maier, 1931; Szekely, 1945). Getting an idea during interruption in work on a problem is called "incubation". A "miniature" example of incubation that we've all experienced is trying to recall a word, giving up for a while, and then having the word suddenly come to mind (Polya, 1957). (This happens all too often after having just walked out of an exam or an interview!)

Stimulus changes during a break can occur in waking life or in dreams. According to legend, at least, the stimulus of his body displacing the bath water suggested to Archimedes a way to determine the gold content of the king's crown without harming it, by comparing its weight to the weight of the water it displaced. The stimulus, in a dream, of a snake biting its tail suggested to Kekule the ring structure of benzene (Stein, 1975).

The stimulus changes that occur in dreams are efficient in that they tend to be related to whatever problem we've been working on that day. This is an effect of priming. The stimulus changes that occur in waking life, however, are reminiscent of the World's Worst Creative Thinking Technique in that they won't necessarily bear any efficient relationship to the problem we're working on. There are two things we can do about this. One is to use the break to work on related problems. The other is to become so deeply immersed in the problem before taking the break that a broad range of everyday experience will be seen as problem relevant.

Make your decision problem a high priority, and then live with it and sleep on it.

Taking a break sounds attractive because it seems to require no effort. This is misleading, since effort is usually required to get deeply enough into the problem for the break to work (Silviera, 1971). As Pasteur said, "Chance favors the prepared mind."

Checklists

Using checklists is one of the easiest of the techniques for getting ideas. you can expose yourself to a large number of stimuli in a short period of time simply by looking through a list of items related to your problem. This is what we do when, in trying to recall a name, we consider each letter of the alphabet in turn and ask ourselves whether it could be the first letter of the name we're trying to remember. It's what the poet does in using a rhyming dictionary to bring to mind words with a particular rhyme pattern. It's what a chess player does when one of his pieces is attacked and he runs through the list: Move the attacked piece, capture the attacking piece, interpose a piece between the attacking piece and the attacked piece, attack a piece more valuable than the attacked piece. Pilots, of course, routinely use checklists before takeoff.

The trick is to discover checklists that are relevant to your problem. We've already presented a Decision Checklist. Later, we'll present specific checklists for thinking about values, alternatives, and uncertainty.

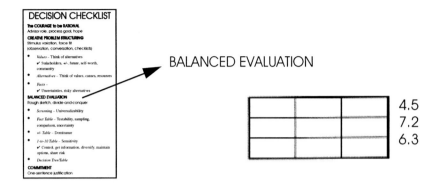

BALANCED EVALUATION

			4.5
			7.2
			6.3

Secret Three: Balanced Judgment

Everything should be made as simple as possible, but not simpler.

Albert Einstein

The third requirement for wise decision making, to be added to the courage to be rational and creativity, is balanced judgment, or judiciousness. Judgment is a matter of weighing various considerations. Good judgment involves attaching an appropriate weight to each of the various considerations, and bad judgment involves inappropriate weighting. The use of the scales as a symbol of justice represents the fact that the function of judges is to weigh considerations, and legal scholars speak of various "balancing tests". Proverbs 11.1 says, "A false balance is an abomination to the Lord: but a just weight is His delight." In social contexts, judiciousness expresses itself as fairness or evenhandedness. In decision making, judiciousness involves assigning appropriate importance to various values and appropriate probabilities to various possible futures. This requires both consistency among ideas and consistency between ideas and observations (Hammond, 1996).

The simple fact that all alternatives, values, and events have been thought about during problem structuring is no assurance that they will be weighed appropriately in evaluating alternatives. The assumption that they won't is at the basis of a strategy a friend of mine uses to influence decisions at meetings. Initially, he remains silent while the others explore the issues in a relatively balanced manner; then he presents his case just before the decision is about to be made. His reasoning is that, of all the considerations discussed, the most recent are the most likely to be in working memory at the time the decision is made and thus the most likely to influence the decision. His success has been remarkable. It'd be considerably less so if good decision practices, such as decision tables, were employed at these meetings.

Creativity identifies the parts of a decision problem: values, alternatives, and events. Its task is qualitative. Judgment evaluates the relative importance of these parts. Its task is quantitative. For this reason, judgment is often aided by numbers and calculation. We'll make use of two kinds of numbers: rankings and ratings.

Recognizing Lack of Balanced Judgment

How can we tell when we're being injudicious, or unfair? This isn't always easy. De Rouchefoucalt observed that, while we hear people complain about their memory all the time, we rarely hear them complain about their judgment. This may be because feedback about failures in memory tend to be so much more clear: When we forget a telephone number, we clearly can't make the call; when we forget a key, we clearly can't open the door. Feedback about failures in judgment tends to be less clear: When a decision turns out badly, we evaluate the situation with the same faulty judgment that led to the decision, in the first place, and can easily blame our failure on external circumstances.

We can improve our ability to recognize injudiciousness or unfairness. Oversimplified representations of decision problems take a limited number of forms; and we can learn to identify them and try to do something about them. The following patterns can function as warning signs.

- *A single alternative.* When we find ourselves considering just a single alternative—perhaps we've heard of a house for sale or have run across an attractive item in a store—we should remind ourselves of the value of comparison shopping.

- *A single value.* When we find ourselves considering just a single value—perhaps when we're thinking about the pro-life/pro-choice issue or the sustainable environment/ economic development issue—we should remind ourselves of the dangers of single-issue thinking. The pro-lifer thinks of the life of the fetus that stands to be lost. Some pro-choicers think of the mother's freedom; others, of the future life of an unwanted child; still others, of overpopulation. Yet all of these values are important, and all should be taken into account in decision making.

- *A single future.* When we find ourselves thinking in terms of just a single future—whether it be an optimistic one, a pessimistic one, or simply the most probable future—we should remind ourselves that planning for a single future is like looking one way when crossing the railroad tracks and that the future we prepare for may well not be the one that occurs.

- *All considerations point to the same alternative.* When we find all considerations pointing to the same alternative, we should remind ourselves that, in this complex world, even the best alternatives usually have drawbacks. Simple problem representations often tell us more about our limited capacity for thinking about a complex world than they tell us about the world, itself.

- *Vacillation.* When we find ourselves inclined toward one alternative on some occasions and other alternatives on other occasions, it may well be because there's too much to keep in mind at one time. After reading a book on shore life, we may be inclined to vacation at the beach; then, after seeing a movie set in the mountains, we may be inclined to go to the mountains, instead; then, after talking with someone who has just come back from the beach, we may be inclined toward the beach again. What causes this vacillation may be the fact that we focus our limited attention on different samples of the relevant considerations at different times (Goldberg, 1968; Shepard, 1964).

Any of the first four patterns could result from a failure in rationality, creativity, or judgment, though the fifth, vacillation, seems to point relatively unambiguously to a failure in balanced judgment resulting from cognitive overload. Take, for example, thinking in terms of a single alternative. The decision maker might not want to think about other alternatives because he or she is already committed to this alternative. The decision maker might not have been able to come up with other alternatives. Or the decision maker might not feel able to think about other alternatives, because thinking about just this one is complicated enough.

The way to tell whether oversimplification reflects a problem with rationality, creativity, or judgment is in the decision maker's response to additional information. *Resistance accompanied by emotionality suggests irrational defensiveness against the new idea; ready acceptance suggests that the decision maker was simply not creative enough*

Cat

to come up with the new idea; resistance accompanied by confusion and cognitive strain suggests lack of capacity to deal with the new idea along with all the others.

In any case, these five patterns can serve as warning signs and stimulate further thought. When any is accompanied by a sense of confusion, a feeling of cognitive strain, and repeated forgetting of important considerations, it suggests a working memory that's too overloaded to represent the problem fairly. Recognition of this can lead us to ask ourselves whether we're excluding information because that information is genuinely unimportant (a good reason) or because it puts us into cognitive overload (a poor reason, and one about which we can do something).

Some warning signs of injudicious, or unfair, thought are:

- Failing to consider multiple alternatives, values, or futures,

- Seeing all considerations as pointing in the same direction,

- Vacillating among alternatives,

- Feeling overwhelmed by new information.

How can we do something about limited capacity and achieve greater judiciousness? We can supplement working memory with external memory or priming, and we can fit the problem to the memory that is available by means of heuristics and decomposition. This is a good point to pick up the discussion of automatic and controlled processes.

Controlled Processes

In the section on creativity, we distinguished between controlled processes and automatic processes and went on to consider the conservative nature of automatic processes ("conservative" in the sense of continuing the past, not in the political sense). Our earlier problem with limited capacity was that it led to reliance on automatic processes, which, because they follow accustomed paths, resist creativity. Our current problem is with limited capacity, itself.

If we've done a creative job of problem structuring, we quite likely have come up with more considerations than can be held in the "mental handful" of working memory. And, if the decision problem is a kind we don't encounter repeatedly, we aren't likely to have chunks in long-term memory to aid working memory and enlarge its capacity. The most important life decisions tend to be ones that we don't encounter repeatedly. For example, we may very well choose a career or a mate or a house just once.

The following problem shows how even a simple task can overload working memory:

> *What day follows the day before yesterday if two days from now will be Sunday?*

Solving this problem "in your head" is like trying to do long division without pencil and paper. With pencil and paper (a form of external memory), such problems become trivial.

Limited capacity contributes to poor judgment, or unfairness, in two ways. First, because we can hold only so much in working memory, much may be simply excluded from consideration. What's excluded from working memory is, in effect, accorded zero weight. This is often not judicious. Second, because our capacity for thinking about what's in working memory is also limited, many of the distinctions among items in working memory may fail to be considered, and items that aren't distinguished with sufficient clarity may be weighted too nearly equally (Slovic, P., & Lichtenstein, S. 1973). This, too, is often not judicious.

A classic example is undervaluing quality products, services, and experiences by failing to attach sufficiently greater importance to benefits that are of long duration than to costs that are of short duration. Henry Royce, of Rolls Royce fame, warned against this, saying, "The quality remains long after the price has been forgotten." Another classic example of inappropriate weighting is overvaluing many "vices" (e.g., getting "high" on alcohol or drugs) by failing to attach sufficiently great importance to costs that are of long duration (a hangover or even addiction) in comparison with benefits that are of short duration (reduction of anxiety, a feeling of belonging, or a "high"), (Varey & Kahneman, 1992).

We tend to adjust to the limited capacity of working memory in a way that seems quite reasonable: We think about just the most important considerations. However, what's most important to us from our current perspective may not be what's most important to us from perspectives we take at other times. In such cases, we find ourselves in a hall of mirrors, vacillating between favoring one alternative at one time and favoring another alternative at another time, entirely unable to arrive at a stable preference.

We turn now to several techniques that can help us attack complex decision problems judiciously, despite our limited capacity. These are external memory, priming, heuristics, and decomposition.

External Memory

External memory can be a powerful supplement to working memory. External memory is the flip side of, "Out of sight, out of mind". We might say, "In sight, in mind." What we keep in view we're likely to remember and think about. Examples of external memory abound. Tying a string on your finger (or, more conveniently, putting your watch on the other wrist) is one form of external memory. In making such changes, you rearrange the world so that it "remembers" for you. A chessboard is another form of external memory. So is a well-arranged desk. Hutchins, a cognitive anthropologist who studied the elaborate external memory of navigators, represented by symbols on charts and settings on instruments, asserts that, "Humans create their cognitive powers by creating the environments in which they exercise those powers" (1996, p. 169).

The most powerful system for creating records in external memory—and one whose power tends not to be fully appreciated—is writing. This includes diagramming, as well as a powerful recent extension of writing, computers, which not only create records in external memory but also manipulate them, doing some of our thinking for us. Written symbols have the power to free us from the limitations of what we know and have learned about the immediate perceptual situation and allow us to contemplate what's not present— the past, the future, and the perspectives of others. As we saw in the story of the residency decision that opened this book, the most important considerations in a decision problem can easily be out of sight and out of mind.

We would all be better decision makers if we wrote our ideas down and diagrammed the relations between them.

Lists. One way of using external memory is making lists of ideas as we think of them, a list of alternatives, a list of values, and a list of future scenarios. For one thing, making lists of alternatives, values, and futures ensures that we don't forget the good ideas we've already come up with. For another, listing ideas encourages us to think of additional ideas. And, finally, writing down old ideas frees controlled processes from reliance on habitual patterns, so they can search with greater flexibility for new ideas (Chambers & Reisberg, 1985; Reisberg, 1996).

Decision tables and decision trees. Decision tables and decision trees are devices in external memory that not only retain ideas we've come up with but also organize them so as to guide further thought in logical directions. Once we have lists of alternatives, values, and events, we should organize them into a decision table. Decision tables will be discussed in detail later. If the uncertainties regarding choices and events in the future are sufficiently great, a decision tree can be of great help. Decision trees, too, will be discussed in considerable detail later.

Without decision tables and decision trees, we frequently fail to make crucial comparisons in reasoning about what we know. In choosing a preferred alternative, we frequently evaluate only one alternative at a time until we find one that's satisfactory, an approach called "satisficing" (Simon, 1955, 1956). This can lead us to stop short of considering superior alternatives. The tendency is to compare single alternatives against intuition, rather than to compare multiple alternatives against one another. (See also Lipshitz, et al., 2001.)

In choosing a preferred explanation, we, similarly, tend to think about only one explanation at a time, thinking about how well just that explanation accounts for the data and not at all about how well other explanations might account for the same data (Dougherty, Mynatt, & Tweney, 1979; Beyth-Marom, R., & Fischhoff, B., 1983). This pattern of thought often results in what has been called confirmation bias (Chapman, 1967; Chapman & Chapman, 1967) and leads to uncritical acceptance of poorly thought-out explanations.

As we shall see, both decision tables and decision trees force comparison of alternatives, and probability trees force comparison of explanations. The result is that we're less likely to accept the first idea that comes to mind.

Removing clutter from external memory. The importance of separating problem-relevant material from problem-irrelevant material in external memory is well illustrated by the "dazzle effect". If two groups of people add up the same columns of numbers but one group has dollar signs placed next to the numbers, the group with the dollar signs will make more errors. Though the dollar signs are irrelevant to the task of adding up the numbers, they demand attentional capacity and take it away from the main task. This is what's behind the principle of maintaining a high "data/ink ratio" in designing graphs (Tufte, 1983): A graph should present the relevant data with a minimum of ink and clutter. For example, three-dimensional bar graphs create more distracting "dazzle" than two-dimensional bar graphs, and those that introduce the greatest amount of distracting information are those that picture people or objects of different sizes.

An organized work space reduces distraction and helps focus attention on the task.

Priming

We have an intermediate-term memory that, like external memory, can make information more available to working memory than it would be if the information had to be retrieved all the way from long-term memory. We all know that recent experiences, such as a new joke, a first kiss, or an unpleasant argument, tend to come easily to mind for the next few days. This is intermediate-term memory.

We can learn to use this memory more systematically. If you're faced with a complex decision problem, such as a financial planning decision, where there are many things to take into account, you may at first feel overwhelmed and inadequate to the task and may tend to procrastinate. It can help enormously to spend some time just going over all the important components first, to get them fresh in mind, before starting work on the problem. If you try this, you'll actually feel smarter when you do start work on the problem. Psychologists used to call this a "warm-up" effect (McGeoch & Irion, 1952). Now, it's called "priming" (Shiffrin, 1988), getting ideas ready to be thought about more easily. It's a simple but powerful trick for expanding our mental capacity.

By now, we've considered a variety of forms of stimulus control, ways to bring automatic processes into the service of controlled processes and higher goals. It should be helpful to review them:

- To get *new ideas*, we vary automatic processes by varying stimuli

- To retain *good ideas*, we reactivate automatic processes by repeating stimuli in the form of external memory aids;

- To make *potential good ideas* more available to thought, we prime automatic processes by thinking about them or associated ideas;

- To get rid of *distracting ideas,* we avoid activating irrelevant automatic processes by removing irrelevant stimuli.

We now turn to two techniques that, while continuing to capitalize on the way the mind is organized also capitalize on the deeper logic of the decision problem, itself. These are heuristic search and decomposition.

Heuristic Search

External memory will get us only so far in dealing with complexity. The full complexity of even modest problems can't be represented on an 8½"-by-11" piece of paper. To get anywhere with complex problems, we have to think efficiently by distinguishing the important from the unimportant and directing our attention to what is essential.

What makes the World's Worst Creative Thinking Technique so bad is that it's inefficient. The ideas that serve as stimuli bear no special relation to the problem. What the technique lacks is any mechanism for searching efficiently.

Mechanisms for efficient search are called "heuristics". You probably know the Greek word "eureka", which means, "I found it", and comes from the ancient Greek word "heureka". A heuristic is an educated guess that helps you find the solution to a problem. The central theme that runs through all heuristics is constraint location, locating those aspects of the problem that constrain further search to regions of the problem space in which good ideas are most likely to be found.

The notion of efficiency in searching for ideas might be made clearer by comparing random search, algorithmic search, and heuristic search. Consider the problem confronting a safecracker who is trying to break into a safe with four dials, each numbered from 0 to 9 (Newell & Simon, 1972).

There are 10,000 possible combinations for this lock. The first dial has 10 positions, 0-9, and *for each of these* the second dial has 10 positions. Thus, there are 10 x 10 = 100 possible combinations of settings on the first two dials alone. Continuing this logic, there are 10 x 10 x 10 x 10 = 10,000 possible combinations of settings on all four dials.

Consider *algorithmic search*. A simple algorithm, or rule, that assures that all numbers will be tried once and only once would be to try them in the order 0000, 0001, 0002, to 0009, then 0010, 0011, 0012, to 0019, and so on up to 9999. This will take a maximum of 10,000 tries, a single sweep through the entire problem space.

Consider *random search*. Random search will be less efficient than algorithmic search, because there's likely to be substantial repetition of combinations already tried. There is no theoretical limit to the maximum number of tries. The probability that the solution will still not be found after 10,000 tries is $(9999/10000)^{10000} = .37$!

Finally, consider *heuristic search*. A heuristic is an educated guess and, as such, goes beyond logic and mathematics to incorporate knowledge about the particular problem or kind of problem one is dealing with. In cracking an old fashioned safe of this type, it's possible to sandpaper your fingertips lightly to increase their sensitivity so that you can feel the tumblers fall into place when each dial is in the correct position. This means that you can divide the problem of finding a four-digit combination that will achieve the goal of opening the door into four *sub-problems* of finding the single digit that'll achieve the sub-goal of causing the tumblers to fall in each dial. This replaces the overall goal of opening the door with the *sub-goals* of getting the tumblers to fall.

The effect on the mathematics is dramatic. Before, we had to try out 10 positions on the first dial and 10 positions on the second dial for each of the 10 positions on the first dial. Thus, the maximum number of combinations for the first two dials was 10 x 10 = 100. Now, however, we try out 10 positions on the first dial until the tumblers fall into place, and then we try out the 10 positions on the second dial only in combination with that one position on the first dial. Now, the maximum number of combinations for the first two dials is 10 + 10 = 20. Instead of 10 x 10 x 10 x 10 = 10,000 possibilities for the entire lock, we now have 10 + 10 + 10 + 10 = 40, an enormous improvement! In general, analysis into sub-problems replaces multiplication signs with addition signs in this way.

These three methods for searching for the solution to a problem differ enormously in their efficiency. In real life, the improvement resulting from various heuristics can be substantially greater than this. Efficiency is something that wise decision makers pay attention to.

The game of chess provides simple illustrations of the most widely useful heuristics. With the number of sequences of moves from start to checkmate or stalemate estimated at more than the number of molecules in the known universe, even computers can't play chess without relying on educated guesses. Three educated guesses used in chess and decision making, generally, are: "Focus on the big picture"; "Think backwards from your goal"; and, "Improve your position". Chess players focus on the big picture by roughing out their plans in terms of the big pieces (king, queen, bishops, knights, rooks) and thinking about the details (pawns) later. They think backwards from the goal by considering desirable intermediate positions they might be able to achieve. Because the ultimate goal of checkmate is too distant early in the game, they try to improve their position by estimating distance from a win in terms of relative strength as measured by number of pieces captured and number of squares controlled. (In the safe-cracking example, distance from opening the door was measured in terms of the number of tumblers that had fallen into place.)

These heuristics are all based on educated guesses. Though they're likely to lead to a win, they may lead to a loss. For example, in capturing a piece to improve your estimated position in chess, you could fall into a trap and lose the game.

Though life is far more complex than chess—so complex that it isn't possible to calculate number of possible "games"—these three heuristics that have been found useful in thinking through chess moves have also been found useful in thinking about life's decisions. In their application to structuring decision problems, they're most often called:

- breadth-first search,

- value-focused search, and

- sub-goal analysis

(Polya, 1957; Newell & Simon, 1972; Wicklegren, 1974).

We'll introduce the concept of breadth-first search in discussing the importance of the relevance criterion for a well-structured value set (Ch. 3). We'll also make use of the concept of breadth-first search in discussing classes of alternatives (Ch. 4) and will return to this concept in arguing for the importance of beginning at the bottom of the Decision Ladder (Ch. 5). We'll make use of the concept of value-focused search in arguing for the importance of analysis of values in thinking creatively about alternatives (Ch. 4). We'll make use of the concept of sub-goal analysis in thinking efficiently about values (Ch. 3).

To think efficiently about your decision problem,

- Get clear about a "rough sketch" before getting mired in details;

- Start the "rough sketch" by thinking about your goals or, if your goals are too distant, by thinking about sub-goals.

Two of these heuristic principles actually shaped the organization of this book. It was the principle of breadth-first search that determined the placement of Values, Alternatives, and Uncertainty as chapters in the main part of the book and Thinking More Deeply About Values, Thinking More Deeply About Alternatives, and Thinking More Deeply About Uncertainty as appendices at the end. Finally, it was the principle of value-focused search that determined the placement of the discussion of values (Ch. 3) before the discussions of alternatives (Ch. 4), decision tables (Ch. 5), and uncertainty (Ch. 6).

Decomposition

To external memory, priming, and heuristic search, we now add decomposition, the decision aid for managing complexity that's most widely discussed by decision practitioners and researchers. What we mean by "decomposition" is analysis of a problem into its components, a strategy of "divide-and-conquer". The problem is broken down into sub-problems; the sub-problems are solved; and then these solutions are put together to solve the original problem. Decomposition employs a logical framework that enables us to think about a small number of ideas at a time and yet arrive at a conclusion that's soundly based on a large number of ideas. In this way, it extends our intellectual grasp. For new and complex decision problems, this logical framework serves the same function that patterns in long-term memory serve for problems with which we've had repeated experience. Moreover, it should do so less fallibly.

A study of differences between developers and environmentalists (Gardiner & Edwards, 1975) shows how decomposition can enlarge our mental grasp beyond what can be accommodated by a familiar perspective and thus reduce differences among parties with conflicting perspectives. A number of environmentalists and developers were asked to evaluate third-party applications for land-use permits in terms of the desirability of the proposed projects. The judgments in the first part of the study were holistic, that is, each participant looked at all the information that was presented and "put it together in his or her head". This, of course, is the way we usually make judgments. Not surprisingly, the developers gave significantly higher approval ratings to the applications than did the environmentalists. At this point, their opinions were in conflict.

The judgments in the second part of the study were decomposed. The environmentalists and the developers went through the applications again, this time evaluating each application on a number of scales that they'd readily agreed upon (number of jobs created, conformity with the building code, etc.) For each developer and environmentalist, a single overall score was then computed for each application, using that participant's own ratings and importance weights. The result was that there was no longer any significant difference between the approval ratings of the two groups. The conflict that was present in the holistic ratings had disappeared in the decomposed ratings. Perhaps most impressive is the fact that this happened without any argumentation! Decomposition, alone, did the trick.

Decomposition enables us to get a complex problem within our mental grasp. Just as it enabled each decision maker to embrace the varied perspectives of a number of decision makers in the land-use permit example, so it can enable a single decision maker to embrace the varied perspectives that he or she—especially when thinking rationally and creatively—may take on different occasions. Decomposition can reduce both intrapersonal and interpersonal conflict. The application of decomposition to decision making is best illustrated by the use of decision tables, which, as we'll come to see later, are far more than simply aids to memory.

External memory representations such as decision tables and decision trees are highly complementary with decomposition in that the full power of decomposition requires some form of external memory—if we're going to break the problem down into pieces, we'll need some way to keep track of those pieces. Used together, external memory and decomposition can enormously expand our intellectual capacity.

Completeness for decision making, simplicity for decision implementation. The navigator may go through many complex calculations to determine the best course, but then give the helmsman simply a star, object, or compass heading to steer by.

We can encourage judicious thought in decision making by

- Using external memory,

- Removing problem-irrelevant clutter from external memory,

- Thinking heuristically, and

- Using a decision table to structure external memory in terms of simpler sub-problems.

In a similar way, once we've made a decision, we should try to reduce the complex reasons for that decision to a single sentence that captures their essence yet is simple enough to motivate our behavior and that of others as we carry our the decision. Such simplification, together with the shift from unbiased evaluation to commitment discussed earlier, should increase the chances of success in implementing a good alternative.

Chapter 3. VALUES: What do I want?

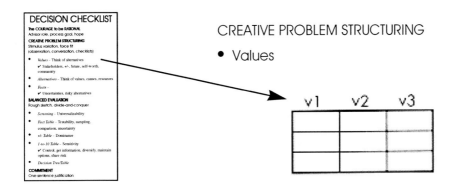

CREATIVE PROBLEM STRUCTURING

- Values

The best place to start thinking about a decision problem is with values. Creative thinking about values can be stimulated by values checklists, analysis of alternatives and events, and value trees. Thinking about values in terms of sub-goals can be more efficient than thinking about them in terms of ultimate goals. The criteria for a well-structured value set are completeness, relevance, meaningfulness, testability/ measurability, non-redundancy, and value independence.

In this chapter and the following chapter on Alternatives, we get down to the business of decision making, beginning with the problem-structuring phase. Problem structuring involves creating a representation of reality, what's sometimes called a "problem space" (Newell & Simon, 1972). Creating this representation is of the utmost importance, because what we think about is necessarily not reality but our representations of reality. We all go through life in "cognitive bubbles", responding to our representations of reality as though they were reality, itself. To the extent that the representations are in error, all subsequent thought is likely to be in error. Ward Edwards, the "Father of Decision Psychology", and his co-author Detlof von Winterfeldt have said that, "Every working analyst we know agrees that good problem structuring is the key to successful analysis" (von Winterfeldt & Edwards, 1986, p. 569).

A simple illustration of the importance of the problem space is the following problem:

Two people were born to the same parents on the same day of the year, but are not twins. How can that be?

Suggested solutions include the day being the same day of different years (which it isn't) and the twins being fraternal, rather than identical, twins (which they aren't). The solution involves an element that, for good reason, people don't tend to put into their problem space—a third sibling. The solution is that the people are two out of a set of triplets! Similarly, in decision making, even the best procedure can't select an alternative that isn't in the problem space or take proper account of a value or an event that isn't in the problem space.

One important part of structuring a decision problem is identifying the relevant values and organizing them logically. Another is identifying and organizing the alternatives. In this chapter, we'll consider ways to put together a list of values. In the next, we'll consider ways to put together a list of alternatives. In the chapter after that, we'll see how to cross these lists to form a decision table. In the chapter after that, we'll return to problem structuring by thinking about sources of uncertainty, at which point we'll introduce decision trees.

It's generally better to begin by thinking about values before alternatives, because values are more general and open the mind to a greater range of possibilities, while at the same time focusing efficiently on just those possibilities that contribute to the values one cares about. This is value-focused search (Keeney, 1992). Thinking about alternatives isn't as likely to suggest alternatives that are widely different from the initial ones as is thinking about values. Trying to "build a better mousetrap" won't stimulate thinking that's as creative as will trying to "find a better way to get rid of mice", which could suggest, for example, something that would work more like a pied piper than a mouse trap—perhaps an ultrasonic tone or an odor that would attract mice out of the house or repel them from the house. Value-focused thinking also enables you to create alternatives that'll satisfy values that wouldn't have been satisfied by any of the original alternatives.

Value exploration can be worthwhile, even in the absence of a decision problem, as a way of discovering decision opportunities. I begin my personal decision making class with value exploration, because it not only helps those who've identified decision problems to work on their problems but also helps those who haven't yet identified decision problems think of some.

The term "value" is confusing to many. Values are positive or negative. Positive values are the attitudes we have about things we want, "good" things; negative values are the attitudes we have about things we want to avoid, "bad" things. An experiential definition of "value" might be "a positive or negative feeling." A more behavioral definition might be "a tendency to approach or avoid." These definitions are consistent, since, in general, we tend to approach things we feel positively about and avoid things we feel negatively about.

Being clear about one's values can make a big difference in life, as indicated by a study of Harvard alumni (McGarvey, 1989). Those respondents who had explicit life objectives were earning three times as much as those with no objectives, and those who'd written their objectives down were earning three times as much again.

In thinking about values, it's probably best to state them initially in a positive way (as goals) rather than in a negative way (as problems). Thinking about positive values gives participants a sense of hope, which contributes to openness and good process. Thinking about negative values, on the other hand, calls attention to external forces and reduces the sense of control and hope. Often, the difference is just one of language: "enhance cooperation" instead of "reduce competitiveness". Eventually, however, negative statements of the same values can be useful in providing additional stimulus variation. For example, "competition" brings a different set of ideas to mind than "cooperation", just as the "rainy" end of the weather variable is associated with different ideas than the "sunny" end.

In this chapter and the next, methods are presented for thinking creatively, efficiently, and critically about values and alternatives in structuring decision problems. The methods discussed in this chapter for thinking creatively about values are the stimulus-variation techniques of value checklists, analysis of alternatives and events, and value trees. The method for thinking efficiently about values is the heuristic of sub-goal analysis. The tool for thinking critically about values is a list of criteria for a well-structured value set.

Now's a good time to meet Amelia. Amelia will accompany us as we go through the book, and the steps she took in making an important decision will illustrate the application of many of the techniques that will be presented. Amelia is a real person (though with a different name), and the decision process described actually took place.

However, while the example is real, it's in one important respect not realistic: No one ever applies as many techniques to one decision as were applied to Amelia's. Though it's good to know a lot of techniques, since different decision problems sometimes have to be approached differently, no single decision problem requires as many as were applied, for the sake of illustration, in Amelia's case. It'd be a mistake, therefore, to let this aspect of the example intimidate you or make you feel inadequate.

I think you'll enjoy getting to know Amelia as we follow her through this important part of her interesting life.

> Amelia is a smallish person, with dark eyes and dark hair falling into a gentle flip. Intelligence and independence flash in her eyes and flow in her crisp English speech. Entering her middle years, she typically wears no makeup, only the earring marks in her naked ear lobes hinting that she might be a dynamite dresser when she has to be. Typically, she might be dressed in a navy blue cardigan, a white men's dress shirt, faded blue jeans, black shoes—and raspberry socks! She's traveled the world—Europe, America, Asia, and the Middle East. Yet she's managed her adventuresome youth in a way that's left her with a stable economic and family life.

Amelia's decision is a career decision. Her initial career decision, made when she was growing up in Chelsea, was to become a high school physical education teacher. Of the career paths that were open to English women at the time and that were encouraged by her family, teaching, she felt, gave her the best opportunity to pursue her dream of traveling to distant lands.

Some twenty years and many countries later, Amelia found herself teaching at a British multicultural high school in the Middle East, married to an airline pilot, with three children, living in very comfortable quarters provided by the government, with a maid, a house boy, and a driver.

In the summer of 1990, Amelia and her family set off on a five-week vacation to England, Ireland, and the United States. Knowing that they both had secure jobs in the Middle East and also had extensive savings there, she and her husband ran their credit cards to their limits. They had a wonderful time! Then, just before they were about to return home, Iraq invaded Kuwait and stationed troops right on the Saudi border. The Gulf War had begun!

Amelia and her husband could have gone back to the Middle East, but the prospect seemed far too risky. Instead, they decided to stay in the U. S. As a consequence, they lost their jobs, their savings, their furniture, and, except for what they had in two suitcases, their clothes. In addition, they owed a great deal of money on their credit cards and were faced with mortgage payments on a house in France that they'd recently purchased as an investment. Amelia couldn't get a job in the U. S. as a teacher, because her United Kingdom credentials weren't valid here, and her husband couldn't get a job as a pilot, because the airline industry was in a slump. Their life had suddenly been thrown into disarray!

As a temporary measure, Amelia waited tables. Once she and her husband had picked up the pieces and started to put their lives back together, Amelia began to see crisis as opportunity. She realized that she really didn't want to go back to teaching but wanted to find a career for herself that would be more deeply satisfying. Here was a chance to redo more thoughtfully a decision that she'd made so long ago. We'll follow the steps she took as she worked on this decision.

Amelia began thinking about her decision problem by thinking about the values she was looking for in a career. She thought of working with people, variety, mentally challenging work, being creative, and making a contribution to society.

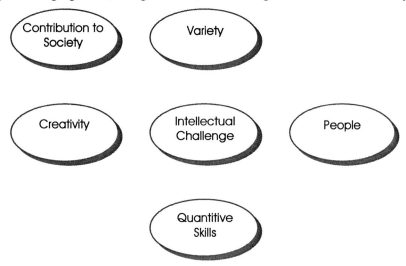

Amelia began with two stimulus variation techniques often used by executive placement services: writing your biography and thinking about people you admire. Since this was an important decision, she bought a ringbinder and started a small notebook. She began by thinking about her life story. Aware of the value of external memory, she started writing down the values she'd come up with.

She remembered a wonderful childhood. She was raised by her grand-parents, with her parents coming and going more as an aunt and uncle would. In retrospect, she recognized the arrangement as unusual, but at the time it'd seemed perfectly natural, and she recalled having been endlessly happy. Everyone doted on her. The values that were important here were not material, for her family hadn't had much money. What was important was Family. Surprisingly, she hadn't thought of values related to her family, though, in the end, they'd turn out to be the most relevant to her decision. She added Family to her list.

Her dad had joined the Royal Marines as a drummer boy at 12 and had traveled the world. Amelia remembered photos of Fijians with spears. Her dad had advised, "Don't get married. See the world." The value here was Travel.

She remembered how upsetting it'd been when her dad died relatively young and when her mum died later. Both were a great loss. The value was Family again.

As an additional stimulus-variation technique, Amelia thought about people she admired: Mya Angelou, Madeline Albright, Margaret Thatcher, Indira Ghandi, Winston Churchill, Hillary Clinton. What she admired most in these people was their persistence and determination to overcome great obstacles and their focus on big problems and unconcern about the little problems associated with convention and propriety. This returned her to her value of Contribution to Society. She also admired Winston Churchill's ability to get people to pull together, to help one another, to think of themselves as one big family. This suggested the value of Community, which she added to Rights to get Community/Rights.

Quite by accident, Amelia had an opportunity to make use of creative conversation.

As Amelia and I were talking over tea about her decision problem, I poured some more tea for each of us and then stepped out for a moment. When I returned, I posed her the problem, "If I wanted my tea to be as hot as possible when I got back, should I have added the cream to my tea before I left or after I returned?"

Her answer was, "After you returned, I suppose."

And my reply was, "Intuitively, that seems right, but I really would have been better off adding it before. Warm bodies radiate heat at a faster rate, the warmer they are. Adding the cream lowers the temperature by the same amount whether I add it before or after, but the tea will radiate less heat while I'm gone if it's at a lower temperature to begin with."

Amelia's response was, "Math is so important. One great regret I have is that I didn't study math more in high school. There are times when I think, 'If only you'd studied harder, Amelia!' I still hope to rectify it."

Here, creative conversation turned up the value Quantitative Skills. Other things being equal, career lines that enabled Amelia to improve her mathematical ability would be preferable to ones that did not.

With this start behind us, let's look at some other stimulus variation techniques useful for thinking of values.

Value Checklists, Analysis of Alternatives & Events, Value Trees

Value Checklists

Ad hoc "checklists", such as positive and negative experiences in your biography or a list of people you admire can be very helpful in bringing values to mind. Below, two formal checklists are provided for thinking specifically about values, a List of Values and a Decision Values Checklist.

The List of Values. A simplification of Maslow's Hierarchy of Needs (Maslow, 1970), this list is intended as a comprehensive list of human values. The needs at the bottom of are basic in that they're present at birth, common to all people, and initially, at least, stronger than those above them. Those at the top are presumed to appear only with maturity and only in those who aren't locked in a constant struggle for survival.

However, these theoretical distinctions, as interesting as they may be, aren't important to the use of the list as a stimulus to creative thought. In particular decisions, these values may take on *any* order of importance, depending on the impacts the alternatives have on each.

- *Cognitive/Aesthetic values* – Experiencing meaning and beauty in life

- *Social values* – Being loved and respected

- *Safety values* – Feeling secure

- *Physiological values* – Being free from hunger, thirst, pain, etc.

In using this list, expect that the values that apply to your decision problem won't be stated directly and that you'll have to do some force fitting before you'll be able to see the relevance of the items to your particular decision problem.

> In an attempt to add to her values, Amelia looked over Maslow's Hierarchy of Needs. Considering "physiological needs" and "safety needs", her first thought was that any job she'd consider seriously would satisfy those needs, so they wouldn't be relevant to her decision. However, force fitting "physiological needs" brought to mind the fact that her son has reading difficulties and that she's planning to go to graduate school to learn about teaching reading to children with special cognitive needs. She added Reading Research to her list of values. "Aesthetic needs" reminded her of a deep concern about Oregon's beauty being destroyed by cheap, ugly buildings. She added Environmental Aesthetics, which she saw as relating to both Nature and Architecture, to her list of values.

The Decision Values Checklist. This list was explicitly designed to bring to mind values that are important but commonly overlooked in decision making.

- Stakeholders,

- Positive and negative consequences,

- Present and future consequences,

- Tangible and intangible consequences, and

- Community values

We'll take these up one by one.

Stakeholders. A stakeholder is anyone who's affected by the decision. In thinking about stakeholders, be sure to consider those not immediately present. A list of stakeholders can serve, in turn, as a powerful checklist for generating values relevant to each stakeholder. A grade-school teacher resolved a conflict with a parent by bringing the child into the stakeholder analysis, saying, "We're all concerned about the best interests of Nancy." This freed the discussion from the associative box that contained only parent and teacher in opposition, the only ones immediately present. Stakeholders that are often overlooked, but that conflicting parties may care about, are those in future generations. One reference of term "big-hearted" would seem to be the number of stakeholders one takes into account. Sociopaths care only about themselves; most of us also care about our families and close friends; and many of us care about all of us. The point of this section is that we can fail to think about even stakeholders whom we care deeply about.

> Amelia looked at the Decision Values Checklist. "Stakeholders" immediately suggested her husband and three children. Up to this point, she hadn't associated her family's values with thoughts about her career. She'd thought about Family and what it meant to her, but she'd not thought to look at her job from their perspectives. As important as her husband and children are to her, it required stimulus variation to bring them to mind in this context.
>
> She added Husband, Girls, and Boy to her list of values. She listed their boy separately from their girls because of his special needs.
>
> She then asked herself what values each of the stakeholders would care about. She felt that her husband's only concern would be how much money she'd be making, since he was about to retire, and also how much the job would take her away from him. The children would care only about her time. She added Money and Time to her values.

Positive and negative consequences. As goal-oriented creatures, we tend to focus on the positive consequences of our actions. We think about intended consequences, not unintended ones. Because we tend to overlook negative consequences, we often need to be reminded of them. One such case is that of a man who completed a Ph. D. in astronomy before it occurred to him that he was committing a good part of his life to the night shift! Another is the case of the law student who was thinking in terms of the upper end of the income distribution of lawyers, until he found himself in the most probable region of that distribution.

> To Amelia, "negative consequences" suggested being poor, not having enough money. When she asked herself what she needed money for, it was for travel, back to England and elsewhere. The children needed to travel, too, since they considered themselves as much English as American. Money was already on the list.
>
> "Negative consequences" also suggested going against her moral standards, which she'd no intention of doing. She added Moral Values.

Present and future consequences. A pernicious failing in human thought is the undervaluing or outright neglect of long-term consequences. A story of a tattooed tear symbolizes this failing well. A woman had had a tear tattooed below her left eye when she was a teen-ager, never thinking at the time how she might feel about that tattoo later in life. As it turned out, she hated it, and for the rest of her life would pay for that brief period of reckless pleasure. What more appropriate symbol for failing to consider future consequences than an indelibly tattooed tear? Urging us in the right direction is an old Chinese saying that the beginning of wisdom is when you plant a tree under whose shade you know you'll never live long enough to sit. A Native American dictum, that's, happily, becoming quite widely known, pushes us even further: Consider the effects of your actions on the seventh generation.

Often conflicting parties, though divided about the present, have a common interest in the future. Jimmy Carter created movement toward the Sinai accord (where the Sinai Peninsula was left in Egypt's hands but without Egyptian troops being stationed there) by passing around family pictures with Begin and Sadat and asking what kind of world the three of them wanted to leave for their children (Fisher & Ury, 1981). In a single stroke, this brought both the future and some important stakeholders into the problem space. Even bright people who've already given a great deal of thought to a problem can benefit from stimulus variation.

> To Amelia, "future consequences" suggested continuing challenge in her career and, eventually, a position of leadership. Future consequences for the children would be going to a good university, something that hadn't occurred to her when thinking about values for the children at their current ages. She added Leadership and Education to her list.

Tangible and intangible consequences. Tangible consequences are easy to think about. By "tangible", we mean touchable, seeable, hearable, etc. These are the consequences that tend to dominate our thinking. It's the intangible consequences that we're inclined to overlook, especially the way implementing an alternative might affect how we feel about ourselves and others feel about us or how others feel about themselves.

A man who was looking for a reliable, safe, attractively designed car at a reasonable price purchased a used Mercedes 240D for $3500. He'd thought about these tangible considerations, but not about how he'd feel about himself, or how others would feel about him, as a "Mercedes owner". He'd always regarded himself as an egalitarian, and his friends had likewise thought of him in this way. So, initially, he felt a little embarrassed to be driving a car with the symbolic value of a Mercedes, and his friends were surprised that he'd own such a car. (Few guessed that it had cost so little.) Though the considerations turned out, on balance, to favor the purchase and didn't incline him to regret his decision, he was surprised to discover that he'd overlooked a whole class of important considerations. The fact that he often mentioned the low price of the car and referred to it as his "economy car" (an example of an appropriate use of the bolstering defense mechanism to maintain commitment to a rationally chosen alternative) suggests that these considerations continued to produce cognitive conflict.

Research on happiness (Myers, 1992) reveals that the best predictor of general life satisfaction is not satisfaction with material possessions but satisfaction with oneself. As Ghandi urged: "You must be the change you want to see in the world." When we become what we value, we value ourselves and are happier.

People who are confident that they're in control of their lives, are making a contribution, and are pleasant to be around tend to be happier. Such people have better health, are less likely to use drugs, tolerate frustration better, and are less conforming. For work to contribute to happiness, it's apparently essential that it be challenging enough to absorb our attention (Czikzhentmihalyi, 1990). What we do should be within our limits yet pushing them. The more we put into life, the more we get out of it. A less expensive activity demands less of others (for example, the manufacturer) and more of us, thus enabling us to exercise our abilities and to feel good about ourselves, rather than about someone else.

Identifying such intangible values often requires being sensitive to your emotional reactions and thinking about them. As Janis & Mann put it (1982, p. 68):

> *Fleeting twinges of emotion may be experienced while the decision maker is writing down specific entries. These affective signals can function as goads to an internal information search, which may bring into the decision maker's consciousness a concrete image of enjoying a specific gratification or suffering a specific deprivation, which he or she can then begin to evaluate objectively. Even when the undifferentiated feelings...can not be pinned down in any way, the decision maker can at least acknowledge having those feelings and take them into account as significant items of self-knowledge.*

Amelia asked herself, "What kind of work would I be most proud to be associated with? What kind would I be least proud to be associated with?:"

She'd be most proud to be involved in research and in human rights. What would make her proud to be a researcher is the ability required to do research. This suggested the value Challenge. What would make her proud to be working on human rights would be the effect she'd have on human lives. This suggested again Contribution to Society.

She'd be least proud to be involved in working for a government agency, enforcing regulations. When she asked herself, "Why?" the answer was that enforcement agencies tend to be so rigid. She remembered that immigration officials had been reluctant to give her and her husband work permits. She felt that it was inconsistent to be afraid of foreigners becoming a burden on social services and, at the same time, be reluctant to give them work permits—if they couldn't work, they'd surely become a burden on social services! She felt that her distaste for rigidity was taken care of by the Creativity value she'd identified earlier.

She'd also be least proud to be involved in clinical work. Why? Doing clinical work with adults, she felt, would be a waste of time, because she'd be dealing with poor problem solvers and, thus, not likely to accomplish much. She added Effectiveness as a value. Doing clinical work with children would be too emotionally involving. She added Emotional Involvement.

Community Values. Community values include pride in being a member of a group, organization, or society that's intelligently and efficiently run; takes care of its children, its elderly, its sick, and its poor; preserves its environment; fosters education and the arts; plans wisely for its future; and has a shared sense of identity. The community, as will be argued later, is more than the sum of its individual members. Failure to take the perspective of the community into account can result in what will later be discussed as "tragedies of the commons". Identification with community values promotes cooperation and can protect us against tragedies of the commons (Dawes, van de Kragt, & Orbell, 1988).

Community values takes us to the topic of ethical decision making. A checklist of values (National Commission for the Protection of Human Subjects of Biomedical and Behavioral Research, 1978; Beauchamp & Childress, 1989) that has been found very helpful in medical ethics is:

- Beneficence

- Autonomy

- Justice

Beneficence refers to the beneficial (or harmful) effects on the patient's health. Autonomy refers to the patient's freedom to choose. Justice refers to fairness in the distribution of benefits and costs through the population. This checklist should be helpful for a broad range of ethical decisions.

Analysis of Alternatives

If you already have some alternatives in mind, as is often the case when you begin thinking seriously about a decision problem, there are a number of ways you can use these alternatives as stepping stones to values.

- *Rank order the alternatives.* Ask yourself which alternative you like best, and then ask yourself what it is about this alternative that you like. These will be values. Next, ask yourself which alternative you like least and what it is about this alternative that you don't like. These, too, will be values, though negative ones. The idea is to begin with an intuitive ranking and then use this to get to an analytic identification of positive or negative features.

- *Consider pros and cons of each alternative.* For each alternative, ask yourself what is its best feature and what is its worst feature. These will be values.

    Since she was starting to come up with the same values again and again, Amelia felt it was time to take a different tack. She thought she'd try thinking about the pros and cons of alternatives. In order to learn more about specific realistic alternatives working in various programs relating to children, she arranged an informational interview with a person who'd founded a local college program in the administration of non-profit organizations and who'd later administered a large child-and-family-services organization. After an intensive hour, she came away with the following list of career areas and a generous list of names and phone numbers to call for further interviews.

- Research

- Enforcement (government agencies)

- Fund-raising/PR

- Administrative (clinically trained)

- Clinical

- Sub-clinical (various forms of day care)

Working with this new set of alternatives, she asked, for each alternative, what its most positive feature was and what its most negative feature was. The most negative feature of research was the time and frustration involved, and the most negative feature of administration was not seeing what's going on. Together, these suggested Tangible Results as a value. She wanted to see the results of her efforts.

Another negative feature of administration was that she'd spend her life sitting in an office all dressed up and keeping regular hours. This was not her cup of tea. This suggested the value Work Culture.

In thinking about it, she realized that she'd rather stay home than be involved in Enforcement, Administration, or Sub-clinical. They'd all be boring. So she screened these out of her list.

In grouping the remaining alternatives, Amelia saw a contrast between Research, on the one hand, and both Fund-Raising and Public Relations, on the other. Research is more closely linked to academic knowledge, which she values. This suggested the value Academic Knowledge. (We'll return to this grouping later.)

Analysis of Events

The outcomes of our decisions are usually not certain but depend to some extent on external events, or what we sometimes call "luck". Thinking about optimistic and pessimistic scenarios is another good way to identify values. (A scenario is a set of events: the timing belt breaks, *and* I'm on a country road, *and* I don't have my cell phone.)

- *Contrast optimistic ("best case") and pessimistic ("worst case") scenarios.* What if everything went wrong? What if everything "went right"? Consider the most optimistic and pessimistic future scenarios you can imagine relevant to your decision problem. What is it that you like and don't like about these scenarios? These differences will be values.

Royal Dutch/Shell got through the last "oil crunch" more successfully than other companies by employing scenario analysis (Schoemaker, 1993). Thinking about concrete, detailed descriptions of fundamentally different futures opened decision makers' minds to possibilities they'd otherwise not have entertained.

Value Trees

Drawing a diagram achieves stimulus variation by changing to a visual mode what may have been thought about in a verbal mode or changing to a single visual representation what may have been thought about in terms of separate visual representations. The effect of representing a problem in graphic terms can be quite powerful. "One good picture," the Chinese proverb tells us, "is worth a thousand words."

We'll make use of three kinds of diagrams in this book: the decision table, the decision tree, and the value tree. We begin with the value tree. All of these diagrams function as both stimulus variation techniques and organizing tools. Almost inevitably, decision makers think differently about decision problems when they're diagrammed. A tree, whether a value tree or a decision tree, is simply a list of lists.

The classic example of a tree structure is the biological classification system, shown on the next page. The distinction flowering/non-flowering applies only to plants and not to animals. We say that this distinction is a "sub-classification" of plants, since it doesn't "cross" the plants/animal distinction. Similarly, the vertebrate-invertebrate distinction is a sub-classification of animals. Values usually have a sub-classification, or tree, structure, also.

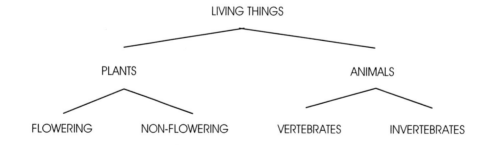

A useful technique for starting to create a tree structure is clustering (Rico, 1977). In clustering, we write each idea on a piece of paper or a Post-It: SELF-ACTUALIZATION, FAMILY, SAFETY, FRIENDS, and HEALTH. Next, we move the pieces of paper around until we've grouped similar ideas together. Next, we label each group with the higher-level value that holds it together. HEALTH, SAFETY, and SELF-ACTUALIZATION can be grouped together and labeled "SELF", and FAMILY and FRIENDS can be grouped together and labeled "OTHERS". Next, we see whether we can group these groups into still larger groups (*moving up the tree*). SELF and OTHERS group into OVERALL VALUE. We also see if we can divide them into still smaller sub-groups (*moving down the tree*). SELF-ACTUALIZATION can be divided into WORK and RECREATION. Another way to add new ideas to a tree is to ask ourselves, for each level in the tree, whether we can think of any additional items at that level (*moving across the tree*). In addition to FAMILY and FRIENDS, we can add SOCIETY. In these ways, a value tree can serve as a powerful tool for thinking creatively about new values.

We can display all of this in terms of the following graphic representation. The bold-faced, italicized terms represent basic values that weren't among the ones we initially wrote down but were brought to mind as we sought to fill out the tree.

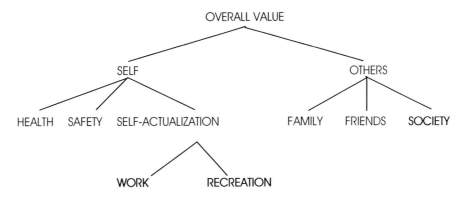

Two mistakes commonly made in creating value trees show up as clearly identifiable visual patterns. It's important to be able to spot them. One is the following:

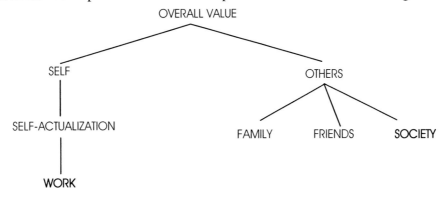

Notice that the path on the left is *unbranched.* Any node that doesn't branch into multiple paths but has only one path coming out of it isn't necessarily wrong but should be a warning sign. Nodes represent categories, and categories typically have multiple members. One of the reasons for creating a value tree is to help you think of additional members of categories. An unbranched path indicates a failure in this respect. This would be like having Plants lead only to Flowering and Animals lead only to Vertebrates. An unbranched path suggests rather strongly that you have more thinking to do.

Another common mistake in creating value trees is illustrated by the following pattern:

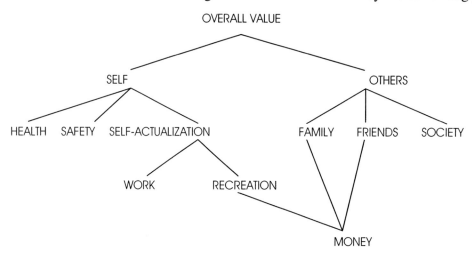

Notice that the paths *converge*—on MONEY, in this case. In a classification tree, branches can only diverge. (Think of a tree in your garden. The branches always split out; they never come together.) Since values take a tree structure, convergence is a clear indication of the presence of something that's not a value. Almost always, what the paths converge on is a *means,* rather than an *end,* or value. In the example, money is seen as a means to greater Recreation, Family, and Society values. Because means can serve many values, it's quite possible for paths to converge on means.

Money has no value, in itself, but derives its value entirely from what can be purchased with it. As such, it has no place in a value tree. Similarly, time is a means, rather than an end value, and derives its value entirely from how it's used.

What should be done with means, like money and time? There are two possibilities. One is to leave them out and have a pure value tree. Often, however, we want to make sure we don't lose sight of important means and want to represent them in some way. In that case, the other possibility is to leave them in but indicate in some clear way that they are means, rather than ends (Keeney, 1992). This has been done below::

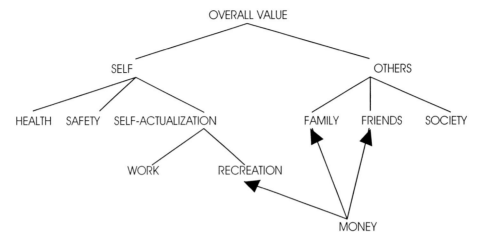

To make clear that Money is not a value, it has been italicized, and its connections to other nodes have been indicated by lines with arrowheads that specify causal direction. The significance of means is in their causal relationships to one another and to values. They're best thought of as being part of an *influence network,* rather than a value tree (Keeney, 1992). The lines in a value tree represent membership in categories, rather than predictive or causal relationships. The line between Work and Self-Actualization, for example, indicates merely that Work is an aspect of Self-Actualization. What we have above, then, is a simple influence network connected to a value tree. Though this influence network has only one node; others could be added, including nodes related to decision alternatives.

> Amelia's value tree is shown on the next page. There are 27 values, in all. Before she'd started using the stimulus-variation techniques, she'd thought of only 5. Of course, she'd eventually have thought of more on her own, but probably nothing close to 27. The shaded nodes represent the values she eventually selected as most relevant to her decision.

In addition to helping us think creatively about values, value trees get us started thinking critically about values by organizing them in a logical manner. As we've seen, they can help us spot means that have gotten mixed up with end values, and they can also help keep us from counting the same value twice under different labels, a common error.

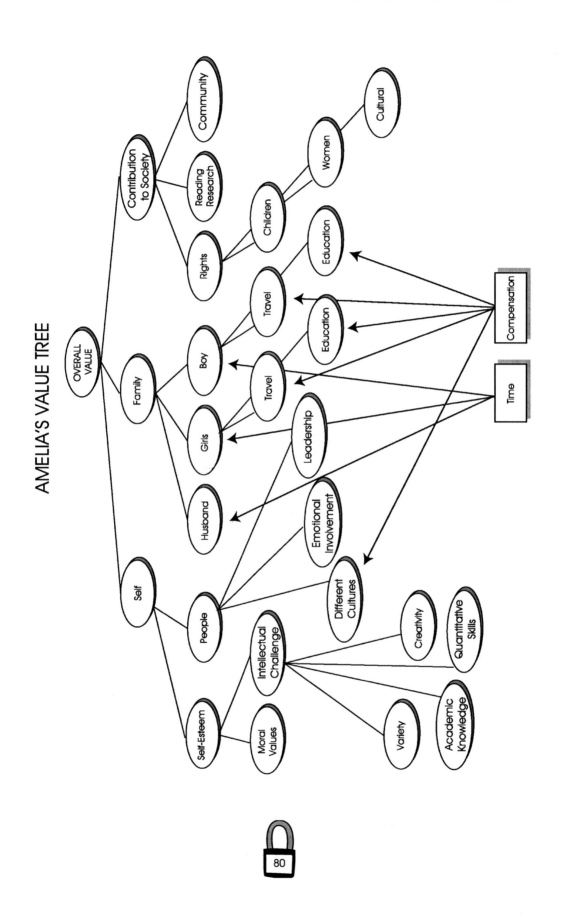

AMELIA'S VALUE TREE

Subgoal Analysis

It can be helpful to think about sub-goals when the goal, itself, is too far off to be able to think about usefully. The sub-goal in the safe-cracking example was the number of tumblers that had fallen into place. The sub-goals in chess were various measures of one's position.

Chess, for example, is sufficiently complex that it would be futile to start planning checkmate positions at the beginning of the game. Even master players think only a few moves ahead. And even moderately good chess players set themselves a variety of sub-goals, for example to capture as many enemy pieces as possible and to move their own pieces so that they attack as many squares as possible. Though achieving sub-goals doesn't guarantee a win, it does make one more likely.

In making major life decisions, as in playing chess, we can't always consider the effects of alternative courses of action on distant goals. Often, the only practical possibility is to consider the effects on sub-goals, such as getting a degree, getting a job, or getting married. Perhaps the most broadly useful sub-goals for this purpose are wealth, time, knowledge, skills, and social contacts. Increasing our wealth, time, knowledge, skills, and social contacts, while not guaranteeing a good life, does make one considerably more likely. Technically, these sub-goals are means and are being used as what are called "proxy values".

In striving to achieve sub-goals, we should never lose sight of the ultimate goals from which they derive their value. Otherwise, we may find ourselves working toward an empty subgoal or ignoring a more direct path to the goal. In a cartoon on my office door, Hagar is asked,

"Do you want power—or gold—or to be truly contented?"

Hagar's answer:

"POWER! Then I'd be able to get the gold...then I'd be contented."

Hagar, forgetting that power is only a means to gold and gold only a means to contentment, chooses the means in preference to its end. We often do likewise, getting so focused on achieving wealth, time, knowledge, skills, and social contacts that we bypass happiness altogether.

To find out whether something you want is a means or an end, ask yourself why you want it. If, like sailing or making love, you want it for its own sake, it's a value. If, like taking a bus or saving money, you want it for where or what it'll get you, it's a means. "Why?" questions move you up from the influence network into the value tree. Of course, some things, like acquiring knowledge and meeting people, can be both means and ends.

To be most efficient, stimulus variation may be better focused on sub-goals, rather than on end values, or at least some sub-goals may have to be included among end values. They should be represented in both the influence network and the value tree.

Consider subgoals, such as income, knowledge, skills, and social contacts.

In Amelia's value tree, Time with Family and Compensation are, of course subgoals, since they're not end values but means to end values.

Aside from their value in increasing efficiency of search, subgoals, since they're easier to achieve than goals, should promote hope and thereby reduce defensive avoidance. If you find yourself avoiding a difficult task, it can help to think in terms of subgoals. Instead of trying to find time to "write a paper"; try to find time to do an outline. Instead of trying to find time to "make a decision"; try to find time to list alternatives. Instead of defining your decision as "deciding on a career", define it as deciding on some courses you might take, or some experiences you might get, that will move you in the direction of a career.

Criteria for a Well-Structured Value Set

Not just any list of values will be appropriate for decision making. Value sets can be well structured or poorly structured. To be properly structured, a value set should satisfy the following criteria:

- Completeness

- Relevance

- Non-Redundancy

- Testability/Measurability

- Meaningfulness

- Value Independence

If you have created a value tree, it's important to be clear that the set of criteria we'll be considering here is not intended to apply to the entire tree. It's intended to apply only to the values (and sub-goals) that you've selected to include in your decision table and upon which your decision will be based.

Completeness

Completeness requires that all important values be included. A decision isn't likely to "stick" if important values are overlooked. it's likely to be a "pseudo-decision" (Tyler, 1969). The Bureau of Reclamation, in one of the most costly mistakes in its history, created plans for an Orme Dam that were never implemented (Brown, 1986). The reason was that such values as impacts on Native Americans and bald eagles weren't fully taken into account. A later plan that was based on a more complete value set has now been successfully implemented.

As we've noted, the values most commonly overlooked are those that relate to consequences to others, those that relate to negative consequences, those that relate to long-term consequences, and those that relate to the ways we and others think about ourselves. Stimulus-variation techniques can be used to bring such values to mind and ensure completeness.

It can help to apply the following test for completeness:

To test for completeness,

- Pick the alternative you would intuitively rank highest;

- Pick the alternative you would intuitively rank lowest;

- Assume that these alternatives are identical with respect to all the values you have identified so far; then

- Ask yourself whether you would still have any preference or would be willing to toss a coin to decide.

If the answer is, "I would care, and I would not want to toss a coin", the follow-up question is, "Then what difference would the choice make?" This difference should call attention to additional values. If, instead, the answer to the first question is, "I wouldn't care, and I'd just as soon toss a coin", the value set passes this test for completeness. The test for defensive avoidance is also appropriate here: "Would I be willing to commit to and actually follow through on whichever of the alternatives the analysis indicates is the best?" Questioning any reluctance here can bring additional values to mind, including ones that are being avoided.

Consider a hypothetical example. You're comparing cars in terms of Cost, Safety, Reliability, and Aesthetics, which you've determined are the important values. You then ask yourself, "If two cars were identical in cost, safety, reliability, and aesthetics, would I be willing to let someone else choose?" If your answer is, "No, I'd want to know how much their trunks hold", you've discovered an additional value. In this case, you may decide that this value isn't important enough to add to your value set, but the technique worked just the same, and you can keep this value in mind in case you need it later to break a tie.

> Amelia selected from her value tree the following set of values as the most relevant to her decision: Contribution to Society, Creativity/Intellectual Challenge, Cultural Diversity, Compensation, Time for Family, Emotional Involvement, and Work Culture. (Notice that Compensation isn't an ultimate value but a means, proxy value, or sub-goal.)

> Amelia tested her value set for completeness by (a) considering the possibility that some variant of Enforcement, her intuitively lowest-ranked alternative, turned out to be superior to all the others in terms of the values she'd selected and (b) asking herself whether she'd then be willing to toss a coin. This question slowed her down; she felt resistance; she realized she wouldn't. When she asked herself why,

her answer was, "If I worked in Enforcement, I wouldn't be in control." Thinking about it, however, she realized that this was Creativity again, and this had been taken into account. When thinking intuitively about the completeness question, she'd been unable to take into account the entire value set that she was easily able to take into account analytically. On reconsideration, understanding now that Creativity had been taken into account, she felt that she'd be willing to toss a coin, and so her value set really did appear to be complete, after all. She didn't need to add any more values. However, in thinking about income, she realized that she'd left out benefits, so she changed Income to Compensation, to take account of both salary and benefits.

Relevance

Relevance requires that no unimportant values be included. An unimportant value is one that is impacted to about the same extent by all alternatives and, hence, of little relevance to a choice among them. Focusing first on only the most relevant aspects of a problem implements the breadth-first search strategy.

In applying breadth-first search to decision making, you first consider a broad range of alternatives taking into account only their most important, or decision-relevant, characteristics. This is what a good artist does in exploring a variety of possibilities with rough sketches, what a good writer does in exploring a variety of possibilities with rough outlines, and what a good chess player does in focusing first on the big pieces, the kings, queens, bishops, knights, and rooks. Later, the most promising alternatives are considered in depth. This is also what we do in creating models and maps, which simplify reality in terms of its most decision-relevant features.

The "20-80 rule" of management science asserts, as a rule of thumb, that 20% of the facts account for 80% of what you care about. These are the "vital few" among the "trivial many" (MacKenzie, 1972, pp. 51ff). Focusing on the vital few is the most efficient way to approach a problem.

If we're to adhere to the principle of breadth-first search in problem formulation, the number of values must be kept to a minimum. A rule of thumb is that usually no more than five to seven values are required for completeness; often, two or three are enough. If alternatives are tied or nearly tied on the basis of just the most important values, less important values can always be brought in later to break the tie. If you already have five to seven values, you should be applying the following relevance test:

How likely is it that information about additional values will change my mind about any decision based on the values already in my set?

Where the completeness test encourages you to add values, the relevance test encourages you to remove them. You should retain a value only if its relevance or importance is substantial in comparison with that of all the other values in the set. A good rough definition for "substantial" is an importance weight (see later) of at least .10.

Sunk costs is a classic example of a value that's entirely irrelevant. As noted in discussing irrationality, we're inclined to stick with an alternative that we've already invested a great deal in, to "throw good money after bad". We tend to think of the sunk cost as applying only to the alternative in which it has been invested. However, the amount invested in any alternative will be "just as gone", no matter which alternative is selected. No matter what you do, you aren't going to get it back.

Let's say that you're planning to buy a piece of land, Parcel A, for $120,000 and that you've given the seller a non-refundable deposit of $2000. You then learn about a comparable piece of land, Parcel B, which is selling for only $117,000. If it weren't for the deposit, you'd purchase Parcel B; however, the possibility of losing the $2000 and getting absolutely nothing for it inclines you toward Parcel A.

	Past Payments	Future Payments	TOTAL PAYMENTS
Parcel A	$2000	$118,000	$120,000
Parcel B	$2000	$117,000	$119,000

However, the $2000 is gone, no matter which parcel you purchase. That's why it's entered in both rows of the table. Past costs are "sunk costs", "water over the dam", or "spilt milk" and shouldn't influence your decision. Only future prospects are relevant to your decision. While the purchaser would have to pay out $118,000, over and above the $2000 that has already been paid, to secure Parcel A, she'd have to pay out only $117,000 to secure Parcel B. If she purchases Parcel B, she'll be $1000 richer than if she'd purchased Parcel A—though she'll have to admit that the initial $2000 was invested in the wrong property. (This admission should be easier—even a source of pride—if she focuses on process and reminds herself that she's managing to resist a seductive decision trap that has led many less able decision makers astray.)

> Amelia considered each of her values and asked herself whether the differences from alternative to alternative were substantial or negligible. All seemed to be substantial, so she didn't drop any She kept relevance in mind, however, in case any alternatives were eliminated along the way, since eliminating alternatives can render once-relevant values irrelevant for deciding among the alternatives that remain.

Testability/Measurability

Testability is the requirement that the valued outcome be describable in objective terms, so that the facts for your decision could be provided *by someone else*. Measurability sets as an ideal the higher standard that each value be not only testable but also quantifiable. The experience of science has shown that numbers provide the most powerful language for expressing facts, and the discussion of value judgments will show that numbers, when they're meaningful, can also provide the most powerful language for expressing values. Although the goal of measurability can't always be achieved, it usually can, and, in any case, it's always a goal worth striving for. Testability, the less stringent criterion, can always be achieved.

The following question is a good check for testability:

Could someone else fill in your fact table for you?

A good test for measurability is to ask yourself what *units* you're using to measure each attribute: dollars, days, number of people, and so forth. A good practice is to specify as part of your labels for values the units of measurement employed.

There are three good reasons for insisting on testability. First, as we saw in the last chapter, it's a safeguard against irrationality. Second, it's a way of getting clear in your own mind just what you mean. (For example, does "income" mean gross income or profit? Before or after taxes?) Third, it makes it easier to get information from someone or someplace else to improve your decision.

Measurability can clarify our thoughts, even in cases where we never get around to doing any arithmetic with the numbers. Dale was deliberating about whether to accept an attractive job offer in California. After some problem structuring, he saw that the principal argument in favor of accepting the offer was the opportunity for personal growth and that the principal argument against accepting it was that he'd have to live farther from his son (who lived with his ex-wife) and would thus become less a part of his son's life.

To prepare him for thinking about the tradeoff between personal growth and involvement in his son's life, I sought a measure for involvement in his son's life. I suggested two: Number of Days with His Son Per Year, and Number of Days Between Visits. Dale saw Number of Days Between Visits as clearly the more meaningful measure, since it didn't take long for him and his son to get out of touch with one another's lives, but it also didn't take long to get back in touch.

I then asked him what'd be the likely number of days between visits if he accepted the job offer, what was the longest time between visits he and his son had already experienced, and what that experience had been like. That did it! The longest number of days between visits that Dale and his son had experienced was only about half what the average number of days between visits would be if he took the job in California—and that had added a strain to their relationship that he wouldn't want to repeat. Without any further analysis, Dale decided to reject the job offer. The rest of the meeting was devoted to exploring ways he might enhance his personal growth without leaving the area.

Quantification, after some preliminary problem structuring, helped Dale see his problem so clearly that he was able to make a choice without performing any calculations. In the medical specialty example that opened the book, quantitative questions had the same effect.

Dollars, hours, number of people, and years are useful measures for quantifying a wide range of values. In choosing among jobs, for example, salary is easy to quantify in dollars. Leisure time can be quantified in terms of hours per week. The responsibility associated with a job might be quantified in terms of number of people supervised. Interesting co-workers might be quantified in terms of hours spent in interactions with co-workers with certain interests or who have college degrees. Opportunity for advancement might be quantified in terms of the average number of years it takes people with your qualifications to reach some specified level. In addition to dollars, hours, number of people, and years, measures of distance and area are also frequently useful for quantifying values.

Certainly, there are cases where quantification makes little sense, for example, color and style of cars, designs of houses, and types of work performed in various occupations. In such cases, where the differences are stubbornly qualitative, we must settle for verbal descriptions of the situations that give rise to positive or negative feelings. However, these descriptions should satisfy testability, in that anyone, regardless of his or her values, could determine whether a particular description is or isn't true of a particular alternative. "Fire engine red" and "cardinal" are testable descriptions, but "a bright red" is less so, and "an attractive red" even less so.

Often values such as job satisfaction or sense of self worth seem, at first glance, to be not only unmeasurable but altogether untestable. Let's look at "self worth", as a particularly difficult example. The key is to think of concrete situations in which the alternatives would result in different levels of a feeling of self worth. For example, what may give you a feeling of self worth on the job is people coming to you to seek your opinion on matters on which you feel you have expertise. Next, try to describe these situations objectively. Let's say that you work in a large architectural firm and that your area of expertise is fire safety. You could then define an objective measure that would be related to your sense of self-worth on the job, such as "the average number of times a week that people would come to you to ask questions about fire safety" or "the percentage of major decisions regarding fire safety on which you would be consulted." In principle, these are measures on which someone else could obtain data, and so they are testable. They happen also to be measurable. Surprisingly often, a value that initially seems inherently untestable will turn out, after some hard thought, to be not only testable but also measurable.

The table below shows the objective descriptions and measures that Amelia came up with for her values.

Value	Objective Description/Measure
Contribution to Society	Number of people/year affected Duration of impact
Creativity/Intellectual Challenge	Percentage of time engaged in activities she has planned
Cultural Diversity	Percentage of time working with people from other cultures
Compensation (Family)	Dollar value of annual salary plus benefits
Time for Family	Days/week with family
Emotional Involvement	Days/week working one-on-one with children with emotional problems
Work Culture	Percentage of time free from a fixed schedule, location, and dress code

Meaningfulness

Meaningfulness requires that each value be stated in terms that are understandable to the decision maker or decision makers and truly expressive of the value in question. To be meaningful, terms should be in plain language and within the experience of the decision maker. In Dale's decision, Number of Days Between Visits was more meaningful than Number of Visit Days Per Year, because it was more closely related to what Dale really cared about. Similarly, a color patch or a photograph provides a more meaningful description of a color than numerical specification in terms of the international CIE Color System.

As another example, the amount of money you earn on a job can be expressed in terms of the number of dollars you earn each hour, the number of dollars you earn each month, or the number of dollars you earn each year. Dollars/hour, dollars/month, and dollars/year are all equally relevant, and they're equally testable and measurable. However, dollars/hour may be more meaningful to a laborer, dollars/year may be more meaningful to a professional, and dollars/month may be easier to relate to your expenses, many of which come due each month. If a professor at another university told me how many dollars an hour he made, I wouldn't likely know, without some mental calculation, whether I'd be pleased or displeased with that salary. While dollars/hour, dollars/ month, and dollars/year are all meaningful, in the sense that you know what the words mean, they're not likely to be equally meaningful, in the sense that you can make equally valid value judgments about them.

Together, testability and meaningfulness assure verbal and numerical specifications of valued outcomes that provide a sound interface between the facts (testability) and values (meaningfulness) in a decision problem.

Non-Redundancy

Non-redundancy requires that no value be represented more than once. Redundancy not only makes the decision table unnecessarily complicated, it also attaches undue importance to any value that's repeated and, hence, works against a judicious, balanced evaluation.

No one is likely to repeat the same value with the same name, but it's common for redundancy to enter into a value set in various subtle ways. For example, income and life style would be redundant values for a job decision, unless "life style" were carefully defined so as to exclude those aspects of life style that depend on income.

Not only double-counting, but triple-counting, entered into a watershed management decision! Quality of Watershed, Quality of Reach, and such more specific measures as Stream Flow are all redundant. The stream flow in a particular reach is one measure of the quality of that reach, and the quality of the reach is one measure of the quality of the watershed that contains it.

A good way to avoid redundancy, as we've seen, is to construct a value tree. In the watershed example, a value tree would have clearly shown that Quality of Watershed, Quality of Reach, and Stream Flow occur at three different levels. One way to avoid redundancy in decisions that affect multiple parties is to organize values in terms of the stakeholders they relate to. Both analyses put values into non-overlapping categories. As noted earlier, a value tree helps satisfy several of the criteria for a value set. By providing a different way of thinking about values, it stimulates creative thought and thus contributes to completeness. By clarifying the relationships among various values, it contributes to non-redundancy. And, as one proceeds down the tree, values tend to become more testable and more meaningful.

Amelia looked over her value tree for indications of redundancy: (a) values that connect in a set-subset relationship and, thus, partially overlap, or (b) means that connect to values that have already been taken into account.

The Time and Compensation means served largely Family values, and these hadn't been taken into account elsewhere, so that was no problem. However, Compensation also served Different Cultures, which had been taken into account. She'd have to be careful when evaluating Compensation to consider only the effects on her family. Any effects of Compensation on her value of Different Cultures she'd have to think about when evaluating Different Cultures. As a reminder, she changed Compensation to Compensation (Family).

Amelia had given some thought to counting Creativity and Intellectual Challenge as separate values. However, although dictionary definitions might distinguish these as separate concepts, she suspected that she was using them interchangeably. To help herself think more clearly about this issue, she gave the alternatives plus/zero/minus ratings on both Creativity and Intellectual Challenge and found that these ratings didn't differ from one another for any of the alternatives. This doesn't mean that Creativity and Intellectual Challenge are necessarily the same, of course, but it was enough to convince her that she was using these concepts pretty much as synonyms. She collapsed them into a single variable and called it Creativity/Intellectual Challenge.

Another problem was Tangible Results, Effectiveness, and Contribution to Society. Tangible Results came up when Amelia was thinking about Administration and saw herself sitting in an office not knowing what was going on in the world outside. This could be a problem with research, also. In either case, she might never see the smiles that resulted from her work. On reflection, however, she realized that what she really cared about was whether she'd be making a difference, not whether she'd see the difference, herself. So she dropped Tangible Results and stayed with Contribution to Society. She renamed it Contribution to Society/Results, however, to make clear that she's concerned about results, whether tangible or not.

Effectiveness simply meant effectiveness in making a Contribution to Society, and Contribution to Society had already taken it into account.

Value Independence

The most difficult of the criteria to understand is value independence. The reason for the difficulty is that thinking about value independence requires us to keep several things in mind at once.

> Value A is independent of Value B if and only if you can make value judgments about A without knowing about B.

You'll have to read this over several times—slowly—and then come back to it after having finished the following discussion.

If your answer to a question as to how much you'd value some change is, "It depends", then you may have a problem with value independence. For example, Nancy might place a positive value on spending Saturday evening with George, and she might also place a positive value on spending Saturday evening with Ron. However, if we try to surprise her by arranging for her to spend Saturday night with both George and Ron, the surprise might not be so pleasant! The value of George's presence may very well depend on whether Ron is present or absent, and vice versa. If so, these values aren't independent.

As another example, the value of highway gas mileage probably doesn't depend on the color of the car or on whether the car has a CD player, but the value of number of air bags probably does depend on braking distance. The longer the braking distance, the greater the value of the air bags (because you'll be more likely to crash into something and need them). Similarly, the value of ease of getting parts depends on the value of reliability; the lower the reliability and the more often you need parts, the greater is the importance of ease of getting them. We hope for values to be independent, for then we can benefit fully from decomposition, first thinking about one value and then thinking about the other. When values aren't independent, we have to think about them both at the same time.

Three quite general cases of failure of value independence are worth mentioning explicitly. One is *quality of a state and duration of that state.* For example, the value of extending a particular health state from, say, one to ten years, depends strongly on the quality of that state. If the state is positive (for example, the removal of a headache), the value of increasing the duration of the pain-free state is positive. If the state is negative (for example, the introduction of discomfort associated with a medical treatment), the value of increasing the duration of the painful state is negative.

Another quite general case of failure of value independence is the *quality of a state and the probability of that state*. If a state is positive, increasing its probability is to be desired; if a state is negative, increasing its probability is to be avoided.

A third general case of failure of value independence involves notions of *fairness* in social situations. For most of us, the positive value we attach to another person's getting a benefit is greater if we also get a comparable benefit. For the many among us who have a sense of fairness, the positive value we attach to our getting a benefit is greater if the other person also gets a comparable benefit.

The easiest way to deal with values that aren't value independent is to combine them into a single value. For instance, number of air bags can be combined with braking distance into a safety value. This solution was applicable to a custody case involving twins, where the happiness of one twin depended critically on what happened to the other. The twins were represented as a single column in the decision table, so they'd be thought about together. It's still important, however, that the combined value be value independent in comparison with the remaining values.

In those cases where the non-independent values are the quality of a state and the duration of that state (*e.g.,* length of life and quality of life), the simplest approach is to represent just the quality of the state as a value attribute and to take duration into account when assessing its importance.

In those cases where the non-independent values are the quality of a state and the probability of that state (*e.g.,* the desirability of getting a job and the probability of getting that job), the simplest approach is to represent just the quality of the state as a value attribute and to take probability into account when assessing its importance. A better approach, however, may be to represent the probabilities explicitly at event nodes in a decision tree and calculate expected value. (See the appendix on Thinking More Deeply About Uncertainty.)

In those cases where the non-independent values relate to notions of fairness, the lack of independence can be handled by creating a separate value to represent fairness, so that the decision maker can think separately about (a) consequences to self, (b) consequences to others, and (c) the difference between consequences to self and consequences to others. Another solution, illustrated by the example of the twins, is to consider all the stakeholders at once.

Note that "value independent" doesn't mean the same thing as "uncorrelated", or "statistically independent". These concepts are frequently confused. Gas economy and ease of parking are correlated, since smaller cars tend to get better gas mileage and to be easier to park; however, it would seem that the value of gas economy wouldn't depend in any way on ease of parking—unless parking were so difficult that one would be in danger of running out of gas during the process! The distinction between statistical independence and value independence is yet another aspect of the important distinction between facts and values.

Value independence is, actually, a matter of degree. It's helpful to distinguish between *ordinal* independence and *interval* independence. The good news is that only ordinal independence is required for much of what we'll be doing later. The bad news is that interval independence, or at least a reasonable approximation to it, is sometimes required.

Consider the problem of deciding where to apply for a job, and consider the relation between the probability of getting the job and the values associated with the job once you've gotten it. This relation almost surely satisfies ordinal independence and almost surely fails to satisfy interval independence. Let's see why.

Ordinal independence would be satisfied for probability, in this example if, no matter what the levels on the values associated with the job, itself, you prefer a higher probability to a lower probability of getting the job. This is surely the case. The *order* of your preference for probabilities is surely independent of which particular job you're talking about. (If there was a job for which you preferred a lower probability of being hired, you wouldn't have included it in the analysis.)

Interval independence would be satisfied for probability, in this same example if, no matter what the levels on the values associated with the job, itself, the *difference* between, for example, a probability of .10 and a probability of .90 had the same value for you. This would surely *not* be the case. You'd surely be willing to pay more to increase the chances of getting your most preferred job from .10 to .90 than to increase the chances of getting your least preferred job by the same amount.

Classic examples of values that aren't interval independent are completing and competing goods (Edgeworth, 1881). As an example of *completing goods* consider surgeons and surgical equipment. The value of increasing the number of surgeons in an area is greater when there is equipment for them to use, and the value of increasing the amount of surgical equipment is greater when there are surgeons to use it. As an example of *competing goods*, consider deer and elk. The value, to both humans and the ecology, of increasing the deer population is greater when the population of elk is low than when it's high, and, similarly, the value of increasing the elk population is greater when the deer population is low than when it's high.

Another piece of good news is that value independence need be only approximate and need apply only over the ranges of impacts involved in the decision. If we're considering small enough changes in the populations of elk and deer, their values may be sufficiently independent for practical purposes.

A properly structured value set permits quantitative judgments. We'll soon be talking about how to put numbers on values, but quantitative judgment is involved, whether we use numbers or not. We take up now some general considerations involved in thinking quantitatively about values.

Thinking Quantitatively About Values

In arriving at quantitative judgments about values, we proceed quite differently from the way in which we arrive at quantitative judgments about facts. For example, in making a quantitative factual judgment regarding the number of sunny days in an area, we think about our sample of experience and whether it's sufficiently large and unbiased to be representative of the population of days in the area we're concerned with. However, in making a quantitative value judgment regarding how we feel about the number of sunny days, we think about *other* areas with which we've had experience, and we may also think about *other values*. In one frame, we might say, "At least it's better than Nome, Alaska." In another, we might say, "I'd always hoped to live in Arizona." The key to quantitative judgments about values is selecting the appropriate value frame (Parducci, 1965, 1968, 1984).

Consider a husband and wife who'd rented a cabin on a mountain lake for a few days. When they found that the cabin had two bedrooms, they decided to invite another couple along. The wife expected that they'd split the costs with the other couple on the basis of the principle that, if they shared the benefits of the cabin equally, they should share the costs equally. The husband expected that they'd ask nothing of the other couple. He was thinking that they'd been invited the previous week to some friends' new beach cabin, and though the cabin had recently cost their friends $150,000, there was never any thought on either side that our husband and wife should pay anything.

As if this were not enough, another possible value frame was that the other couple should pay just the incremental $10 per night that their presence would add to the cost, and yet another was that the cost should be split except for a finder's fee reduction for the couple who'd made the arrangements.

Clearly, the issue here is not one of fact but of an appropriate value frame. The value frames in this example appear to be highly case-specific. One way to think about case-specific value frames is to think of *comparable cases*. In law, this approach is called *case law,* and, in ethics, it's called *casuistry* (Beauchamp & Walters, 1994). The hope is that you'll find comparable cases that are easier to evaluate since, "Hard cases make bad law."

Thinking about particular cases helps us deal with similar cases, but, if we could derive some general principles, the general principles should be able to help us with a much greater range of decisions in the future. There are several concepts that can guide us as we test value frames by comparing them with clearly understood reference situations. These relate to attributes, measures, and zero points. Choices of attributes are involved in deciding on a value set, and choices of measures and zero points are involved in satisfying measurability.

Attributes. When Henry Royce, designer of the Rolls Royce, said, "The quality remains long after the price has been forgotten," he was adding a time perspective to the initial value frame. He was calling attention to the perspective of the distant future and to the cumulative effects of cost and benefit streams over time.

Consider the case of a student in a course on personal decision making who chose for his class project whether or not to commit suicide! Initially, he'd placed greater weight on his intense personal pain than the possibility of complete relief and had judged suicide to be the least unattractive choice. In discussing the paper with him, I pointed out that he'd restricted himself to a very short planning horizon. If he didn't commit suicide, there was at least a possibility that his problems would eventually become resolved. Assuming, pessimistically, that they'd become resolved in five years (which was well beyond his planning horizon) and given his young age, that'd be five years of pain in exchange for over 50 good years. (Clinicians refer to suicide as "a permanent solution to a temporary problem"!) This suggestion changed the student's perspective dramatically. He abandoned the plan to commit suicide and decided to seek counseling.

The effect of adding a value to or subtracting one from a value frame is related to the completeness criterion for a well-structured value set.

Measures. We think differently about amounts and percentages (Savage, 1954, p. 103; Thaler, 1980). Many people who'd be willing to go across town to save $10 on a $30 calculator wouldn't be willing to go across town to save $10 on a $300 VCR. However, the essential question in both cases is, Would you be willing to go across town to save $10? Though the value of $10 is the same in both cases, it's perceived as less in the second case, because we tend to think of it as a percentage of the selling price. This is why we're so willing, as car dealers well know, to accept expensive add-ons to a car with a high selling price. Since percentages can lead to this kind of inconsistency, we should generally use scales with real units, unless there's a very good reason for doing otherwise.

This relates to the meaningfulness criterion for choosing among possible measures.

Zero points. Consider a photograph of a pile of scrap metal, identified in the caption as a crashed World War II plane, with a healthy pilot standing next to it, whom the caption quotes as having said, "Any landing you can walk away from is a good landing!" The pilot is providing a rather persuasive argument for valuing this landing positively. However, his argument is in no way based on the scientific method. There's no talk of anything like sample size or sample bias. This isn't an issue of fact.

What the pilot's argument consists of is extending the range of our value frame to include the possibility of his having been killed. We don't ordinarily include the possibility of being killed in our value frame for evaluating landings. A flight instructor in evaluating a student's landing would never say seriously, "That was a really good landing! You didn't kill us."

Kahlil Gibran wrote:

> *"The deeper that sorrow carves into your heart, the greater the joy it can contain";*

and

> *"Comfort enters our house a stranger, soon becomes guest, and finally master."*

The psychological mechanism that underlies these poetic verities is evaluation in comparison with a neutral reference point, specifically a neutral reference point that adjusts to our current experience. Sorrow lowers this reference point, so that much of what we used to take for granted now brings us pleasure; comfort raises this reference point until comforts that used to bring us pleasure now are required to maintain neutrality and avoid pain. (This is also the way drug addiction works.)

The zero on our value scale tends to adjust to what we have, so that the status quo comes to have neither positive nor negative value, and we compute gains and losses from a new neutral point. We are, thus, on a "hedonic treadmill". Initially, we think that if we made just a few hundred dollars more a month, we'd be happy. However, once we reach that level and have been there for a while, our value scale zeroes at what we have, and the cycle repeats itself. We want ever more.

One way to be happier is not to leave our reference point to automatic processes but to take control of it and adjust it closer to what we believe to be a true zero. This is what's meant by the time-worn, but well-founded, advice to "count your blessings". If we lower the zero on our "blessing counter" to a genuine zero, we'll inevitably count more genuine blessings.

Stephen Hawking, the brilliant English physicist who has very little control over his body because of Lou Gehrig's disease, said, "When one's expectations are reduced to zero, one really appreciates everything that one does have." This is probably why people in wheelchairs give themselves a higher life satisfaction rating than the average person (Meyers, 1992, p. 48): What they've lost apparently makes them all the more aware of what they still have. The expression, "No big deal!" seems to be a way of saying, "Your zero point is too high. On my scale, what you're complaining about isn't so bad." (The benefits of lowering your zero point wouldn't seem to extend to *traumatically* painful experiences. There are, after all, experiences that are negative in an absolute sense, not just a relative one.)

One reference of the term "big-hearted" would seem to be the number of outcomes one counts as positive. A common notion of a happy person is one to whom good things happen; a more accurate notion may be one *who sees as good* the things that happen to him or her. A person who "drinks life to the lees" values even the "sediment" of life positively enough to "drink" it.

If we can afford luxury and excess only rarely, it may be better to avoid it altogether, since even infrequent exposure can detract from the lesser, but real, pleasures that make up most of our life. Similarly, we can add to the experience of ordinary pleasures by exposing ourselves at least occasionally to reminders of how bad things can be (Parducci, 1968, 1984).

The sorrow that enlarges your heart may be your own, or it may be someone else's. Those who are concerned about people who are less well off than they adjust their value scales downward and thus should be happier with their own lives, and those who compare themselves with people who are better off adjust their value scales upward and can be expected to be less content with their own lives.

Another way to say all this is to say that there's a cost to pleasure and a benefit to pain (Solomon, 1980). The person who spends his or her days experiencing pleasure can be left with a feeling of emptiness, while the person who exerts effort toward some goal tends to be left with a feeling of satisfaction.

Because expectations work this way, a steadily improving life should bring greater happiness than one that's at a consistently high level.

As the prayer of St. Francis suggests, there seem to be two routes to happiness.

> *Lord, grant me the courage to change what can be changed, the serenity to accept what can not be changed, and the wisdom to know the difference.*

These two routes to happiness are changing the world to fit our desires, and changing our desires to fit the world. The approach taken in this book is the first of these, thinking about our values, thinking creatively of ways to achieve these values, and selecting and implementing the most promising of these. Once we've done our best in this regard, however, we should consider relaxing our goals, enlarging our perspective, and letting ourselves enjoy our share of the miracle of life. Perhaps this is why, as we near the end of our life span and reflect on our past efforts to live a good life, we find that a spiritual or philosophical perspective is increasingly important to happiness. (Again, there are limits to acceptance. We don't want to accept evil or injustice.)

We think differently about gains and losses, that is, changes upward and downward from the zero point defined by the status quo. One difference that we'll be concerned with is that losses loom larger than gains (Kahneman & Tversky, 1979). If you ask someone how much they'd pay for an item, say a lottery ticket, they'll indicate a lower price than if you give them the item and then ask how much they'd take for it. Such differences are attributable in part to strategy, of course; but they also appear to be attributable in large part to an honest difference in the way values are perceived. Moving up one lottery ticket from the status quo doesn't seem as large a change in value as moving down one lottery ticket from the status quo. This asymmetry poses a problem for conflict resolution, since an exchange that restores a fair balance may appear unfair to both of the parties: The seller feels that a fair price is too low, and the buyer feels that a fair price is too high.

A related problem is that the location of the zero point affects our attitude toward risk, a topic taken up in the appendix on Thinking More Deeply About Uncertainty.

A general solution to the problem of gains and losses is, as suggested, adjusting the psychological zero toward a true zero. Just as earlier we argued for measures in terms of real units, such as dollars, rather than relative units, such as percentages, we're now arguing for real zero points, rather than relative zero points. The fight, in both cases, is to keep our representations of reality from getting too far removed from the reality they're representing.

Chapter 4. ALTERNATIVES: What can I do?

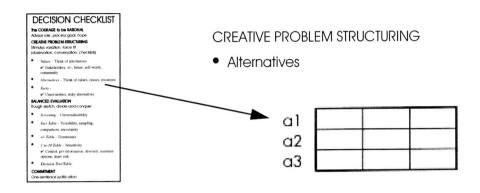

DECISION CHECKLIST

The COURAGE to be RATIONAL
Advisor role; process goal, hope
CREATIVE PROBLEM STRUCTURING
Stimulus variation, force fit
(observation, conversation, checklists)

- *Values* – Think of alternatives
  ✔ Stakeholders, +/-, future, self-worth, community
- *Alternatives* – Think of values, causes, resources
- *Facts* –
  ✔ Uncertainties, risky alternatives

BALANCED EVALUATION
Rough sketch, divide-and-conquer

- *Screening* – Universalizability
- *Fact Table* – Testability, sampling, comparison, uncertainty
- *+/- Table* – Dominance
- *1-to-10 Table* – Sensitivity
  ✔ Control, get information, diversify, maintain options, share risk
- *Decision Tree/Table*

COMMITMENT
One-sentence justification

CREATIVE PROBLEM STRUCTURING

- Alternatives

The more satisfactory the alternatives considered, the more satisfactory should be the consequences of the decision. The most satisfactory resolutions of decision problems are achieved by the creation of win-win alternatives, which require no value tradeoffs. Creative thinking about alternatives can be stimulated by analyses of values, causes, resources, or alternatives and by alternatives checklists. The search for alternatives can be made more efficient by the heuristics of classification and analysis into sub-problems. The criteria for a well-structured set of alternatives are that there be a sufficient number of alternatives, that they be mutually exclusive, and that they differ significantly from one another.

Once you've identified your values, you should turn your attention to alternatives. If your decision appears to be a simple "go-no go" choice, you probably haven't thought enough about alternatives. Going beyond a simple "go-no go" choice is the principle behind comparison shopping. For decisions of any importance, comparing a wide range of diverse alternatives is a good idea. And, while thinking about alternatives, you should always keep your mind open for additional values.

An *alternative* is a possible course of action. Various courses of action can often be represented by verbs: "buy", "sell", "wait". Sometimes courses of action are distinguished by verb phrases: "Buy Car A", "Buy Car B". (Usually, of course, the verb is simply understood in such phrases as: "Car A", "Car B".) The alternatives "Ob/Gyn" and "EM' are abbreviations for "Specialize in Ob/Gyn" and "Specialize in EM". Sometimes alternatives are distinguished by adverbs: "break off the relationship gradually", "break off the relationship quickly". However, verbs are always at least implicit, because action is always involved. The key question in a decision is what to *do*.

Even in classic problem solving situations, which are thought of as having only one satisfactory solution, it can pay to press on and seek additional alternatives. Consider the famous nine-dot problem:

The problem is to draw four contiguous straight lines (that is, without lifting your pencil from the paper) in such a way that they go through all nine dots. Two solutions are shown at the bottom of the following page. You may wish to try solving this problem before reading further. [1]

Notice how each of the solutions shown requires relaxing unstated assumptions. The 4-line solution requires relaxing the unstated assumption that the lines must remain within the square implicitly defined by the nine dots. The 3-line solution requires relaxing the unstated assumption that the dots are geometric points, without area. (There's also a 1-line solution, which requires relaxing the implicit assumptions that the line is a geometric line, without width, and another that requires relaxing the assumption that the paper on which the dots are drawn can't be folded.)

The importance of seeking additional alternatives in real-life decision problems is well illustrated in Arthur Schlesinger's account (1965, pp. 803-4), considered earlier, of the meeting of President Kennedy's Executive Committee on the first day of the Cuban missile crisis. You'll recall that most of the members initially thought that the best alternative would be an air strike to destroy the missile sites. Then Attorney General Robert Kennedy urged them to seek additional alternatives. As it happened, the alternative that was finally chosen, a naval blockade, was one of those generated in response to his suggestion.

Following the pattern established in the last chapter, methods are presented for thinking creatively, efficiently, and critically about alternatives. The methods for thinking *creatively* about alternatives are various stimulus-variation techniques: analysis of values, alternatives causes, and resources; and alternatives checklists (Keller & Ho, 1990). The methods for thinking *efficiently* about alternatives are the heuristics of value-focused

1.

The accepted solution to the nine-dot problem requires going outside the square implicitly defined by the nine dots.

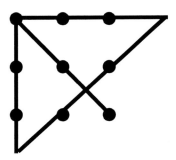

Better solutions are possible, however. Since the dots aren't points but occupy area, it's possible to connect all nine with *three* lines. The areas of the dots have been exaggerated in the drawing below to make this solution clearer:

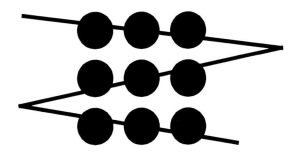

(Given the diameter of the original dots, of course, the lines would have to be quite long.) Solutions with one line are possible. Adams (1986) claims that at least 27 solutions exist.

search, classification, and analysis into sub-problems. The tool for thinking *critically* about alternatives is a short list of criteria for a well-structured set of alternatives.

Analysis of Values, Alternatives, Causes, & Resources; and Alternatives Checklists

Analysis of Values

The first step in value-focused thinking was to think of values; the second step is to use these values to suggest alternatives. Value-focused search is an example of the general problem-solving heuristic of working backward from the goal (Polya, 1957; Wicklegren, 1974). There are many practical examples where working backward is more efficient than working forward. Planning a climbing route up a mountain is one, since a mountain has many places to start up but only one place, the top, to start down. The most efficient way to find the few routes that reach all the way from the bottom to the top is to start at the top and work down. Writing a line of poetry is another, since there are many ways to begin a line of poetry but, if the last word is to rhyme, few ways to end it. Preparing a report is another, since there are many ways to prepare a report but few that'll be of real use to the recipient. Before starting in on a report, it's wise to be clear as to the audience for which it's intended and the purpose to which this audience will put the report.

In decision making, focusing on the values and working backward to events and alternatives is usually more effective than working in the other direction (Keeney, 1992; Pearl, Leal, & Saleh, 1982; Pitz, Sachs, & Heerboth, 1980; Keller & Ho, 1988). The general principle is:

Start by getting clear about where you want to go and then look for ways to get there.

It's easier to generate alternatives, if you try to satisfy one value at a time (Pitz, Sachs, & Heerboth, 1980). Not only do people generate more alternatives when they try to satisfy one value at a time, they also generate higher quality alternatives (Butler & Scherer, 1998). (Since alternatives generated in this way aren't likely to satisfy the other values well, some force fit may be required.) It's also easier to generate alternatives, the more specific you are about your values (Jungermann, von Ulardt, & Hausmann, 1983). One way to introduce efficiency in using values to come up with alternatives is to focus on the value or values that eliminate the greatest number of unsatisfactory alternatives. For example, when the values relate to different stakeholders and one of the stakeholders is more difficult to satisfy than the others, you narrow your search most quickly by generating alternatives that'll satisfy the stakeholder that's the most difficult to please and then check later to see which of these will also satisfy the others. If you're going out to dinner with some friends, one of whom has dietary restrictions, the efficient way to proceed is to begin by putting together a list of places that'd be satisfactory to the person with dietary restrictions. Another, related way to introduce efficiency into using values to come up with alternatives is to focus on the most important value or values (Keller & Ho, 1988), even though none eliminates any alternative.

Analysis of values led to a creative win-win alternative when a husband and wife were in conflict over who should get the shower. A closer look at the husband's needs revealed that he didn't need a shower. He had taken a shower just before taking a nap and certainly didn't need another one just after getting up. The problem was that sleeping on hair that wasn't fully dry had created a mess that couldn't be corrected with a comb alone. So the husband would shampoo in the kitchen sink, and the wife would get the shower. Then came a conflict over who'd get the shampoo. Analysis into attributes again led to a win-win alternative. The husband's hair was clean. He didn't need to shampoo it; he just needed to wet it and re-dry it. So the wife got both the shower and the shampoo, and both were happy.

Analysis into value attributes also led to a creative win-win alternative when a husband and wife were in conflict over throwing out some imperfect family snapshots or putting them in the album. Analysis into attributes revealed that what they both liked about these snapshots were the faces, and what they both disliked were the backgrounds. The win-win solution was to cut around the faces, throw away the backgrounds, and paste just the faces in the photographs in the scrapbook, a solution that also added variety to the page layout.

In an attempt to generate more alternatives, Amelia focused on the two most important values in her value set, Contribution to Society and Creativity/Intellectual Challenge, and asked herself what careers could contribute most directly to these values. For Contribution to Society, she thought of being a Member of Parliament or the U. S. Senate, where her actions would affect a great many people. Force fitting this idea more realistically to her situation, she thought of education and, in particular, of University Teaching. This seemed worth adding to her list of alternatives.

Turning to Creativity/Intellectual Challenge, she thought of research. Force fitted to her situation, this became Research on Reading. Her son had great difficulties in reading, and the remedies tried in school had been based more on politics than science.

Analysis of Alternatives

We're often able to think of additional alternatives if we think about the attributes of the alternatives we've already thought of (Crawford, 1964; Manning, Gettys, Nicewander, Fisher, & Mehle, 1980; Glucksburg & Danks, 1968; Glucksburg & Weisberg, 1966). Combining attributes of alternatives to create new alternatives often results in alternatives that are superior (Zwicky, 1957, 1969; Keppner & Tregoe, 1965; Macrimmon & Taylor, 1976; Starr & Greenwood, 1977).

A person who was going to school full time and working part time was debating whether to work full time and go to school part time, in order to make ends meet. After thinking about the possibilities, he saw that either school or work could be zero time, part time, of full time. Any of these three levels under "SCHOOL" can be thought about in connection with any of the three levels under "WORK", thus creating nine possibilities out of the original two. The combination Zero Time School and Full Time Work, for example, suggests dropping out of school for a while to save up money.

As a final example, a student of mine was uncertain as to whether to major in psychology, English, or physical education. I asked her what attributes of each field most attracted her. She said that she liked the fact that psychology enabled her to understand people, but that she didn't want to help people with problems or to do research; that she liked writing, but not literature; and that she liked sports activities, but not the more scientific side of physical education. Putting the positive attributes "writing", "about people", and "in sports activities" together, I asked whether she'd considered sports writing. She lit up and said, "No, but that's a great idea!" and left to try the idea out by working as a sports writer on the school paper.

In applying this method, you should expect to come up with combinations that don't make sense. Some of these you'll have to reject—but don't forget to try force-fitting them first.

Analysis of Causes

While analysis of values specifies what we like and don't like, causal analysis specifies factors that promote or prevent what we value. The philosopher David Hume (1888) called causation "the cement of the universe", so important is it to holding together the universe, or at least our understanding of it. The link between causes and alternatives is both simple and powerful: Good alternatives cause good outcomes.

Good alternatives cause good outcomes.

Thinking backward from outcomes to causes can greatly enrich our view of the problem (Axelrod, 1976; Sevon, 1984).

Once we've a clear understanding of the causes of our problem, ideas for solving it often come quickly to mind. Once we've determined that at least one reason we haven't gotten the call we've been waiting for is that the phone is off the hook, we know right away what to do about it. Once we've determined that the reason our car is sluggish is that the compression is falling, alternative ways to deal with the situation come quickly to mind: put up with the problem, fix the car, or sell it. The connection between causal analysis and alternative generation is especially clear in medicine, where a given diagnosis typically brings to mind appropriate treatments.

A faulty causal analysis can direct thought to inappropriate alternatives or restrict thought to an overly narrow range of alternatives. If we want to generate *good* alternatives, we should start with *genuine* causes.

A correct causal analysis by a couple with a leaky basement suggested a better and cheaper alternative than had been suggested by a national franchise that had had extensive experience in basement waterproofing. The solution proposed by the franchise was installing a drain gutter all around the inside walls of the basement. The quoted price was $3850. The couple decided to wait a year or so (taking a break) to think about it. During that time, one of them noticed (thoughtful observation) that a rain gutter they'd just had installed was leaking *at the top*. A little more thought led to the following causal analysis:

Clearing out the storm drain for $160 solved the problem and saved the couple well over $3000. Sound causal reasoning is not just for scientists!

A restricted causal analysis resulted in a restricted set of alternatives when looking for solutions to the problem of crowding in a county jail. An obvious cause was the size of the jail, and early discussion centered on ways to expand the jail. A more careful analysis revealed, in addition, a more subtle cause, a bottleneck in the courts. More people were arrested each day than were processed through the courts, creating a backup that held no promise of ending. So new jail space was built, and additional judges were also hired.

Thinking of the causal chain that connects research to the teaching of reading, Amelia identified the following five links:

She realized that she could work to enhance the impact of research on the teaching of reading by intervening at any of these five points. When she asked herself where the weak links in the chain might lie, she realized research might well not be the most important place to intervene. She wasn't interested in teaching at the K-12 level, because she'd done that already and wanted something higher on

Creativity/Intellectual Challenge. So she broke the old Research alternative into two, Conducting Research and Disseminating Research, understanding the latter to include disseminating research to school policy decision makers, teachers, and parents.

A common error in reasoning about the causes of behavior is what's called the Fundamental Attribution Error (Ross, 1977). When we make the Fundamental Attribution Error, we falsely conclude that the reasons for a person's behavior have to do with the *kind of person* he or she is, when, in reality, they have to do with the *kind of situation* he or she is in. For example, many attribute Nazism to the German national character and anti-Negro racism to the character of Southerners. Yet some analyses (Arendt, 1963) have concluded that many Nazis were ordinary people responding to extraordinary pressures and that Southerners are no more authoritarian than Northerners, their attitudes toward blacks having changed substantially once the legal situation had changed (Pettigrew, 1959). In Milgram's (1963, 1974) famous study, 65% of a sample of normal subjects were willing (much to the surprise even of experienced clinicians) to inflict "450 volts" of "dangerous" and "painful" electrical shocks, when pressured by a legitimate authority, on a subject who supposedly had a heart condition. Prior to this study, clinicians would have seen such behavior as indicative of personality disturbances. The conclusion from all this is that, if we wish to change behavior, we'd do well to consider alternatives that focus on changing the context in which the behavior takes place.

We tend to perceive as causes changes that occur closely in time to the event we're trying to explain, especially ones that are similar to the event or that we have some other reason to believe are related to the event (Einhorn & Hogarth, 1986). Thus, a health treatment is often thought of as causing a complaint to go away, even though it may well have gone away "by itself". And when the crime rate goes either up or down, people seem able to identify any number of "causes" among the many social and economic changes that are correlated with the crime rate.

The key to a sound causal analysis is the principle of *controlled comparison:*

> To justify the claim that *A* causes *B*, you must find that *B* changes when *A* is changed *and nothing else is changed.*

In decision terms, before you should believe that Alternative A1 has a better impact on Value B than Alternative A2, you must be sure that the difference is attributable to the alternatives, rather than to the persons implementing them or the situations in which they were implemented. This principal can be applied in actual experiments, where you gather the data yourself, or in mental experiments, where you think about data gathered by someone else or about life experiences. In the previous chapter, I provided a framework for thinking quantitatively about values; here, I provide a framework for thinking quantitatively about facts, which is elaborated on in the appendix on Thinking More Deeply About Uncertainty.

There are many psychological barriers to the correct application of this principle (Einhorn & Hogarth, 1986). Implicit in the principle of controlled comparison is the assumption that some comparison is made. Often we fail to make any comparison at all, controlled or otherwise. A particularly dramatic case is the Challenger disaster. When considering that there might be a causal relationship between cold temperatures and malfunctioning of the O-rings, the engineers were asked to graph the temperatures at launch time for the flights in which problems have occurred (Russo & Schoemaker, 1989, p. 197). The graph showed no relationship between temperature and O-ring failure. When, however, a comparison was made between launches in which problems had occurred and launches in which problems hadn't occurred, a clear relationship emerged (Russo & Schoemaker, 1989, p. 198).

Comparison alone is not sufficient to justify conclusions about causality. Such conclusions also require that the comparison be controlled. According to the National Safety Council, deaths per million boat passenger hours in one year were:

Canoe (no motor)	1.66
Canoe (motor)	0.14
Sailboat (no motor)	0.52
Sailboat (motor)	0.44

Here, explicit comparisons can be made between boats with motors and boats without motors, and, clearly, the death rates are higher in canoes and sailboats not equipped with motors than in canoes and sailboats equipped with motors. The conclusion seems inescapable: Motors provide a safety factor. This causal analysis suggests a course of action for improving the safety of your canoe: Put a motor on it.

Despite its seeming inevitability, however, this conclusion doesn't follow. Before we can say that the presence of a motor is causally related to death rate, we must be sure that the class of boats with motors on which data were obtained differs in no other important way from the class of boats without motors on which data were obtained. Because we've taken no such precautions and have no reason to believe that the National Safety Council has, we can't justify this conclusion.

Indeed, it's quite likely that canoes with and without outboards are engaged in different activities. Canoes with outboards don't run white water, the most hazardous of canoeing activities. This difference could be a possible cause of the difference in death rate. Furthermore, a sailboat with an auxiliary is more likely to be a large sailboat, and large sailboats are less likely to capsize. This difference also could be a possible cause of the difference in death rate. If we used this faulty causal analysis to suggest putting an outboard on our white water canoe, we'd likely *increase* the danger.

A Oregon State Supreme Court justice inadvertently provided us with another example of generating alternatives on the basis of faulty causal reasoning. His line of reasoning went as follows:

> *Most of those who use hard drugs started out with marijuana. Therefore, in order to curb the use of hard drugs, we should have more severe penalties for using marijuana.*

Although, no comparison was made with those who don't use hard drugs, let's grant the judge the assumption that there's a relationship between the use of marijuana and the later use of hard drugs. But is this necessarily a causal relationship? Remember our test: To justify the claim that *A* causes *B*, you must find that *B* differs when *A* is changed *and nothing else is changed*. Are there likely to be no other important differences between marijuana users and non-users besides their use of marijuana? Personality factors and social factors come to mind. Perhaps people who aren't "turned on" by life tend to seek mechanical turn-ons, like drugs; and perhaps people who have such people for friends tend to follow their example.

If factors such as these are the real causes, then increasing the penalties for using marijuana could actually *increase* the use of hard drugs. Because increasing the penalties for using marijuana would do nothing about the real causes, people would be as inclined as ever to use drugs. The only question would be which drugs to use. One reason for using marijuana may well be that the penalties are not severe. Increasing the penalties for using marijuana would remove this reason for not using hard drugs. Because the judge started with faulty causal reasoning, he was inclined towards a course of action that could have brought about the *opposite* of what he desired.

Another example is that of the teacher who attempts to curb the disruptive behavior of Johnny by scolding him when he acts out. Her causal analysis is that Johnny hopes to get approval for his behavior, not scolding. When the school psychologist points out that the attention provided by the scolding may, in itself, be reinforcing to a child starved for attention, the teacher tries ignoring future misbehavior, and it gradually disappears. A better causal analysis leads to a better decision and a better outcome.

And then there's the case of a couple whose parents (his parents, who are not too happy with his choice of a wife) were constantly buying them things and dropping by for visits during which they'd fix up the house and yard, all at their own expense. The couple, in attempts to stop this annoying behavior, had frequently objected, had tried to get things done before his parents could get to them, and had insisted on paying, but all to no avail. A psychologist, on the basis of a different causal analysis, suggested that, on the next visit, they just loaf around and let the husband's parents do all the work. The result was that his parents cut that visit short, telling the couple that, in the future, they'd have to learn to do more for themselves (Watzlawick, Weakland, & Fisch, 1974, pp. 116-124). Because of a faulty causal analysis, the couple, like the teacher, had been exacerbating the problem in their very efforts to ameliorate it!

Causes can be excellent stimuli for thinking creatively of alternatives, but they have to be genuine causes.

Analysis of Resources

In a lot of practical problems where you have to make do with limited resources, thinking about what you have to work with can be an efficient and effective way to generate alternatives (Duncker, 1945). The following story illustrates the principle nicely:

> *I still don't know whether it was fast thinking or whether Grandmother figured it out in advance. Anyway, she certainly did the right thing when our vicious ram suddenly lowered his horns and rushed at her.*
>
> *It happened in the sheep pasture, a big cut-over field that was full of knee-high stumps. Here our ram ruled a flock of ewes and made war on anybody who ventured into his domain. That ram always terrified me, especially after I saw him hit a hired man hard enough to snap a bone in his leg. From then on, afraid to cross the pasture, I always walked around it.*
>
> *Not Grandmother! She just ignored the ram, and that's what she was doing this time I speak of. She'd been picking wild plums on the other side of the pasture and was now carrying her filled pail back toward the house. She was halfway across the field when the ram spied her. He advanced a few slow steps—and then, while I watched fearfully from behind the fence, he put down his head and charged furiously.*

How did Grandmother trick the ram and get safely from the pasture? The answer, if you're ready for it, is:

> *Stepping behind the nearest tree stump, Grandmother faced the oncoming ram. She picked up her ankle-length skirt and apron and dropped them over the stump, concealing it completely. The ram crashed into the hidden stump with a sickening force; then, badly dazed, he wobbled away...while Grandmother took up her pail and walked on (Saturday Evening Post, 1949).*

That field didn't provide Grandmother with much in the way of resources, but she certainly did a good job of thinking about what was there in coming up with her solution.

Vocational planning is an obvious place where the decision maker should take into account, not only his or her desires, but also his or her abilities and other resources when generating alternatives. In thinking of places one might live, similarly, one should think not only about what one desires but also about what's available, given one's location and income. Other important resources to think about are people you know.

Amelia thought about the strengths she'd bring to a job. The major ones seemed to be:

- Communication skills: writing, speaking

- People skills

- Adaptability to different cultures. Ten years in the Middle East, one year in Germany, six months in Italy, plus shorter stays in Asia.

- Experience in working with children. Had taught children in different cultures.

- Experience working with reading disabilities.

- A knowledge of applied developmental psychology (to be acquired in graduate school)

The resource she knew the least about was the training she'd be receiving in applied developmental psychology. To learn more, she arranged to meet with a couple of professors in the program she'd be applying to.

A checklist that's been found broadly useful for these purposes is the one used in a SWOT analysis:

- Strengths

- Weaknesses

- Opportunities

- Threats

This checklist systematically calls attention to both positive and negative resources within oneself (strengths and weaknesses) and outside oneself (opportunities and threats). Many people have found it helpful in thinking about a variety of practical problems.

Alternatives Checklists

Perhaps the most famous checklist for alternatives is that provided by Osborn in his book *Brainstorming* (Osborn, 1963). This checklist suggests that you put to other uses, adapt, modify, minify, substitute, rearrange, reverse, or combine.

We've already considered a checklist for coming up with alternatives that address defensive avoidance, in ourselves or in others:

- Reduce importance

- Reduce uncertainty

- Increase hope

And, in the chapter on uncertainty, we'll consider a checklist for coming up with alternatives that address uncertainty:

- Control

- Diversify

- Keep options open

- Share risk

- Obtain information

Classification, Analysis into Sub-Problems

In addition to value-focused search, there are two other things you can do to promote efficiency in search and keep the set of alternatives from becoming unmanageably large. One is evaluating broad classes of alternatives, and the other is analyzing your problem into subproblems.

Classification

The set of alternatives can often be simplified by thinking in terms of broad classes of alternatives, rather than specific, detailed alternatives. You can consider whether you want to go to law school, medical school, or graduate school in psychology without bothering yourself at this point with distinctions among specialties or particular schools. You can consider whether you should look for a second family car, a sports car, or a motorcycle before thinking about specific makes, models, and years.

If you can reject an entire class of alternatives as unsatisfactory on the basis of general characteristics without searching within that class, you'll have saved yourself time. If you find that motorcycles, in general, are too dangerous for you, you don't have to establish that fact about every motorcycle. This is breadth-first search again.

> Amelia screened out Enforcement, Administration, and Sub-clinical immediately on the basis of their not being sufficiently challenging.

Analysis into Subproblems

Another way to simplify the set of alternatives is to analyze the decision problem into two or more simpler subproblems. This is an application of the *subgoals search heuristic*, also considered earlier. The educated guess, in this case, is that the subproblems are relatively independent, so that you can first solve one and then solve the other.

Analysis of a decision problem into subproblems is simple when the values of the alternatives in each subproblem don't depend on the alternative chosen in the other subproblem. Over a broad range of alternatives the desirability of various items on the dinner menu doesn't depend on what I'm wearing, nor vice versa. So I can treat the decision as to what to wear as a separate problem without having to worry about what I might have for dinner. Fortunately, most of our decisions are separable in this way. For a more complex example, see the appendix on Thinking More Deeply About Alternatives.

It gradually became clear to Amelia that she had two sub-problems, a Work-Experience Decision and a Career Decision. Since she was planning to go to graduate school, there'd be plenty of time to make her final Career Decision, and there was much to be said in favor of putting this decision off until she'd acquired more information. Before entering graduate school and during graduate school, however, she could be gaining valuable experience working in different positions. This experience could suggest specific alternatives to consider in her Career Decision and also prepare her for obtaining work and achieving success in those areas. The sub-problem that she had to work on immediately was the Work-Experience Decision.

Criteria for a Well-Structured Set of Alternatives

There are few criteria for a well-structured set of alternatives. The first is that there be at least two alternatives. If you don't have at least two alternatives, you don't even have a decision problem. You may have a second alternative in the back of your mind, but at least two alternatives must be explicitly represented to ensure a proper analysis. However, while two alternatives gives you a decision problem, it usually doesn't give you a very thoughtful representation of the problem. It's wise always to search for at least a third alternative. Once you get this far, you often find that there are several alternatives that hadn't occurred to you.

The second requirement is that the alternatives for each choice (except in resource allocation problems, discussed later) be mutually exclusive. It should be possible to go out one path and only one path. Sometimes people intend alternatives to be mutually exclusive but don't represent them that way, with the result that the analysis is flawed and could indicate a preference for the wrong alternative.

A good set of alternatives will have

- At least two alternatives (preferably more),

- Alternatives that are mutually exclusive, and

- Alternatives that differ substantially from one another.

The third, more a desirable feature than a requirement, is that the alternatives differ substantially from one another. If your choice among cars is restricted to one make, or your choice among careers is restricted to one field, you may be well-advised to widen your search. Ideally, they should all achieve high levels of value but in different ways.

The criteria for a value set and those for an alternative set are summarized together in this diagram:

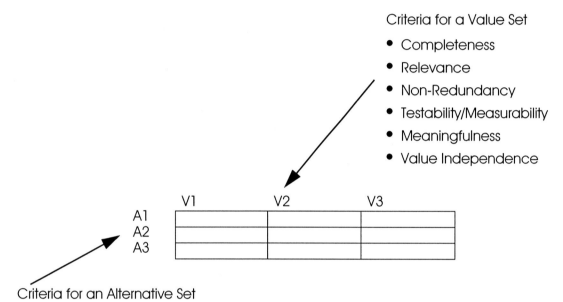

Criteria for a Value Set

• Completeness
• Relevance
• Non-Redundancy
• Testability/Measurability
• Meaningfulness
• Value Independence

Criteria for an Alternative Set

• Multiple Alternatives
• Mutually Exclusive Alternatives
• Varied Alternatives

Chapter 5. THE MIGHTY DECISION TABLE: How do I choose?

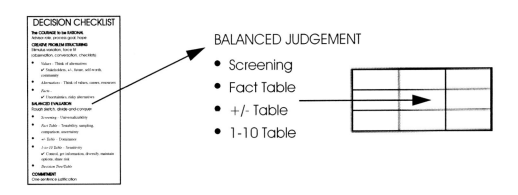

There are a variety of ways to make choices, which can be thought of as a Ladder of methods. At the lowest rung of the Ladder, a prioritized list compares a number of alternatives with one another on the basis of an intuitive criterion. It's the only intuitive method on the Ladder. At the next rung, screening compares a number of alternatives with one another on the basis of a set of analytic values taken into account one at a time. Screening is the first of the analytic methods. Whenever analysis is used, analysis and intuition can provide useful checks against one another.

The key rung on the Decision Ladder is the decision table. A decision table compares a number of alternatives with one another on the basis of a set of analytic values taken into account simultaneously. Decision tables can enhance rationality, creativity, and judgment and are especially helpful in identifying and creating win-win alternatives. Analysis into facts and values separates a decision problem into components that are appropriately dealt with in different ways. The soundest basis for fact judgments is the scientific method. The soundest basis for value judgments is a thorough exploration of various value frames, or perspectives. A fact table is a decision table with factual information entered in the cells. A plusses-and-minuses value table, which is adequate for most decisions, is a decision table with +/0/- evaluations of the facts entered in the cells. Where finer distinctions are required, a 1-to-10 value table can be used, with numerical value ratings of the facts entered in the cells. Such 1-to-10 tables permit sensitivity analysis.

The highest rung on the Decision Ladder is the decision tree/table. The decision tree portion represents both choices (e.g., take umbrella, don't take umbrella) and uncertain futures (e.g., rain, no rain) as paths in a diagram.

Resource allocation decisions and commons decisions are important special cases.

There are a variety of ways to evaluate a number of alternatives on the basis of a number of values (Beach & Mitchell, 1978; Payne, 1982; Payne, Bettman, & Johnson, 1993; Schoemaker & Russo, 1991; Spetzler & Zamora, 1974). An easy way to think about the most important of these is in terms of a *Decision Ladder*, with the simpler methods at the bottom and the more complex methods at the top. (See figure on next page.) We'll introduce all five steps on the Ladder in this chapter and cover the first four in detail. A detailed consideration of the highest step will be left until the chapter on Uncertainty.

A good way to approach a decision problem is to start at the bottom of the ladder, with the simplest method. If this is inadequate, then proceed just far enough up the ladder to get a sufficiently clear picture of the problem to be able to make a sound decision. For problems that are simple, relatively unimportant, or both, there's no need to go beyond the first rung. As the importance and complexity of the problem increase, methods farther up the ladder become more appropriate.

Start with simple methods and proceed to complex methods only as necessary.

Even for problems that require going to the top of the ladder, it's a good idea to start at the bottom and work your way up, in the spirit of *breadth-first search*. You'll recall that we've already encountered breadth-first search in discussing the importance of the relevance criterion for a well-structured value set and in discussing classes of alternatives. Here, we make use of it once again, in the logic of the Decision Ladder.

The Decision Ladder

- **Decision Tree and Table**

	Value A	Value B	Value C
	.50	.30	.20
	10	8	1
	4	8	10
	0	10	10

.60

.40

- **1-to-10 Decision Table**

	Value A	Value B	Value C
	.50	.30	.20
Alternative I	10	8	1
Alternative II	6	1	7
Alternative III	0	10	10

- **Plusses-and-Minuses Decision Table**

	Value A	Value B	Value C
Alternative I	+	+	-
Alternative II	+	0	+
Alternative III	0	+	+

- **Screening**

	Value A	Value B	Value C
Alternative I	+	+	
Alternative II	+	0	
Alternative III	0		

- **Prioritized List**

    Alternative I

    Alternative II

    Alternative III

123

Uses of diagrams, maps, and models all involve breadth-first search, since all retain only the most important aspects of the problem situation. All of these approaches enable us to stay "on top of the problem". The general principle is:

Start with the important considerations, bringing in details only when and if needed.

As we make decisions in various areas of our lives, it's appropriate to go up the ladder for decisions at the major turning points, such as accepting a job or buying a house, and to stay low on the ladder for minor adjustments to these decisions, such as moving within the organization or remodeling the kitchen (Etzioni, 1967).

Even in major decisions, rejecting the least promising alternatives is often a simple matter easily handled with the methods at the bottom of the Decision Ladder. It's choosing among the final contenders that may be more difficult and require moving up the Ladder to more powerful methods.

You should be careful not to go so far up the Ladder, however, that you're in danger of a fall. Never rely on a method that you aren't sure you're able to use correctly.

You're better off using a simple method well than a complex method poorly

We'll work our way up the Ladder, a rung at a time.

Prioritized Lists

A course I used to teach provided seniors an opportunity to apply what they'd learned about group process and decision process by serving as consultants to school-based "site councils", parent-teacher decision making bodies established by Oregon law. Students in this course were struck by how often decisions were made by (a) someone suggesting a single alternative, (b) a few comments being made (usually all supportive), and (c) the alternative being adopted unanimously!

The concept of lists has already come up. We've encountered lists of values, lists of alternatives, checklists for creative thinking, lists of criteria for critical thinking, and even lists of lists in the form of a value tree. The most fundamental list for decision making is a list of alternatives, since we can't engage in serious decision making with a single alternative. A list of alternatives arouses cognitive conflict and engages us in a decision process, even if that process is no more than prioritizing the list intuitively.

Just making a list of alternatives appears to introduce judiciousness into the decision process (Jones, Frisch, Yurak, & Kim, 1998). When we consider an isolated alternative as an opportunity to be accepted or rejected, we tend to accept alternatives with predominately positive features (*e.g.,* buy a CD) and reject alternatives with predominately negative features (*e.g.,* get the car repaired). Listing additional alternatives can get us to reject alternatives with predominately positive features when the other alternatives have even more positive features and to accept alternatives with predominately negative features when the other alternatives have even more negative features. An example of the latter is Winston Churchill's famous quip that "Democracy is the worst form of government—except for all the others."

Intuition vs. analysis. There are, basically, two ways to prioritize items on a list: intuition and analysis. Intuition is what we ordinarily use. We just look at the items, think about them, and form an impression of the overall value of each. Often, one alternative stands out fairly clearly as the best. Whereas intuition considers everything at once, analysis breaks the overall problem into sub-problems. The higher rungs on the Decision Ladder represent various methods for approaching a decision analytically.

Which is better, intuition or analysis? Intuition and analysis differ in a number of respects (Hammond, Hamm, Grassia, & Pearson, 1987). Intuition is quicker, takes less effort, and requires no training. This makes it more appropriate for most everyday decisions. Analysis is more conducive to complete problem structuring and balanced judgment. For important and difficult decisions, some analysis is usually a good idea. But analysis takes longer, requires effort, and requires training. Thus, reading a book like this should enable you to do a better job of it. In general, we tend to use intuition for preliminary screening and analysis for the final choice (Potter & Beach, 1994).

If you have developed a level of expertise in an area, intuition can be a very good guide (Lipshitz, et al., 2001). However, expert decision making is based more on habit than on thought (Chase & Simon, 1973; Simon & Gilmartin, 1973; Newell & Simon, 1972), more on experience with the subject matter than on training in decision processes. For many important decisions, such as choosing a college, a career, a mate, a house, we tend not to repeat the decisions or, at least, not to repeat them often enough to develop any area-specific expertise in making them. And even expert decision makers can be greatly in error in their areas of expertise (Meehl, 1986; Redelmeier & Shafir, 1995; Redelmeier & Tversky, 1990.) As a general rule, if the decision is important, you should consider the kinds of analytic approaches presented in this book.

While analysis can be a valuable supplement to intuition, it should never replace it entirely, however. The results of analysis should always be checked against intuition. *Once the decision analysis has indicated a preferred alternative, you should return to intuition and ask yourself, "Does this really make sense? Does it seem right?"* If intuition and analysis are in agreement, you're done. If they disagree, however, there are three distinct possibilities:

- The analysis is in error;

- Intuition is in error; or

- Both are in error.

Analysis could be in error in a number of ways. The analysis could have left out an important value or event, or there could be an error in calculation. Intuition could also be in error in the very same ways.

When intuition and analysis are not in agreement, it requires further thought to tell whether it is intuition, analysis, or both that is in error.

Intuition could be failing to take into account an important value or event, or it could be combining the information inappropriately. You shouldn't draw any conclusion as to whether it's intuition or analysis that's in error until you've identified the specific error or errors. Then you should correct either your analysis, your intuition, or both, so that, in the end, they're in agreement.

No matter how far we proceed up the Decision Ladder, we should never leave intuition behind. Even the Nobel Prize winning physicist Richard Feynman relied heavily on concrete modes of thought to check the validity of abstract modes. "I had a scheme, which I still use today when somebody is explaining something that I'm trying to understand: I keep making up examples" (Feynman, 1985, p. 85).

On the other hand, we shouldn't treat intuition as the "answer book". Many people take intuition as the ultimate criterion and simply reject any analysis that doesn't agree with it. This has led to serious errors in the past and is likely to do so in the future. Intuitively, it seems perfectly clear that the earth is flat and that it's the sun that moves. Intuitively, it seems that sunk costs do matter. We'll have occasion to consider numerous examples of the failure of intuition as we move on through the rest of the book.

Reasons vs. outcomes. In choosing from among a set of alternatives, you can look for either (a) an alternative that's likely to have good consequences, or (b) an alternative that you'll be able to give good reasons for having chosen—that you can justify to yourself and others (Montgomery, 1983; Montgomery & Svenson, 1983; Simonson, 1989; Tversky & Shafir, 1992; Shafir, Osherson, & Smith, 1993). Often, these will be the same alternative, but not always.

In justifying their votes in the Presidential election of 2000, one friend of mine focused on consequences and the other on reasons. The one who focused on consequences said that he'd have voted for Nader if he felt that his vote wouldn't have affected the choice between Bush and Gore, since he wanted Nader's views to be heard more widely. Because he felt that his vote would've affected the choice between Bush and Gore, however, he voted for Gore, since he felt that a Gore presidency would have better impacts on society and the environment. The other friend who focused on reasons said that he liked Nader and that, because it's a free country, we have a right to vote our preferences. Although these two people had similar values, they approached their voting decisions in quite different ways.

The reasons we give to justify our decisions often take the form of *rules of thumb.* Perhaps the simplest way to make a decision is to do what's worked in the past. If you've always bought Fords and Fords have always given you good service, you could certainly do worse than buying a Ford the next time. For situations in which we've had little or no direct experience, ourselves, we can try to bring the experience of others to bear by applying common rules of thumb, such as: "Neither a borrower nor a lender be"; "If you want to have a friend, be one"; "When the sky looks like its been scratched by a hen, it's time to reef your topsails then"; "Honor thy father and thy mother"; "A bird in the hand is worth two in the bush"; "Be willing to compromise"; "Don't send good money after bad."

It's certainly wise to pay attention to what's worked in the past, and, when our own past experience is inadequate, it's certainly wise to look to the experience of others. However, rules of thumb are a very clumsy way to access experience. Rules of thumb tend to take the form: Do X. They rarely tell you *when* to do X or *why* you should do it. Rules of thumb are imprecise, ambiguous, and even contradictory. Thus, we have the inconsistent advice: "Look before you leap", but then, "Don't cross bridges until you get to them"; or "Two heads are better than one", but then, "Too many cooks spoil the broth."

If you're choosing a mutual fund, for example, you might prefer one that's performing well and that gets favorable reviews in the finance literature. You could easily justify such a choice by invoking the principle, "Buy quality." However, you've also heard that you should, "Buy low, sell high." Purchasing a high-performing fund will violate at least the first part of this prescription and, many (e.g., Dreman, 1982) say, it's likely to violate the second part, as well. The "buy low" part suggests that we should buy a fund that is *low-performing*. Thus, we have two sets of reasons, justifications, or rules of thumb, and they appear to be in conflict. This can easily happen with reasons of this sort, since they're so imprecise.

There are better ways than rules of thumb to bring our experience and that of others to bear on our decisions. These are incorporated in the steps on the Decision Ladder above the first, all of which involve thinking about the outcomes, or consequences, of the various alternatives. When two rules of thumb are in conflict, the ultimate test for deciding between them has to lie in a consideration of consequences (Mill, 1861/1957, pp. 69-72). Let's move on, then, to the main part of the ladder, where all methods are based on the ultimate test—the consideration of consequences. We can evaluate consequences by means of screening, decision tables, or decision trees.

Screening

The first step in winnowing down a list of alternatives, especially if it's long, is screening. In one sense, screening takes account of less information than intuition, in that it considers only one attribute at a time and doesn't consider tradeoffs. In another sense, however, it may take account of more information in that the total number of attributes it can consider is larger. Screening is appropriate for rejecting those alternatives that are so clearly unacceptable that it's possible to reject them by considering one attribute at a time.

It may be good enough to consider one value a time, using each to evaluate as many alternatives as have not yet been rejected. So long as more than one alternative remains, continue to consider additional values. As soon as only one alternative remains, accept it.

Screening is easy, not only because you have to think of only one value at a time but because you often have to think of only a small number in all. In buying a VCR, you might first decide what vendors you're going to check out. Then you might eliminate those of the brands carried by these vendors that don't have good reliability ratings in *Consumer's Report.* Then you might eliminate those of the remaining brands that you can't afford. If this hasn't narrowed the alternatives to one, you might make the final choice on the basis of appearance or certain special features, such as a high-speed rewind. Screening enables you to make a decision "in your head", without writing anything down.

> As we saw earlier, Amelia screened out Enforcement, Administration, and Sub-clinical immediately on the basis of their not being sufficiently challenging.

The trouble with considering only one value at a time is that, once an alternative has been screened out on the basis of a deficiency in a value considered early in the process, there's no opportunity for it to compensate for that deficiency by a strength in a value considered later. For this reason, screening is referred to as a *non-compensatory* decision process. A VCR that just missed the cut on reliability might come with the best warranty and in other respects give you the most for the money—but you'll never know, because, once it's been screened out, you'll never look at it again.

Two secondary rules decrease the chances of such errors and increase the chances that screening will result in a good choice:

Screen on the most important value first, then on the next most important value, and so on. Also, when in doubt as to whether to screen out or retain an alternative, retain it. When only one alternative remains, accept it.

In this way, if you make mistakes, they're likely to be small ones. The second rule, to retain alternatives about which there's any doubt, might result in a number of alternatives remaining at the end of the process, tied for first place. To choose among these, you should move up the Decision Ladder.

Screening is the decision method of choice when values of overriding importance are involved, characteristics that you *must* have rather than simply *want* to have. Ethical considerations are, perhaps, the best example (Etzioni, 1988). Screening out unethical alternatives rarely, if ever, screens out alternatives we'd have preferred. Normal people don't even *think* of the most seriously unethical alternatives. For example, if your neighbors don't mow their lawn as often as you'd like, you might consider various persuasion and conflict resolution approaches, but you wouldn't consider burning their house down to drive them out of the neighborhood, even if you thought you could get away with it!

There are two other general cases where screening may be the decision method of choice. One is low decision importance, and the other is high processing costs. If you're simply deciding what movie to go to, the importance of the decision doesn't justify any more time-consuming process than intuitive judgment or screening. If you're an emergency medical worker deciding on whom to treat immediately, whom to treat later, and whom to let die, decision importance is high, but so, too, are the costs of processing. The last thing you want to do at a time like this is think through a decision table. A recommended decision rule for making first aid decisions is screening on the basis of the following criteria: Bleeding, Breathing, Poisoning, Broken Bones. Begin with the most urgent condition, bleeding. If there's any serious bleeding, attend to it immediately. Then check for absence of breathing, and so forth.

Simple screening performs surprisingly well in comparison with methods higher up on the Decision Ladder (Thorngate, 1980; Russo & Dosher, 1980). In one study (Russo & Dosher, 1980), a simple screening rule reduced decision time from two minutes to 15 seconds yet increased error rate only from 8% to 14%.

It's actually possible to screen in a *compensatory* manner (Keeney, 1980, *pp. 92ff*). A simple rule for compensatory screening is:

Set each rejection level sufficiently low that no rejected alternative would be acceptable *even if it had the highest possible levels on all values not yet examined.*

Fifty applicants had to be evaluated for admission to a graduate program which could accept no more than seven. Six kinds of information were considered important: Verbal GRE, Quantitative GRE, School awarding bachelor's degree, GPA, Statement of Purpose, and Letters of Recommendation. Without some form of screening 50 x 6 = 300 items of information would have had to be processed. Screening was based on the sum of the two GRE scores. A cutting point was decided upon below which no one would be admitted *even if at the top of the range on all other measures.* The applicants that passed this screening were then evaluated on all measures. As it turned out, 30 applicants could be rejected on this basis. This saved processing of over 40% (30 x 4 = 120) of the items of information without any loss in decision quality.

Even when you plan to use a decision table, screening can play an important role, as in this example. Some alternatives that come to mind have such serious deficiencies that they can be easily and safely rejected by screening before you make up the decision table. The only alternatives that need be included in the decision table are those that are so attractive that none can be easily rejected. You eliminate what alternatives you can at this rung of the Decision Ladder then move up a rung to look more closely at those that remain.

Decision Tables

Like screening, a decision table decomposes the overall problem of comparing alternatives into the more manageable sub-problems of comparing them in terms of one value at a time. Unlike screening, however, decision tables allow for ultimately taking into account more than one value at a time, so that tradeoffs can be evaluated.

Also, unlike screening, a decision table ensures that the same values will be used to evaluate all alternatives. A person looking for a used car may quickly narrow down to recent model Toyotas because reliability is the most important value and *Consumer's Report* gives very high reliability ratings to Toyotas. However, when comparing Toyotas with one another, he or she may attend entirely to, say, aesthetics and convenience, even though recent model Toyotas may still differ importantly in reliability (Van Zee, Paluchowski, & Beach, 1992; Van Zee, 1989). A decision table assures that all alternatives will be evaluated consistently against the same set of attributes.

We sometimes apply different criteria to favored and unfavored alternatives. For example, whether Christians or Muslims, we're inclined to think about the community values associated with our own religion and the fanaticism associated with the other. As another example, and one that we touched on earlier, we tend to think of sunk costs as associated with the alternative that incurred the costs, even though these costs are just as irretrievable no matter which alternative is selected.

A decision table imposes a rational symmetry on our thought that should result in more balanced judgment. In the Christians-and-Muslims example, the table might look like this:

	Community Values	Fanaticism
Christians		
Muslims		

This table forces attention to all four cells, whereas Christians might think just of the upper-left and lower-right cells and Muslims might think just of the upper-right and lower-left cells.

As an example of a decision table, consider the analyses often presented in such publications as *Consumer's Report*. Each value distinction crosses the entire set of alternatives in that each alternative has a value on each attribute. For example, in a car purchase decision, every car has a value on Cost, Safety, Comfort, and Reliability.

	COST	SAFETY	RELIABILITY	COMFORT
Toyota Camry				
Subaru GL				
Volvo 760				

Each column can be thought of as a simple decision problem. The first column, for example, represents the problem of evaluating three cars that differ only in cost, a much simpler problem than the overall problem we started with. This is the divide-and-conquer strategy at work.

In entering data in a decision table, it's important to try to achieve the ideal of controlled comparison. This ideal wouldn't be well approximated if, in evaluating the above cars on Comfort, for example, your evaluation of the Toyota were based on having owned one; your evaluation of the Subaru were based on having read an article; and your evaluation of the Volvo were based on having talked with an owner. You'd better approximate the ideal of controlled comparison if you test drove the Subaru and the Volvo. Even then, you might have to make a mental adjustment for the fact that you'd still have had considerably more experience with the Toyota. Only a controlled comparison is a fair comparison.

Two special problems can arise in setting up a decision table: how to represent impacts on multiple stakeholders, and how to represent impacts at multiple points in time. Many of the decisions we make in life involve a number of people, either as decision makers or just as stakeholders whose values will be impacted by the decision. There are two ways to take multiple stakeholders into account in a decision table. You can let each stakeholder have his or her own columns and, when it comes time to assign importance weights, allow each an equal weight to divide among his or her own columns. Or, if the decision has greater impacts on some stakeholders than others, stakeholders might be given differential weights.

A way to take multiple stakeholders into account that would seem less divisive and more encouraging of group cohesion would be to treat the problem as a shared problem and use a single set of columns for everyone, implementing what has been called the "single text" approach to conflict resolution (Fisher & Ury, 1981). An effort would then be made to come to consensus on the weights, and sensitivity analyses would be performed on any ranges of disagreement.

Many decisions involve consequences that occur at different points in time. There are two ways to take present and future consequences into account in constructing a decision table. If these consequences are essentially the same, and your thinking about the future has simply called attention to their duration, note that duration in your fact table, so you can take it into account in judging importance weights. If present and future consequences are fundamentally different, such as an immediate cost and a delayed benefit or beginning salary and ultimate salary, you can create one column for the present consequences and another for the future consequences. In that case, also, you'll want to keep track of duration, so you can take it into account in weighting these columns.

Crossing the list of alternatives and the list of values to form a table accomplishes a number of surprisingly helpful things. For one, *a decision table calls attention to cells that might otherwise be overlooked,* and, in this way, it can enhance creative thinking. This is a form of stimulus variation. You can demonstrate this effect to yourself in a dramatic way. The next time you're getting advice from an expert (e.g., a medical doctor), try taking notes in decision table form. The expert will certainly suggest some alternatives; make these rows. The expert will also mention pros and cons; make these columns. Then, every time the expert makes a statement associating a particular alternative with a particular value (e.g., "Surgery will require that you be out of work for a month"), note that fact in the cell where the appropriate row and column intersect. What you'll undoubtedly find is that the expert won't consider even half of the cells! Without the help of a decision table, the expert will almost surely not give you enough information to get you any higher up the Decision Ladder than screening.

As we'll see shortly, a decision table can greatly increase the power of our thought in two other ways. First, when you look down columns, *a decision table calls attention to values in terms of which the alternatives are about equally desirable.* Such values can be eliminated entirely from further consideration. Second, when you look across rows, *a decision table makes it easy to identify alternatives that are* dominated *by another alternative.* "Dominance" will be defined shortly, and we'll see that dominated alternatives can be eliminated entirely from further consideration. Without a table, it's more difficult to identify irrelevant values and dominated alternatives.

It's always a good idea to draw a decision table out, perhaps on a handy napkin or the back of an envelope. It's hard enough to think of separate *lists* "in your head", and it's even harder with *crossed lists*, or tables. Just drawing the table can free up your mind enough to be able to consider the table in different ways and achieve important insights.

Because Amelia intended to conduct a number of informational interviews in order to get her facts straight, she prepared her decision table in the form of a data sheet that she took around to the interviews. This data sheet specifies the objective measure for each of her values and also includes reminders of the various things she wanted to keep in mind when thinking about each value. A data sheet like this can be very helpful in keeping discussions conducted at different times with a variety of people all focused on precisely the same decision problem.

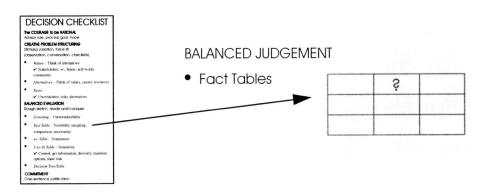

Fact Tables

So far, we've said nothing about what to put in the cells of a decision table. What we put in the cells depends on whether we're putting together a fact table or a value table. It can be of great help in decision making to separate facts from values, since, as already noted, we deal with them in quite different ways (Hammond & Adelman, 1976). Generally, we'll need both a fact table and a value table. We assemble the facts in a fact table and evaluate them in a value table.

"Facts" and "values" are both best thought of as statements or assertions. The term "fact" is used in this book, and commonly in the decision literature, to refer to an assertion of *belief,* or opinion: "I believe that it will be windy tomorrow." The term "value" is an assertion of *preference*: "I'd prefer that it be windy tomorrow" (because I plan to go sailing then). The important point to make here is that "fact" is *not* meant to imply, as it does in everyday language, that the statement of belief is *true*. (The weather prediction, a statement of fact rather than value, may be for wind tomorrow, yet there may turn out to be no wind tomorrow.) The label "fact" is meant to imply only that the statement, unlike a value statement, can be verified by others. This is the testability criterion encountered earlier.

Because of their logical priority, we begin our discussion with fact tables. However, in making decisions, sometimes we start with a fact table, and sometimes we start with a value table. In most problems, we need to start by doing some "research". We need to learn something about what consequences are associated with each of the alternatives. For example, a person considering various treatments for a health problem needs to begin by familiarizing herself with the efficacy and side effects of these treatments. A fact table is a good way to organize this "research", so she prepares a fact table first and then proceeds to a value table. Similarly, a person purchasing a product needs first to learn something about the characteristics of the alternative brands and models.

In other problems, we already know many or all of the facts and just need to get our thinking clear about our values. Consider a husband and wife trying to decide whether to charter a boat or rent a mountain cabin for their vacation this year. Since they've done each before, there's little question about facts. Their problem is to think through how various members of their family and some friends they often vacation with might feel about each alternative. They begin with a value table. Thinking about the value table may bring them to the realization that they need to get clearer about some of their facts; however, they're not likely to need a complete fact table.

Getting the facts straight is often crucial in decision making. As pointed out earlier, a causal analysis can suggest alternatives that are worth exploring or solutions that are obviously satisfactory. If you learn that the brown spots on your lawn were caused by using too much fertilizer, you know immediately what to do to avoid brown spots in the future. If you know that using high-wattage bulbs in your ceiling fixtures is what caused the insulation to dry and crack, you know right away what to do to keep this from happening again. Facts can both suggest alternatives and help us evaluate their effectiveness.

The role of facts is especially important where there are multiple decision makers and interpersonal disagreement. Fact-value separation identifies a portion of the problem that can be submitted to an external criterion (sometimes called "fact finding"). Once the fact issues have been cleared up, the scope of the conflict is often sufficiently reduced that the remainder of the problem resolves itself.

A group that I was working with came up against a decision that threatened to introduce serious conflict. People took strong positions, so strong that they started attributing the views of those who disagreed with them to the "kind of people" they were. They put off discussing the matter for months. When they finally did sit down to discuss it, they avoided dealing with it directly and took up, instead, the issue of whether a two-thirds majority should be required to settle the matter.

I made three simple suggestions. First, people should write down their beliefs (thus introducing testability into the picture). Second, they should examine the factual basis of these beliefs. Third, they should be open to the possibility of a creative alternative that would be better than the simple "yes" and "no" they'd been thinking about. I also had the temerity to predict that, if they did these things, they'd likely achieve consensus and not even need a vote.

The prediction was borne out. They arrived at a unanimous conclusion. They didn't even need to come up with a creative alternative; the first two suggestions were enough to do the trick. These suggestions are, in essence, the suggestion to create a fact table.

In using fact tables, we should never forget that beliefs can serve either a representational function or a self-enhancing function. If you or others are reluctant to agree on testable value attributes or an impartial arbiter for your beliefs, such as observation, a publication, or an expert opinion, those beliefs may be self-enhancing and may have to be approached differently. In cases where there's reluctance to put beliefs to a test, it's wise to try to ensure that all involved have reason to hope that they'll be able to feel good about themselves and the outcome in the event that that important beliefs are disconfirmed. The fact table can enhance decision making only if we feel secure enough to be able to put our beliefs about matters of fact to an objective test. Otherwise, it becomes a sham, serving only to rationalize our initial inclination, as do so many "decision analyses" done for powerful people.

Beware of self-enhancing beliefs in fact tables. In doubtful cases, ask, "Would I be willing to test my belief against observations, a publication, or an expert opinion?"

Amelia further summarized the data she had obtained in the fact table on the next page. (Her ranges of uncertainty are discussed in Chapter 6. Uncertainty.) In arriving at these summary figures, she didn't simply take averages but came up with her own best guess, taking into account what she felt to be the experience and credibility of her various sources of information. Amelia dropped Contribution to Society from the analysis, because she didn't feel that the alternatives could be reliably distinguished on this basis. She left the column in her table, however, to remind herself to keep trying to find some way to make this distinction reliably.

	Contribution to Society (children's/women's/cultural rights, reading, community)	Intellectual Challenge (creativity, academic knowledge, qualitative skills, variety)	Cultural Diversity	Compensation (Family)	Time for Family	Work Culture
	Number of people/year affected (also duration of impact)	*Percentage of time engaged in self-planned, skilled activities*	*Percentage of time working with people from other cultures*	*Dollar value of annual salary plus benefits*	*Hours/week with family*	*Percentage of time free from fixed schedule, location, and dress code*
University Professor		75%	55%	$45,000	30 hrs/wk	80%
Other Research		60%	55%	$40,000	15 hrs/wk	80%
Other Dissemination		65%	30%	$32,000	40 hrs/wk	50%
Fund-Raising/PR		35%	25%	$60,000	50 hrs/wk	5%

139

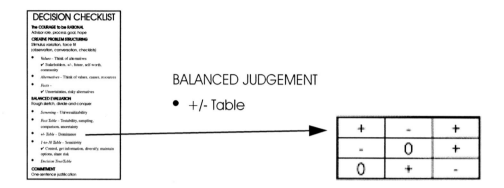

DECISION CHECKLIST

The COURAGE to be RATIONAL
Advisor role, process goal, hope

CREATIVE PROBLEM STRUCTURING
Stimulus variation, force fit
(observation, conversation, checklists)

- Values – Think of alternatives
  ✔ Stakeholders, +/-, future, self-worth, community
- Alternatives – Think of values, causes, resources
- Facts –
  ✔ Uncertainties, risky alternatives

BALANCED EVALUATION
Rough sketch, divide-and-conquer

- Screening – Universalizability
- Fact Table – Testability, sampling, comparison, uncertainty
- +/- Table – Dominance
- 1-to-10 Table – Sensitivity
  ✔ Control, get information, diversify, maintain options, share risk
- Decision Tree/Table

COMMITMENT
One-sentence justification

BALANCED JUDGEMENT

- +/- Table

+	-	+
-	0	+
0	+	-

Plusses-and-Minuses Value Tables

The simplest way to enter values in a value table is by means of plusses, zeroes, and minuses. If you've started with a fact table, the plusses-and-minuses table should have exactly the same rows and columns. Even if you plan to proceed to 1-to-10 ratings, it's helpful to begin with plusses and minuses to get a feel for the problem.

Amelia created the following plusses-and-minuses table to help her think about what she'd learned.

PLUSSES-and-MINUSES TABLE

	Soc	Intel	Cult	Comp	Fam	Work
U Prof		+	0	0	0	+
Research		0	0	0	-	+
Dissem		0	-	0	+	0
FR/PR		-	-	+	++	0

There are two ways to define plusses, zeroes, and minuses: in terms of absolute values or in terms of relative values. In absolute terms, a plus represents a positive experience; a zero, a neutral experience; and a minus, a negative experience. In relative terms, a plus may represent an improvement over the status quo; a zero, no change; and a minus, a worsening with respect to the status quo. Another way to define plusses, zeroes, and minuses in relative terms is to use a plus for the highest value in each column and a minus for the lowest.

Amelia preferred the absolute definitions. This is consistent with the advice given in Chapter 3 to adjust the zeroes on our value scales toward true zeroes, though the real force of this advice applies to thinking about attitude toward risk, a topic taken up in the appendix on Thinking More Deeply About Uncertainty.

In any case, multiple plusses and minuses can be used to make finer distinctions. Fund Raising/PR allowed so much extra time for family that Amelia used double plusses for this cell. Double plusses indicate the ordering of values in this column, but there's no reason to believe that double plusses in this column are any more positive than the single plusses in any other column. Evaluation at this stage is attribute by attribute. Evaluation at this stage is also only *ordinal*; it indicates only order of preference and tells us nothing, even within an attribute, about relative differences, or *intervals,* for example, whether the difference between a minus and a zero is equal to that between a zero and a plus. For plusses-and-minuses tables, value independence is required only at the ordinal level (p. 103).

Plusses, zeroes, and minuses are all we need to screen out irrelevant values and dominated alternatives. If an *attribute* is all plusses, for example, (or all zeroes or all minuses), it may be irrelevant and not worth considering further. If an *alternative* has too many minuses, it may not be worth considering further. More specifically, what we look for in rejecting alternatives is *dominance.* The following definition of "dominance" requires careful reading.

Alternative B *is dominated by* Alternative A if there is at least one difference in A's favor and no difference in B's favor.

Note that dominance does not apply attribute by attribute. When dominance is involved, it's an *entire alternative* that dominates another *entire alternative.* In the following table, for example, Alternative A does *not* dominate Alternative B:

Alternative A	+	+	+	+	+	+	+	+	-
Alternative B	-	-	-	-	-	-	-	-	+

The following example from an actual career decision illustrates how both dominated alternatives (the shaded rows) and unimportant attributes (the shaded column) can be eliminated.

	Satisfaction	Independence	Security	Income	Family
Attorney	0	0	0	+	-
Law Professor	+	+	0	+	+
Legal Consultant	0	0	0	0	+
Criminology Professor	+	+	0	+	+
Criminologist	0	0	0	0	+
Social Studies Teacher	+	0	0	+	+

In this example, we can begin by considering eliminating Security from the set of values, since all alternatives have approximately the same impact on this attribute. In this case, the decision maker, on reflection, agreed with the implications of her zero ratings, that there were no important differences in Security. Although security may have been important to her in some abstract sense, it was not important to this decision. This reduced the size of the set of value attributes.

To see how dominance works, let's compare Attorney and Law Professor, value by value. We notice right off that Attorney is inferior to Law Professor on Satisfaction. This means that Attorney will be dominated by Law Professor unless it's superior on one of the other values. We see that Attorney is also inferior to Law Professor on Independence, so that changes nothing, and they're tied on Security and Income, so that changes nothing, either. Finally, Attorney is inferior to Law Professor on Family. So, attorney is inferior to Law Professor on three values and superior on none and is therefore dominated by Law Professor.

In dominance, it's as though all the values took a vote, and the vote was unanimous, except for possible abstentions (ties). None of the values "voted" in favor of Attorney. Another way to say it is that, where there are differences, the differences are all in the same direction. Since the values don't disagree, we don't have to worry about which should have the greatest "vote". We can reject Attorney without having to think about tradeoffs and importance weights.

At this point, we can take a shortcut in evaluating dominance. Noticing that Law Professor and Criminology Professor have all plusses, we can, therefore, eliminate all alternatives that don't have all plusses as being dominated by these two. Each of these two alternatives is superior to each of the others in at least one respect and inferior in none. We've thus reduced a table of 6 x 5 = 30 cells to one of 2 x 4 = 8 cells, which should be much easier to think about.

Since Law Professor and Criminology Professor both have all plusses, the decision maker must consider whether these alternatives really differ in value or whether he or she'd be willing to let the toss of a coin decide between them. Getting beyond the rough sketch, a closer look at the plusses may reveal important differences among them. *However, important differences among plusses should have been represented by double or even triple plusses, and important differences among minuses should have been represented by double or triple minuses. Otherwise, alternatives might be rejected as dominated that wouldn't be dominated on the basis of 1-to-10 ratings.*

> Amelia saw that Other Research was dominated by University Professor and that Other Dissemination was nearly dominated by Fund Raising/PR. Suddenly, she realized that the alternatives fell into two qualitatively different groups, with University Professor and Other Research satisfying her personal values and Other Dissemination and Fund Raising/PR satisfying her family's values. University Professor dominated in the first category, and Fund Raising/PR dominated in the second, though no dominance occurred across categories. This turned out to be the crucial insight in her decision analysis.

We hope to find dominance, but when we find it we should be cautious. Dominance may indicate a superior alternative, but it may also indicate irrationality or lack of creativity. This is especially likely to be the case when one alternative dominates *all* the others. The most extreme case I've seen was a table in which one alternative had all plusses, another had all zeroes, and the third had all minuses! This is possible but quite unlikely. If these were, indeed, the true values, why would the person have felt any decisional conflict, in the first place? There must be a hidden value.

When one alternative dominates all the others, it'd be wise to spend some time trying to think of negative features of that alternative and positive features of its nearest competitor or to apply the rationality test to the alternatives that are not in first place:

Would I be willing to commit to and follow through on any one of these alternatives if the analysis indicated that it was the best?

Though we seldom *find* an alternative that dominates all others, we can sometimes *create* one; it's always worth putting a good deal of effort into trying to create an alternative that dominates all others before proceeding. Nothing can make a decision easier, or should make a decision maker happier, than such a win-win, alternative.

If you're unable to identify an alternative that dominates all others, try to create one.

The success of visionary companies has been attributed (Collins & Porras, 1994) to finding win-win solutions, rejecting "the tyranny of the OR" and embracing "the genius of the AND". The "tyranny of the OR" is accepting tradeoffs as inevitable, forcing you, for example, to choose between high computing power or portability. The "genius of the AND" is creatively thinking of win-win alternatives, alternatives that dominate all others, allowing you, for example, to have both high computing power and portability.

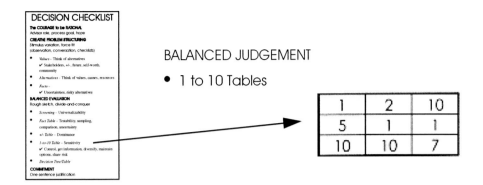

1 to 10 Value Tables

In those relatively few cases where the decision is not clear from the plusses-and-minuses table, we move up the Decision Ladder to the 1-to-10 table. Except for the elimination of any dominated alternatives and irrelevant values, the 1-to-10 table should have exactly the same rows and columns as the fact table and the plusses-and-minuses table. What we're about to do now is replace the plusses, zeroes, and minuses we've been using with numbers, specifically, value ratings.

Why do we need numbers? Usually, we don't. We try to make decisions without numbers, but, when things are sufficiently complex, introducing quantification can be an enormous help. Quantification enables us to combine our thinking about different parts of a decision problem with the least possible loss of information. And quantification opens the door to the power of sensitivity analysis, which, as we'll see, can provide great insight into a decision and also put to rest immediately and permanently both an individual decision maker's doubts and conflict among multiple decision makers!

In putting numbers on values, we first rate and then weight. There are four steps, in all.

- Rate

- Weight

- Multiply down

- Add across

Rate. The idea of value ratings isn't esoteric. Olympic diving, gymnastics, and ice skating are routinely given value ratings. In the movie, *Ten*, a 1-to-10 rating scale was used for evaluating feminine beauty. And often in conversation about some item of interest, we'll say, "On a 1-to-10 scale, how good would you say it is?"

Though we'll be talking about 1-to-10 scales throughout, some people prefer 1-to-5 scales because there's less to think about. So long as you don't feel that a 1-to-5 scale forces you to give the same rating to items that differ to any important degree, a 1-to-5 scale will work fine. Some people prefer 0-10 scales, because 5 provides a nice midpoint on such a scale. These are fine, too, so long as you realize that zero doesn't have to represent the absence of any value at all. It *can* represent a very low value or even a high value that just happens to be the lowest value associated with any of the alternatives under consideration. Zeroes confuse many people, however, and that's why we use 1-to-10 scales here.

In the table below, each attribute is rated on a separate 1-10 scale. Each column in the table is thus treated as an independent subproblem. Interval value independence allows us to do this.

	Cost	Safety	Reliability	Aesthetics
Car A	10	1	1	6
Car B	1	10	7	10
Car C	7	3	10	1

It's a very good idea at this point to compare your 1-10 ratings with your plusses and minuses. While people sometimes mistakenly assign a 10 to a high cost, they rarely mistakenly assign a plus to a high cost.

Evaluation at this stage indicates the relative differences between what had previously been indicated as plusses, zeroes, and minuses. Relative differences can be very important. Buying insurance, for example, involves choosing a small minus (the premiums) to protect against a large minus (the cost to recover from the loss). Investing involves foregoing a small plus (the amount invested) to achieve a larger plus (the principal plus the return on the investment).

For each value attribute, 1 is ordinarily assigned to the least preferred end of the range, and 10 is ordinarily assigned to the most preferred end. However, there are, basically, two kinds of ranges, local ranges and global ranges. In using *local ranges*, you assign a 1 to the lowest level (or levels, if there are ties) in each column and a 10 to the highest level (or levels, if there are ties) in each column. In using *global ranges*, you assign a 1 to the level on each attribute that you consider to be very low, regardless of whether any of the alternatives actually has a value this low, and a 10 to the level on each attribute that you consider to be very high, regardless of whether any of the alternatives actually has a value this high. The first method uses ranges that are problem specific; the second uses ranges that are more general. When there's a difference, global ranges are necessarily broader than local ranges. The distinction is similar to that between relative and absolute bases for assigning plusses and minuses. Local ranges were used in the car example.

Local ranges may be easier, because it's easy to remember that there must be at least one 1 and at least one 10 in each column. as in the table above. Using local ranges should also make it absolutely clear that the numbers in different columns are on entirely different scales. It's quite all right that an unimportant impact in one column gets an 8, while a more desirable impact in another column gets a 2. The weights will correct this later.

Global ranges may result in somewhat more valid judgments, because the scales are anchored on lows and highs that are meaningfully related to the decision maker's general experience. Also, because global ranges are beyond the ranges involved in the decision at hand, they should also result in value judgments that are more stable from decision to decision (Brown, 1981; Gabrielli & Von Winterfeldt, 1978; Morrison & Slovic, 1962; Tversky & Simonson, 1993). Earlier, I suggested that the superiority of real units, such as dollars, to relative units, such as percentages, and of real zero points to relative zero points pointed to a general principle of keeping our representations of reality as close as possible to the reality they're representing. This same principle would seem to argue for global ranges in preference to local ranges.

Since differences are important, it's a good idea to spend some time thinking about them. Is each 5 or 6 really about halfway in value between the 1 and the 10 in its column? In other words, if you were going to get the outcome rated 1 and got the outcome rated 5 or 6 instead, would the improvement in value be about the same as if you were going to get the outcome rated 5 or 6 and got the outcome rated 10 instead?

The following are Amelia's ratings. Because she used global ranges, not every column will have a 1 for its lowest value or a 10 for its highest.

1-to-10 Table

	Soc	Intel	Cult	Comp	Fam	Work
U Prof	7	8	6	5	8
Rsch	5	8	4	1	8
Dissem	6	3	2	8	5
FR/PR	3	2	10	10	1

Weight. Each attribute is assigned a weight that reflects its relative importance. Weights for the car problem have been inserted into the table below:

	Cost .10	Safety .30	Reliability .40	Aesthetics .20
Car A	10	1	1	6
Car B	1	10	7	10
Car C	7	3	10	1

Weighting involves three steps: preparing a range table, ranking the values in importance, and weighting the values. It should help to see how Amelia went through these steps.

Amelia's range table is shown below:

Range Table (with Rankings)

	Contrib-ution to Society	Intellectual Challenge B	Cultural Diversity C	Compen-sation B	Time for Family A	Work Culture B
10		100%	70%	$60,000	15 hrs	100%
1		10%	10%	$25,000	50 hrs	0%

A range table has the same columns as the 1-to-10 table, but only two rows. The top row represents the high ends of the ranges (rated "10") on all the values, and the bottom row represents the low ends of the ranges (rated "1"). Since it's unlikely that any alternative will be all 1's (it would have been rejected with little thought) or that any will be all 10s (it would have been selected with little thought), each of the rows in the range table will represent a hypothetical (not real) alternative.

The first step in assigning weights is to *rank order* the attributes in terms of importance. It's at this point that we start to compare "apples" and "oranges". If you were offered your choice from a bowl of apples and oranges, you wouldn't find the task of comparing them overwhelmingly difficult and could quickly choose one or the other. The logic of rank ordering the attributes is similar, in that it's based on *choices* you make. I call this the "magic wishes" technique. The decision maker begins by assuming the least preferable level on all attributes and then changes each to the most preferable level by making a series of "magic wishes", beginning with the wish that would result in the greatest improvement, then proceeding to the wish that would result in the next greatest improvement, and so forth.

> Amelia began by asking herself magic wishes questions to rank order the values in importance. She imagined she was in the situation depicted by the bottom row in the range table: doing work she'd decided on only 10% of the time, associating with people from other cultures only 10% of the time, earning $25,000 a year, working 80 hours a week, and having no time free from a rigid dress code and time schedule. The first magic wish was easy, to reduce the hours worked per week, so she could spend more time with her family. After that, the values were all about the same, except for Cultural Diversity, which was the least important. Hence, her ranking for Intellectual Challenge, Cultural Diversity, Compensation, Time for Family, and Work Culture, respectively, was B, C, B, A, B, where A represents the most important category, B represents the next most important category, and C represents the least important category. There were three B's, because Amelia couldn't rank these values. Ties are acceptable in weights, as well as in ratings. Contribution to Society got no weight, because there was still no clear difference among the alternatives in this regard.

There are a number of considerations that can help in thinking about importance: magnitude, duration, probability, and number of people affected.

In thinking about relative importance, it can help to think about relative

- Magnitude of impact,

- Duration of impact,

- Probability of impact, and

- Number of people impacted.

The third step in thinking about attribute importance is to assign numerical weights to the attributes. The easiest way to do this is to distribute 100 points over them in such a way that the relative numbers of points reflect relative importance. This method of assigning weights is called the *point-allocation method* (Metfessel, 1949). The idea is that all of the attributes together make up 100% of the importance of the difference between the hypothetical alternative that is all-1s and the hypothetical alternative that is all-10s.

It's worth repeating that the importance weights should not reflect the importance of the *attributes* but the importance of *full-range (1-to-10) changes* on the attributes (see Anderson, Deane, Hammond, McClelland, &, Shanteau 1981.) For example, most people would say that "safety" is more important than "cost", yet the relative importance of these two values depends entirely on the particular decision and the ranges involved. In purchasing a painting for your living room, safety would probably get zero weight (and not even be thought of), since paintings don't differ in safety, yet cost might get a very high weight, since paintings can differ enormously in cost. The point-allocation weight of any attribute can be thought of as the importance of making a full-range change on that attribute as a percentage of the importance of making full-ranges on all attributes.

When weighting sub-goals, such as wealth, time, knowledge, skills, and social contacts, there's a danger that you'll under-weight them, because they're more abstract than specific goals (Prelec & Herrnstein, 1991; Tversky & Koehler, 1994). A corrective for this tendency is to try to think concretely about ways in which the sub-goal in question might benefit you. If time is the sub-goal, for example, how might you spend that time?

Amelia did not use the point-allocation method, but preferred one of the tradeoff methods presented in the appendix on Thinking More Deeply About Values. Her use of this method is described there.

Amelia placed her weights along the top of her value table:

Weights and Unweighted Ratings

	Soc	Intel	Cult	Comp	Fam	Work
	0	0.19	0.05	0.19	0.38	0.19
U Prof		7	8	6	5	8
Rsch		5	8	4	1	8
Dissem		6	3	2	8	5
FR/PR		3	2	10	10	1

Since it's a good idea to perform consistency checks on importance weight judgments, Amelia noted that the weight for Time for Family, .38, was about twice as great as that for Intellectual Challenge, .19 and asked herself whether the impact of a full-range change on Time for Family would really be about twice as great as a full-range change on either Intellectual Challenge, Compensation, or Work Culture. She felt that it would, thus confirming her weights for these values.

It's most important to perform a consistency check on the extremes of the importance range, the highest weight and the lowest weight. If these extreme weights aren't in the correct ratio, then other weights will probably have to be adjusted proportionately, as well. Additional consistency checks can be especially helpful for weights about which a single decision maker is most uncertain or with respect to which multiple decision makers are in substantial disagreement.

Multiply down. Up to this point, the attributes have been measured on separate 1-10 scales. These numbers are "apples and oranges" and can't be compared. Adding them would be like adding 12 inches and 1 yard. We'd get 13, but the 13 would be nonsense—the same nonsense we'd get by adding 12 yards and 1 inch. One way to add 12 inches and 1 yard is first to multiply yards by 3 to get feet and inches by 1/12 to get feet and then to add the feet together, "apples and apples". Following this same logic, the ratings in each column are multiplied by the importance weight for that column, to put everything on a common scale of value. In the car example, the rating of 10 for Car A on Cost is multiplied by the .10 weight for Cost to yield a *part value* of 1.0, which has been placed right in bold italics below the unweighted rating of 10.

	Cost .10	Safety .30	Reliability .40	Aesthetics .20
Car A	10 *1.0*	1 *0.3*	1 *0.4*	6 *1.2*
Car B	1 *0.1*	10 *3.0*	7 *2.8*	10 *2.0*
Car C	7 *0.7*	3 *0.9*	10 *4.0*	1 *0.2*

Add across. Now that everything is in terms of "apples", or comparable part values, all the part values in each row are added to get a *total value rating* for that alternative.

	Cost .10	Safety .30	Reliability .40	Aesthetics .20	TOTAL
Car A	10 *1.0*	1 *0.3*	1 *0.4*	6 *1.2*	*2.9*
Car B	1 *0.1*	10 *3.0*	7 *2.8*	10 *2.0*	*7.9*
Car C	7 *0.7*	3 *0.9*	10 *4.0*	1 *0.2*	*5.8*

Decision makers will almost always be uncertain about the ratings and weights. Usually, uncertainty about weights is greater than uncertainty about ratings. This is probably because rating requires thinking about only one value at a time, while weighting requires thinking about at least two values at a time. In the case of multiple decision makers, discussion may produce agreement on some of the numbers, but there will virtually always be disagreement on others. Whether the uncertainty is within or across decision makers, we tentatively enter the average ratings and weights in the table—a statistical compromise. But we keep track of the ranges of uncertainty, so that later we can perform sensitivity analyses on them to see whether the extent of the uncertainty would have any effect on which alternative has the highest total value rating. Sensitivity analysis is discussed in the next chapter.

Amelia multiplied down to get the part values in the cells of the following table and then added across to get the total value ratings at the right end of each row.

Weights and Weighted Ratings

	Soc	Intel	Cult	Comp	Fam	Work	Totals
	0	0.19	0.05	0.19	0.38	0.19	1
U Prof		1.3	0.4	1.1	1.9	1.5	*6.29*
Research		1.0	0.4	0.8	0.4	1.5	*4.01*
Dissem		1.1	0.2	0.4	3.0	1.0	*5.66*
FR/PR		0.6	0.1	1.9	3.8	0.2	*6.56*

Because they have been adjusted by their column weights, all numbers in this table are on the same scale and can be compared with one another. As in the plusses-and-minuses table, it can be seen that Other Research and Other Dissemination are substantially inferior to University Professor and Fund Raising/PR. Also, as in the plusses-and-minuses table, it can be seen that University Professor is highest on Amelia's own values, while Fund Raising/PR is highest on her husband's and children's values. In Amelia's case, the plusses-and-minuses table was really all she needed in order to see what to do.

If Amelia had been making a career choice at this point, she might simply have gone with the highest alternative, Fund Raising/PR. She'd almost surely have done this if she had two outstanding job offers and had to choose within a short time. However, she wasn't making a career choice, but simply deciding how best to learn more about career alternatives and also, hopefully, to create career opportunities. Since graduate school would already give her an opportunity to learn about and create opportunities in the area of University Professor, she decided to look for part-time work in the area of Fund Raising/PR. Gaining experience in each of the two most attractive areas should put her in the best position to make a choice later and, even better, it might enable her to discover or create a win-win combination that'd satisfy both the personal values of University Professor and the family values of Fund Raising/PR.

We're almost done, but not quite. We should finally compare the results against intuition, asking ourselves, "Does this feel right?" If it doesn't, we'll have to examine both analysis and intuition to find the basis for the discrepancy, so we can correct it.

Amelia felt good about this result. It certainly didn't feel like an alien result imposed by an artificial method. Rather, she felt that it gave her a deeper insight into things she'd known, though only in a fragmentary, disconnected fashion, all along.

Commitment and Follow-Through

Once we've arrived at a balanced judgment and our decision has been made, it can then be helpful to find a one-sentence justification for the decision. A one-sentence justification is useful for reminding ourselves of our reasoning, making it easier to justify a good decision to both ourselves and others and thus maintain commitment in carrying it out. At this point, simplistic "bumper sticker" slogans can serve a useful function, so long as they honestly express the essence of a sound decision analysis.

> Amelia was able to justify her decision to herself easily: Gaining experience in each of the two most attractive areas should put her in the best position to make a choice later and, perhaps, to discover or create a win-win combination that would satisfy both her personal values and her family values.

Finally, as you plan to implement your decision, think about the steps involved. When should they be accomplished? Who should be responsible for each? What resources will be needed? Then monitor your progress to make sure you're on course, being prepared to make course corrections and even to re-evaluate the initial decision, if things don't go as planned.

Resource-Allocation Decisions

All the decisions we've considered so far are decisions that involve *mutually exclusive alternatives,* that is, decisions in which the decision maker intends to choose one and only one alternative. The shopper usually buys only one car; the couple usually buys only one house; the patient usually chooses only one surgeon. Such decisions seem to be, far and away, the most common; however, not all decisions are of this kind.

In *resource allocation* decisions, the decision maker intends to choose more than one alternative, as many as can be "paid for" with a limited resource. A couple has $10,000 to spend fixing up their house. How should they spend it? A dieter has 2500 calories a day to "spend" on food. What foods will maximize nutrition and taste? A single parent who's working part time and going to school part time has 100 hours a week to allocate to her children, studying, workouts, and leisure. How should that time be allocated? A mountain climber has 3500 square inches of backpack space to allocate to food and equipment. What should come along, and what should be left behind? A couple can invite about twenty people to a party. Whom should they invite? For such decisions the mutual exclusiveness requirement for an alternative set is obviously not applicable.

The general procedure for making resource allocation decisions is as follows:

- Analyze the problem just as you would if you were choosing a single alternative, but *don't include the limited resource (dollars, time, space, etc.) in the analysis.*

- For each alternative, take total value as the measure of *benefit* and the amount of the limited resource that the alternative requires as the measure of *cost,* and divide benefit by cost to obtain a *benefit/cost ratio.* (In a simplified version, you can evaluate total benefit intuitively, rather than using a decision table.)

- *Rank* the alternatives in order of their benefit/cost ratios.

- Select the alternative with the highest benefit/cost ratio, and subtract its cost from the total amount of the limited resource. Then select the alternative with the next highest benefit/cost ratio, and subtract its cost from what's left of the limited resource. Continue on down the ranking.

- Stop when (a) the limited resource is exhausted, or (b) you get to a benefit/cost ratio so low that you don't feel that the benefit is worth the cost.

This sounds complicated, but here's an example to show how simply these general principles can be approximated in application.

> *While travelling, I went into a tie store with about $100 to spend on ties and very little time to devote to the decision. I first looked around the store, screening out unacceptable ties and taking acceptable ones off the rack. Then, using external memory, I arranged the ties I'd selected on the counter, so that the left-to-right positions of the ties represented increasing benefit. Next, maintaining these left-to-right positions, I distributed the ties from front to back in decreasing order of cost. Finally, I started in the back right-hand corner, with the high benefit, low cost ties, and selected three ties that were sufficiently different from one another to constitute a varied set. It took only a minute or two to lay out the ties in this way and make the selection. The clerk's comment was, "Most people take longer than that to decide on one tie!", and my thought to myself was, "And, I'll bet, they don't take account of nearly as much information." Good decision processes don't have to be cumbersome.*

Here's a numerical example. Every year, the Psychology Department reviews its journal orders, adding new ones and dropping old ones so as to maximize the benefit obtained from its library budget. The following procedure was developed for this process:

- *Each faculty member rates each publication on a 1-5 value rating scale.* The instructions point out that value should be considered from the point of view of the department as a whole, so that the upper end of the scale will presumably be anchored by American Psychological Association journals. This instruction addresses the *commons dilemma* problem (discussed in the next section), which could, in the extreme case, incline everyone to put the highest ratings on journals in their special areas, leaving it to others to give high ratings to the APA journals, with the result that important APA journals get deselected.

- *Mean ratings are divided by costs to obtain benefit/cost ratios.* This is easy to do in a spreadsheet.

- *Publications are ranked in decreasing order of benefit/cost ratio, and funds are allocated in that order until the budget is expended.* This, too, is easy to do in a spreadsheet, using the Sort command.

- *Finally, a search is made among the rejected journals for any that were rated highly by one or more faculty members, so that their rejection may be reconsidered.* This, too, is easy to do in a spreadsheet. This instruction helps guard against a tyranny of the majority. At this time, *portfolio effects* (discussed in the appendix on Thinking More Deeply About Values) are also considered.

To use a phrase that's been around for a while, what benefit/cost ratios measure is "bang for the buck." This phrase was first used by the nuclear physicist Edward Teller when trying to persuade President Truman to support the development of the atom bomb. The atom bomb, Teller argued, would give more "bang for the buck". The use of a benefit/cost ratio is appropriate here, since Truman had limited resources to commit to the war effort and would certainly pursue as many of the best alternatives as he could with those resources. However, "bang" seems an inadequate measure of benefit. An appropriate measure of benefit, even in war, would be multiattribute and would include along with "bang" such negative "benefits" as unnecessary loss of life and long-term biological, psychological, and political effects. In any case, the proper application of benefit/cost ratios assures the greatest benefit for the amount of the limited resource spent.

Commons Decisions

Commons decisions are surely the most important decisions humankind faces and the most important to understand correctly. The striking fact is that *the principle we've come to regard as the very foundation of wise choice—selecting the alternative with the highest total value rating—can actually get us into trouble in commons decisions!*

Consider the example that gave the "tragedy of the commons" its name (Hardin, 1968, 1993). A number of herders share a common grazing area. In terms of community values, all would prefer a well-regulated and prosperous commons in which no one grazes more than his or her share. In terms of individual values, however, each realizes that he or she would be better off to graze just a few extra animals. These few extra animals would make little difference to the commons but a great difference to the individual decision maker. (An urban example is the choice to drive or take the bus during a pollution alert.)

The decision tree below shows the pattern of payoffs typical in commons decisions. Decision trees will be explained in the chapter on Uncertainty. For the moment, it will suffice to know that the square represents the herder's choice, with the branches coming out of it representing alternatives, and that the circles and the branches coming out of them represent the herder's uncertainty about the choices that other herders will make. In the herder's case, "Cooperate" means don't graze, and "Not Cooperate" means graze.

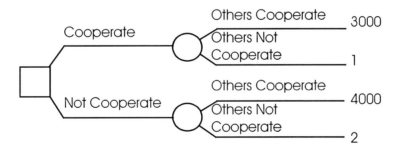

The 1, 2, 3000, and 4000 represent only ordinal relations. Any numbers can be substituted for these numbers, so long as the number substituted for the 4000 is greater than the number substituted for the 3000, the number substituted for the 3000 is greater than the number substituted for the 2, and the number substituted for the 2 is greater than the number substituted for the 1. If you cooperate, it's better when others cooperate (4000 is better than 3000); and, if you don't cooperate, it's also better when others cooperate (2 is better than 1).

The crucial point is that each individual is better off to graze extra animals no matter what the others do (a kind of dominance). When others cooperate, it's better not to cooperate (4000 is better than 3000); *and*, when others don't cooperate, it's also better not to cooperate (2 is better than 1). Yet it's better for all to cooperate (3000) than for all not to cooperate (2). *If all follow the compelling logic of individual rationality, the commons will eventually be destroyed, and all will suffer!* Those who, in such situations, are seduced by the limited logic of individual rationality have been aptly dubbed "rational fools" (Sen, 1977).

Consider another example. From the perspective of individual rationality, the negative impact of having a third child—adding one more person to a world population that, as of this writing, stands at over five billion—is certainly negligible in comparison with the joy the parents would receive. Yet, if everyone acted in this "rational" way, the sum of the negligible impacts would be disastrous.

The decision rule proposed by the philosopher Immanual Kant is helpful in commons decisions, that is, decisions involving community goods: Decide only in ways that would be appropriate for everyone in similar circumstances. This rule is called the *Principle of Universalizability*. The key question is, "What if everyone did this?" Thinking about decisions in terms of universilizability quickly leads to general ethical principles that apply across situations. Ethical actions are universalizable; unethical actions are not. An emphasis on ethics and "community rationality" can help us to avoid tragedies of individual rationality.

As a check, before choosing the alternative with the highest total value rating, ask, "What if everyone did this?"

The Golden Rule and the Platinum Rule, as useful as they may be, are no substitutes for the Principle of Universalizability. If our herder had considered the Golden Rule, "Do unto others as you would have others do unto you," he or she might have thought, "My few extra animals will have no real impact on the others. I wouldn't care if they did something that had an undetectably small impact on me, so they shouldn't care if I do something that has an undetectably small impact on them."

The Platinum Rule is more sophisticated than the Golden Rule in that it's open to the possibility that others have different values from you: "Do unto others as *they* would have you do unto them." A good part of the art of diplomacy is treating people from other cultures as people in *their* culture would have you treat them (Platinum Rule), and not making the social gaff of treating them as people in your own culture would have you treat them (Golden Rule). However, even the Platinum Rule can't be counted on to avoid the tragedy of the commons.

The reason neither the Golden Rule nor the Platinum Rule works is that both focus on individual decisions. It's also important to think about the multiple decisions that would result if the same decision policy were repeated. The Principle of Universalizability calls attention to the consequences of generalizing the contemplated action to everyone.

Actually, a similar problem can arise in decisions that affect only oneself (Prelec & Herrnstein, 1991). In deciding whether to smoke or eat a rich dessert on a single occasion, the benefits might well outweigh the costs; yet, in repeated decisions, the costs might outweigh the benefits. In deciding whether to exercise or put money in savings on a single occasion, the costs of saving might outweigh the benefits; yet, in repeated decisions, the benefits might outweigh the costs. An extension of the principle of universalizability would seem helpful here, also. We should ask ourselves: Would it be acceptable if in similar circumstances I repeatedly decided as I'm now thinking of deciding?

The following joke shows with unusual clarity that the best choice for an individual decision is not necessarily the best choice for a series of such decisions:

> Some kids were in the habit of teasing one of their group by repeatedly offering him a choice between a nickel and a dime. He always chose the nickel, "because it's bigger."
>
> One day, a friend took him aside and asked, "Don't you know that a dime's worth more than a nickel?"
>
> The kid answered, "Yeah, but if I picked the dime they'd stop doing it!"

Community values can keep us from making poor decisions in commons dilemmas, but, because the commons problem is more a matter of logic than values, we have to be careful. Commons dilemmas can arise in situations where selfishness doesn't seem to be an issue. Imagine that everyone made a perfectly rational decision to send his or her charitable contributions to the charity that would provide the greatest benefit for the dollar.

The consequence would be that that charity would have more money than it could use efficiently, and the others would have none! The decision might make sense for one person, but it certainly doesn't pass the test of universalizability. This is exactly what happened when, following the September 11th tragedy, many generous, public-spirited Americans made the "rational" decision to send money to the Red Cross. While community values provide a good rough test, the ultimate test appears to be universalizability.

Chapter 6. UNCERTAINTY: What could happen?

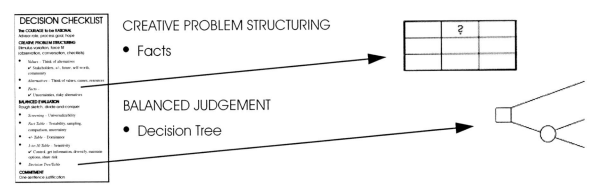

DECISION CHECKLIST

The COURAGE to be RATIONAL
Advisor role, process goal, hope

CREATIVE PROBLEM STRUCTURING
Stimulus variation, force fit
(observation, conversation, checklists)

• *Values* – Think of alternatives
   ✔ Stakeholders, +/-, future, self-worth,
      community
• *Alternatives* – Think of values, causes, resources
• *Facts* -
   ✔ Uncertainties, risky alternatives

BALANCED EVALUATION
Rough sketch, divide-and-conquer

• *Screening* – Universalizability
• *Fact Table* - Testability, sampling,
   comparison, uncertainty
• *+/- Table* - Dominance
• *1-to-10 Table* – Sensitivity
   ✔ Control, get information, diversify, maintain
      options, share risk
• *Decision Tree/Table*

COMMITMENT
One-sentence justification

CREATIVE PROBLEM STRUCTURING

• Facts

BALANCED JUDGEMENT

• Decision Tree

Awareness of uncertainty can be enhanced by a number of idea-stimulating questions. Regret is an expression of poor judgment in thinking about uncertainty and should be resisted as a basis for evaluating decisions. There are a variety of ways to "uncertainty proof" alternatives and make them more robust over a range of possible futures: control, obtaining information, keeping options open, diversification, and sharing risk. Sensitivity analysis determines whether a given source of uncertainty is important to the decision. It can greatly simplify a decision problem by freeing attention from unimportant aspects of the problem. Decision trees are the most sophisticated way to represent decisions involving uncertain events to which the decision is sensitive and also for representing sequences of decisions.

"There's many a slip 'twixt cup and lip." "Life is uncertain. Eat dessert first." These sayings—along with terms like "uncertainty", "chance", "luck", "risk", "gamble", "venture", "speculation", "accident", "possible", "likely", "unlikely", and "random"—all call attention to the fact that we seldom, if ever, really *know* what the future will bring. How then, if we can't be certain about the future consequences of the alternatives, can we have any confidence that we've chosen the best of the alternatives? We'll consider three answers to this question:

- *"Uncertainty-proofing" alternatives.* Creating "uncertainty-proof" alternatives is applicable anywhere on the Decision Ladder and is the only one of the three approaches that isn't at all quantitative. It involves such strategies as diversification and sharing risk. It's the most robust approach in that it assumes little about our ability to predict the future.

- *Sensitivity analysis.* Sensitivity analysis identifies important uncertainties for further consideration. It requires working with 1-to-10 ratings.

- *Maximize expected value.* Maximizing expected value requires moving up to a new rung on the Decision Ladder. It's the most involved of the three approaches, requiring (a) a 1-to-10 decision table, (b) a decision tree, (c) a probability for each possible future, and (d) calculation of expected value for each alternative. Maximizing expected value is discussed in the appendix on Thinking More Deeply About Uncertainty. However, there's little point in taking this last step up the ladder, until the first two approaches have been thoroughly explored, and it's not a step you should take unless you understand it well.

Following the pattern of the chapters on values and alternatives, methods are presented for thinking creatively, efficiently, and critically about uncertainty. The methods for thinking *creatively* about uncertainty are a checklist of questions for identifying sources of uncertainty and a checklist of "uncertainty proofing" operations. The method for thinking *efficiently* about uncertainty is sensitivity analysis. The tools for thinking *critically* about uncertainty are the rules for creating decision trees and for performing probability and expected-value calculations.

Awareness of Uncertainty

We begin our consideration of uncertainty with ways to think creatively about it. No one who's unaware of uncertainty is likely to consider *any* of the approaches for dealing with it. We tend not to be sufficiently aware of uncertainty, often thinking of a single future and one that's much like the present. We tend to be overly confident in our beliefs, perhaps because it requires effort to doubt our automatic processes. Sir Francis Bacon (1620, First Book, Aphorism 45) said:

> *The human understanding is of its own nature prone to suppose the existence of more order and regularity in the world than it finds [and] when it has once adopted an opinion, draws all else to support and agree with it.*

More recently, and in a more down-to-earth way, the humorist Artemus Ward (Stevenson, 1949, p. 1055) has said much the same thing:

> *It is better not to know so much than to know so many things that ain't so.*

Or, as I prefer to say it:

> *It ain't the things we don't know that get us into trouble so;*
> *It's the things we know that ain't so.*

Even the far-sighted Malthus (1826), who predicted as early as 1798 the effects of population growth that we're just now beginning to experience, anticipated only effects similar to those experienced in the past, such as mass starvation, and was unable to anticipate effects much different from those experienced in the past, such as global warming, acid rain, and the destruction of the ozone layer.

In investment decisions, people are often lulled into complacency by the term "risk-free investment", yet a "risk-free" investment is risk-free only in terms of the *nominal* dollars that'll be returned at the end of the investment period. Because of inflation risk, there's considerable uncertainty as to how much those dollars will be able to buy. If we think in terms of eventual purchasing power, or *constant* dollars, "risk-free" investments are *risky*. Indeed, some recent analyses even suggest that "risk-free" bonds may be riskier, in terms of purchasing power, than stocks (Siegel, 1994, p. 32).

As a consequence of expecting no surprises, we often are surprised (perhaps you were surprised by what was said about "risk-free" investments in the preceding paragraph), and life's surprises can be costly. The expectation that the future will be like the past is what leads people to build in flood plains. It's what inclines the healthy to put off getting medical insurance and the young to put off planning for retirement. It's what initially led U. S. automobile manufacturers to discount foreign economy cars and Swiss watch makers to discount digital watches as significant competitive threats.

A common stance with respect to such dangers as smoking, earthquakes, global warming, or overpopulation is expressed in words like: "Scientists are still in disagreement, so there's no reason to change my behavior." Such comments seem to assume, perhaps as a defense mechanism, perhaps as a failure of creative thinking, that there's no risk associated with business as usual. In the case of smoking, for example, the greatest suggested risk is associated with continuing to smoke, and a better stance would seem to be to *refrain* from smoking until scientists are "in agreement". Similarly, in the case of potential catastrophic damage to the environment, the better course would seem to be to *refrain* from any potentially risky behavior until scientists are "in agreement" that it's safe.

Anticipating uncertainty is part of problem structuring and requires creative thinking. The following questions can provide effective stimulus-variation to help with this task.

- What entries in the fact table am I most uncertain about?

- What entries in the value table am I most uncertain about?

In filling out the fact table, you were likely fairly certain about some cell entries yet quite uncertain about others. In trying to come up with 1-to-10 ratings, or even just plusses, zeroes, and minuses, for your value table, you may have asked yourself, "How can I be sure how I feel about this value?" Perhaps you recorded confidence intervals in your table. Now's the time to think further about the entries you were uncertain of. Although uncertainty about the future is all that we care about when choosing among alternative courses of action, we should also be sensitive to uncertainty about the present and the past, since such uncertainty can result in uncertainty about the future. We should also be sensitive to both uncertainty about the facts and uncertainty about the values we place on those facts. You may know for sure that the car you're considering has a sun roof, but are you sure just how much you'll like a sun roof?

Often, one or two alternatives will seem more risky than others. If you're trying to decide whether to stay with your current job or accept a new job offer, to stay in your current house or move to a new one, to stay married or get a divorce, the status quo alternative is usually the more predictable of the two. It's alternatives that involve changes that tend to be less certain and more risky. It's the uncertainty of the consequences of change that deterred Hamlet from suicide. "To sleep, perchance to dream. Aye, there's the rub!" Hamlet knew what life was like, but he wasn't at all certain what death might bring. The following question, too, can help identify uncertainties:

Which alternative represents the greatest gamble?

Two other such questions focus on events or scenarios (collections of events):

- What things could go wrong?

- What things could "go right" and provide a lucky break?

It can be helpful to make a *list of events* that could affect, favorably or unfavorably, the outcomes of the alternatives you're considering (Keller & Ho, 1988). Thinking of optimistic ("best case") and pessimistic ("worst case") scenarios and ways in which they differ is a powerful method for thinking of such events. Another is thinking, for each option, what event would make it turn out best and what event would make it turn out worst (Keller & Ho, 1988).

As noted earlier, the most sophisticated approach to thinking in terms of scenarios was developed by Royal Dutch/Shell and has now been used by over 50 percent of *Fortune* 500 companies (Schoemaker, 1993). Briefly, the process is to:

- Construct two *extreme scenarios* by placing all positive outcomes of key uncertainties in one scenario and all negative outcomes in the other;

- Derive *plausible scenarios* from these by backing off from combinations that could not occur; and then

- Use these scenarios as *stimuli for further thought*, for example, by thinking about how key stakeholders might behave in them.

The scenario method doesn't attempt to predict the future, but to bound it. Perhaps more important, the scenario method doesn't represent uncertainly directly, but as differences between scenarios that are, themselves, thought of as certain. By making the improbable vivid, it corrects the tendency to ignore it altogether. These features of the scenario method, representing uncertainty in terms of certainty and making the improbable believable, presumably make it easier to think well about this difficult topic (Schoemaker, 1993).

Reliance on automatic processes is one reason for the tendency to think in terms of a single future, and we've considered four stimulus-variation questions that can help with this problem. But mental habits aren't the only reason for failure to take proper account of uncertainty.

Because of limited processing capacity, it's difficult to think about more than one possible future. Like multiple values, multiple futures can complicate a decision problem greatly. A good part of this chapter presents decomposition methods that, in effect, expand our mental capacity and thereby enable us to think more adequately about multiple futures.

A final reason for thinking in terms of a single future is, of course, motivational. Defensive avoidance can *motivate* us to think in terms of a particular restricted range of futures that we're comfortable with. What we should look for here is excessive *emotionality* and any *unwillingness* to think through certain futures. The remedies, as before, are realistic hope that we can deal successfully with the uncertainty, an appropriate emotional distance from the problem, and process orientation. This chapter can provide some measure of realistic hope by increasing your ability to deal adequately with multiple possible futures, and the formal methods for thinking about uncertainty can help achieve some emotional distance from the problem.

Regret

There's a special circumstance in which people tend to think in terms of a single future that merits separate comment. This is after the decision has been made and the future has arrived. In deciding whether to take an umbrella, for example, you consider two possible futures: (a) it will rain enough that you'll want to have an umbrella, and (b) it won't rain this much. Let's say that there's little chance of rain, so you leave your umbrella home. Then it rains, and you're angry with yourself for not having brought your umbrella. This is regret. The intensity of the regret seems to increase with the seriousness of the loss (Bell, 1982).

The experience of regret is generally a consequence of poor judgment—but often poor judgment at the time you're experiencing the regret, rather than poor judgment at the time the decision was made. At the time the decision was made, we're assuming, you considered both possible futures, rain and no rain, and weighted each by its probability. Now, however, you're considering only the future you're vividly experiencing and entirely forgetting that, at the time you made the decision, there was another possible future that was, in fact, far more probable. This is hindsight bias, the belief that the way things actually turned out was easy to foresee (Fischhoff, 1975). We experience less uncertainty in foresight that we should, but we experience even less in hindsight than in foresight.

A "therapy" for regret is to remind ourselves of what we knew *at the time we made the decision*. If we considered the future that's now the present and attached a reasonable probability to it, that's all that can be expected of anyone. (In the case of extremely unlikely events, even that may be too much to expect.) If, however, we somehow failed to take account of this future when we could have, that's another matter.

Even better than "therapy" is "inoculation." You can "inoculate" yourself against regret by (a) preparing yourself to live with the worst-case scenario and also (b) preparing to remind yourself of what little was known at the time you made the decision. To the extent that fear of regret motivates decision avoidance, this may also function as a "therapy" for that potentially costly malady.

Creating "Uncertainty-Proof" Alternatives

The following checklist provides a stimulus-variation technique for creating "uncertainty proof" alternatives (MacCrimmon & Taylor, 1976).

> To create "uncertainty proof" alternatives:
>
> - Control,
>
> - Obtain information,
>
> - Keep options open,
>
> - Diversify,
>
> - Share risk.

Obtaining information and control reduce our *uncertainty about the event* in question. For example, if you're considering making rain hats to sell at the football game on Saturday, you could obtain information about the probability of rain, or you could (in principle, if not in practice) seed the clouds to increase the probability of rain. Keeping options open, diversification, and sharing risk leave uncertainty about the significant event unchanged but reduce *uncertainty about the consequences of that event*. Making hats that could be used either as rain hats (by making them waterproof) or sun hats (by adding a large brim) would leave a profitable option open whether it rains or not. Going into business with someone who sells sunscreen would be sharing risk and diversifying and, in a different way, creating a possibility of profit whether it rains or not. Riskier than this would be going into the original hat business with someone else, so that you wouldn't invest as much and also wouldn't stand to either gain or lose as much. Let's have a closer look at each of these strategies.

Control. A person was planning to travel through Europe with three friends and was concerned about whether they'd get along. Taking uncertainty into his own hands, he raised the issue with the others and got them to agree to take a "shake down" trip together beforehand. His idea was that, by taking control of things, he could increase the probability that things would go well.

As in this example, control usually increases the probabilities of desirable outcomes or decreases the probabilities of undesirable ones, rather than providing any guarantees. If you're looking for a mate, join a lot of organizations and participate in a lot of activities. If you're looking for a job, start looking early, and let a lot of people know. If you're looking for a parking place, drive slowly, and keep an eye out for brake lights and people walking to cars. Also, know when to drop a low-probability lead. People who make "cold calls" over the telephone often waste a lot of their own precious time trying to convince someone who just isn't going to be convinced. Recently, at a fund-raising phone bank, I raised considerably more money than any of the other callers, simply by quickly accepting each "no" and moving on.

Control of uncertainty is an important consideration to keep in mind when designing decision alternatives. In deciding whether to implement control, or any other of the "uncertainty proofing" techniques, however, you should take account of its costs in time, money, and risk to personal feelings.

Obtain information. Yogi Berra said, "I don't like surprises unless I know about them in advance!" There are, basically, two ways to obtain information, wait for it or seek it out. The idea in *waiting for information* is not to "cross bridges until you get to them". The idea in *seeking information* is to "look before you leap". Delaying a decision can sometimes be attributable to the defense mechanism of procrastination, but not always. Politicians and executives, who operate in highly unpredictable environments, frequently delay decisions as long as they can and for perfectly rational reasons. The advantage of waiting for information, rather than seeking it out, is that the cost tends to be lower. There's an important caveat, however: don't wait so long that you foreclose important options. In considering whether to wait for information, you have to weigh the benefits of the information against the costs of waiting.

For any important decision, it's a good idea to ask, "When would be the best time to make this decision?"

A common problem takes the following form. You have to meet someone across town. You're uncertain as to how long the trip will take and, consequently, how soon you should stop doing what you're now doing and leave. If you're able to bring your work with you, drive to your destination first. Then, having resolved the uncertainty as how long it will take to make the trip, you'll know precisely how much time you have left to put into the work you brought with you, sitting in the car or in a nearby coffee shop. The same principle applies when you have an important project to complete by a deadline, even though no travel is involved: Get the important uncertainties resolved first.

When uncertainties can be resolved at different points in time, get the important uncertainties resolved first.

You can seek information by looking, asking advice, doing library research, or trying things out. Sometimes you can arrange a "test drive" to try out an alternative and get a better idea of how you'll feel about it before committing to it. A couple was planning to retire early. They knew that their retirement income would be less than if they worked to 65, but they felt that it would be adequate. To be more sure, they tried actually living on this amount of income for a year, investing the rest. Finding that they could, indeed, live comfortably on this amount of money, they went ahead with their plan.

Often, an important time to obtain information is as you're implementing the chosen alternative. In a career decision, for example, it's wise to attend to feedback on how you're doing, so you can make course corrections before too much damage has been done.

Keep your options open. One way to keep your options open is to have a specific fall-back plan, a "Plan B". A wise pilot selects a route that maintains a good altitude (allowing time to respond) and that includes some emergency landing fields. A wise sailor selects a route that's well upwind of any lee shore (allowing time to respond) and that includes some emergency harbors. A wise sky diver carries an extra chute.

A good question to ask is, "What do I do if this doesn't work?"

The Saturday before we were about to fly to Sweden, I found that our passports were not in our desk at home where I thought I'd put them. They were probably still in our safe deposit box, but there was no way to check over the weekend. Since our plane didn't leave until Monday evening, there'd be time to check on Monday morning—but if they weren't there, we'd have to cancel our trip!

Rather than panic, I assumed (against my true beliefs) that the passports wouldn't be in the safe deposit box and started creating a Plan B. I first prepared myself to accept the worst, to make sure I stayed rational. "This was only a vacation, we didn't have to go. We could go later. True, we'd be out about $3000 for plane tickets and deposits, but that wouldn't be the end of the world." Then I considered what I'd do if I didn't find the passports in the safe deposit box. They'd have to be somewhere around the house, so I'd have to drive back home and check the house. That was something I could do over the weekend, and I did, very carefully. Then I asked myself what I'd do if the passports were neither in the safe deposit box nor at home. We were flying out of Seattle; Seattle is the nearest place that issues passports; and I'd heard that passports can be issued on short notice in emergencies. Another thing I could do that weekend, then, was look up the address and phone number of the passport office and locate it on the map. Then, as soon as I found on Monday that the passports weren't in the safe deposit box, I could notify the passport office, so the passports would be ready when we got to Seattle.

When I opened the safe deposit box on Monday morning, the passports were, as I expected, sitting right on top, and we were able to go ahead with Plan A. What I did on the weekend was worthwhile, however, in realistically preparing a Plan B that might have been needed and in virtually eliminating anxiety.

A general way to keep your options open is to maintain "prudent person reserves". Having money set aside can enable you to respond to a wide range of unforeseen financial emergencies. Allowing extra time when working on a project can enable you to respond to the many time crunches that come up when carrying out a complex task. When proxy values like money and time appear in your decision table, it'd be wise to consider giving them extra weight because of their value in "uncertainty proofing".

When proxy values like money, time, skills, and contacts appear in your decision table, consider giving them extra weight because of their value in "uncertainty proofing".

Saving some of your energy when engaged in a physically demanding task, such as climbing a mountain or swimming a body of water, can enable you to respond to unanticipated demands for strength or endurance. At the public policy level, maintaining a greater reserve of natural resources than is required for dealing with the current population (or, which is much the same thing, keeping the population well below what can be supported by existing resources) can enable us to respond to unforeseen threats to the ecology—and it's perfectly foreseeable that *there will be unforeseen threats.*

Another way to keep your options open is to seek *reversible alternatives.* As the saying goes, "Don't burn your bridges behind you." It's all right to decide not to do business with someone, but break off the relationship in a way that'll make it easy to resume, should that become desirable. Reversibility is a relevant consideration in many decisions. Avoiding drugs is a more reversible alternative than using them. On a grander scale, not paving over topsoil is a more reversible alternative than paving over it; not cutting down a forest is a more reversible alternative than cutting it down; not building a nuclear power plant is a more reversible alternative than building one.

Diversify. "Don't put all your eggs in one basket." If you literally put all your eggs in one basket, and the probability that the bottom will fall out of the basket is (to keep the arithmetic simple) 1/100, then the probability that you'll lose all your eggs is (very roughly) 1/100. If you divide your eggs between two such baskets, the probability that you'll lose all your eggs is 1/100 times 1/100 or 1/10000. If you add just one more basket, the probability of a total loss plummets to 1/100 times 1/100 times 1/100, or one out of a million! This is the way diversification works.

Diversification is an extremely important principle in financial investment, where the future is notoriously difficult to predict. If you invest all your money in one company (perhaps the one you work for, as some Enron employees did), and the probability that that company will fail is 1/100, then the probability that you'll lose all your money is 1/100. If you invest all your money in two such companies, whose behavior we'll assume is uncorrelated, then the probability that you'll lose all your money is 1/100 times 1/100 or 1/10000, a considerably less disturbing figure. If you place your money in an index fund that diversifies your investment over some 500 to 1000 such companies, you can forget about the possibility of losing *all* your money, and you'll greatly reduce the probability of losing any.

Happy people tend to have well diversified emotional investments. People who have emotional investments in a variety of areas are less troubled by a setback in any one area (Myers 1992). For example, successful artists frequently get invested in a new work of art before they find out whether the work they've just finished is well or poorly received. That way, a bad review will attack less of what they base their self-esteem on and will be less devastating. If you have just one good friend, you'll suffer a serious loss if something happens to the friend or the friendship. If you have a number of good friends, your emotional future will be more secure. If you put all your hopes in becoming a professional musician or a professional athlete, things will work out well only in the event that you achieve professional status. If, on the other hand, while investing most of your time in music or athletics, you also get a college education, you'll be better prepared for a range of futures.

> Amelia's solution achieved a measure of diversification, for it involved "investing" in both the University Professor/Research area and in the Fund Raising/ PR area.

Share risk. If you're contemplating an investment that isn't diversifiable, such as buying a rental property, considering going in with other investors. This is one of the values of extended families. it's also the principle behind volunteer fire departments.

If you find yourself in a position of leadership, where you make decisions on the behalf of a group, involve others in the decisions. If you make a decision entirely on your own, you'll get all the credit if it succeeds, but you'll also get all the blame if it fails. If you involve others in the decision, you share the credit, but you also share the blame. This is less risky. In addition, involving others in the decision has the advantages that the decision is likely to be better, that it should be easier to implement, and that people will give you credit for having respected their views.

Obtaining insurance is just a special way of sharing risk. You pay into a pool that then assumes your risk. Insurance premiums can be as low as they are because only a few in the risk pool are likely to need the insurance. Greater diversification is one argument for universal health care. Buying a rebuilt engine, rather than having your own rebuilt, is an interesting way of sharing risk. Engine rebuilders spread the costs of unusual damage, such as a warped cylinder head, over many customers.

Sensitivity Analysis

Sensitivity analysis isn't as mysterious as it may sound. When you get in a car that you haven't driven before and get the "feel" of the steering, accelerator, and brakes, you're really just performing a sensitivity analysis.

Sensitivity analysis simply tests the sensitivity of the output of a process to variations in the inputs.

In getting the "feel" of a car, you test the sensitivity of the direction in which the car is moving to changes in the position of the steering wheel and the sensitivity of the speed at which the car is moving to changes in the amount of pressure you put on the gas or the brakes.

You can—and should—do the same thing with a new decision table, to make sure that it, too, is "safe" to use. You can do this by changing factual estimates or value judgments. You then look to see whether these changes have the expected effects on the overall evaluation of alternatives, either the pattern of plusses and minuses or the total value ratings. By performing sensitivity analyses in this way, you can refine and gain confidence in a new decision table using the same logic you use to gain confidence in a car. After all, it isn't an understanding of the engineers' mathematics that gives most of us enough confidence in our cars to trust them with your lives; it's the understanding we've gained through what is, in effect, a sensitivity analysis.

Actually, sensitivity analysis has two applications. One is the application just discussed: to test the model against intuition and refine it until you can trust it. Often, the focus here is on the direction of change. For example, if you find that increasing the cost of an item you're thinking of purchasing *raises* its 1-to-10 rating, then you've gotten your ratings wrong. You should be giving high ratings to *low* costs.

The second application is to guide further work on the problem efficiently. The focus here is on the amount of change. You shouldn't spend time thinking about uncertainties to which the decision isn't sensitive.

To use sensitivity analysis to evaluate the importance of uncertainty or disagreement about a quantity, *calculate total value twice, once using one estimate and once using another.* Very often, you'll find that, while one or more total value ratings will change, the changes won't be enough to affect which alternative is in first place. The decision is then said to be insensitive to this variation When this is the case, there's little point in trying to resolve the uncertainty or any disagreement about the proper estimates, and you can feel more comfortable about your estimates.

If a difference makes no difference, there is little point in giving it further thought.

An efficient search procedure to follow in performing a sensitivity analysis on a decision table is as follows:

- Identify the one or more columns with high importance weights;

- Identify the two or more rows with the highest total value ratings;

- Focus on the cells at the intersections of these rows and columns about which you're most uncertain; and

- Within each of these cells, focus on changes in the direction that could change the decision.

Amelia didn't need such a search procedure. She already knew her areas of greatest uncertainty. The shaded cells in the table below are those about which Amelia was most uncertain, and the ranges indicate her ranges of uncertainty.

Ranges of Uncertainty in Fact Table

	Soc	Intel	Cult	Comp	Fam	Work
U Prof		75	55	45	60	80
Research		35-70	25-70	40	75	80
Dissem		65	30	32	50	5-80
FR/PR		10-40	25	60	40	5

Sensitivity Analysis

	Soc	Intel	Cult	Comp	Fam	Work	
	0	0.19	0.05	0.19	0.38	0.19	1
U Prof		7.2	7.5	5.8	5.0	8.0	*6.27*
Research		5.6	7.5	4.3	1.3	8.0	*4.27*
Dissem		6.1	3.4	2.1	7.5	5.0	*5.53*
FR/PR		2.8	2.6	10.0	10.0	0.6	*6.48*

Amelia recalculated the total value ratings of alternatives with uncertain cells to see whether this would change their ranking. She used only the ends of the ranges that could change the ranking, that is, the low end of the range for an alternative that was currently ranked high and the high end for an alternative that was currently ranked low. This is what she learned.

- Changing Intellectual Challenge for Other Research from 60% to the high end of the range, 70%, raised the 1-10 rating from 5.6 to 6.7 and the total value to 4.48. Since this was still the lowest of all the total values, the decision was insensitive to this range of uncertainty.

- Changing Cultural Diversity for Other Research from 55% to the high end of the range, 70%, raised the 1-10 rating from 7.5 to 10.0 and the total value to 4.40. Since this was still the lowest of all the total values, the decision was insensitive to this range of uncertainty. (She might have guessed that this wouldn't make any difference, since the importance weight was only .05.)

- Since Other Dissemination was in the middle of the ranking, it was tested in both directions. Lowering Work Culture from 50% to 5% lowered the 1-to-10 rating to 0.6 and total value to 4.69. Raising Work Culture from 50% to 80% raised the 1-to-10 rating to 8.0 and total value to 6.10. Neither change affected Other Dissemination's position in the ranking, and so the decision is insensitive to this range of uncertainty.

- Finally, Intellectual Challenge for Fund Raising/PR was changed from 35% to 10%, lowering the 1-to-10 rating from 2.8 to 1.0 and total value from 6.48 to 6.13. This places Fund Raising/PR below University Professor but not below Other Dissemination. If the decision were of the usual kind where the decision maker selects the highest alternative, the decision would be sensitive to this range of uncertainty. However, since the decision was to pursue the highest alternative in each of the two categories—the personal values category and the family values category—this particular decision is not sensitive to this range of uncertainty.

In short, Amelia's decision is not sensitive to any of the uncertainties in her fact table, a happy result.

As a final example of a case where the decision was insensitive to uncertainty regarding a key factor, consider a disagreement among the members of a committee trying to decide whether to alert individual employees to the possibility that they might have to be laid off in nine months. The key issue was the likelihood that anyone would have to be laid off, at all. The committee members were intelligent, well-intentioned people who weren't troubled by emotional or communication blocks and who'd been giving their best to the problem all along but who, nevertheless, had been wandering, confused, through a mental hall of mirrors for weeks. Their thinking was that, if the probability of a layoff were high, people should be notified so they could make plans; but, if the probability of a layoff were low, a false alarm would do more harm than good. They'd come to agreement on all other aspects of the problem. It was this one issue, the probability of a layoff, that had held them up and that had made it impossible for them to take action.

The usual approach to dealing with such a conflict would be to marshal the arguments on either side and begin to sort them out, looking for corroborations and inconsistencies. This could take a long time. Indeed, it already had. The approach of sensitivity analysis is to try to dispense with the issue in a single stroke. Sensitivity analysis asks whether the difference in opinion makes any practical difference.

Once the problem had been quantified (which took less than an hour), it became clear that one could assume a probability of a layoff more pessimistic than the most pessimistic assumed by any member of the committee or one more optimistic than the most optimistic assumed by any member of the committee, and they'd take precisely the same course of action! In fact, the probability of a layoff could vary all the way from 0 to 1.00 without changing the preferred course of action! Though the committee hadn't been able to see this without the sensitivity analysis, all clearly saw it with the sensitivity analysis.

Sensitivity analysis settled this conflict immediately and permanently. The committee members never did resolve their differences about the probability of a layoff—but they didn't need to, and so they rightly didn't care!

Of course, in some cases unlike those of Amelia and the committee, sensitivity analysis will reveal that the decision *is* quite sensitive to the extent to which the parties disagree and that further attention is required. This attention could take the form of further discussion. Sensitivity analysis is a superb way to set an agenda. Or this attention could take the form of modeling the sensitive factor by incorporating it in a decision tree, as an *event node*). Sensitivity analysis is a good way to identify event nodes for decision trees (Spetzler & Zamora, 1974).

Value of information. A classic calculation in decision analysis determines the value of information. Value of information is addressed whenever you perform a sensitivity analysis. An approximate rule of thumb is: *Whenever a decision is insensitive to a source of uncertainty, information that would help resolve that uncertainty is of no value in helping make that decision.* A more general approach is to ask, Is the increased comfort the information would provide enough to justify its cost?

If a difference makes a difference, ask, "Is the increased comfort that information would provide enough to justify the cost of the information?"

Destruction testing. In manufacturing, engineers frequently test products by trying to destroy them. The same concept can be applied to decision analysis. Up to this point, we've been talking implicitly about judging and testing unbiased confidence intervals. If your decision still looks good, this may be a good point to *introduce* bias.

Try to push your confidence intervals as far as you realistically can in the direction that could *change* your decision.

Try to think of values and events that you haven't yet taken into account that could *change* your decision.

This is a good point to seek outside expertise and apply the giant fighter's stratagem. If you can't change your decision in this way, then you can certainly have a great deal of confidence in it. If you can change it, then try destruction testing in the opposite direction. Destruction testing is a way of returning—as we should always be prepared to do—to the problem-structuring phase of decision making and expanding our view of the problem.

Decision Trees

In most cases, it will be a sensitivity analysis that suggests adding a decision tree to your decision table in order to represent uncertainty explicitly (Spetzler & Zamora, 1974). This is the sequence depicted on the Decision Ladder. In other cases, such as investment decisions, insurance decisions, and certain medical decisions, uncertainty is such an overwhelming consideration that it may be more natural to start with a decision tree, in the first place, and then add a decision table if necessary.

In either case, decision trees are excellent ways to represent uncertainty. Decision trees consist of *act nodes* and *event nodes*, with *branches* at each node. Let's return to the umbrella example.

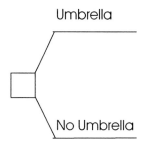

Act nodes are drawn as squares or rectangles. Each act node represents the question, "What can I do at this point?" The branches represent possible answers to this question, here, Umbrella and No Umbrella. Event nodes are drawn as circles or ovals. Each event node represents the question, "What could happen at this point?" The branches represent possible answers to this question, here, Rain and No Rain.

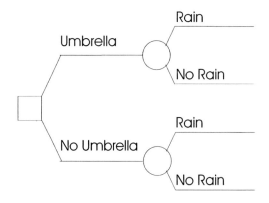

Since this uncertainty is important whether you take an umbrella or not, this event node is placed at the ends of both the Umbrella and the No Umbrella branches. (If the decision had been whether to have a party indoors or outdoors, an event node might have been required only for the outdoors alternative.) Note that branches radiate from both act nodes and event nodes in a left-to-right direction. Decision trees are conventionally "grown" from left to right.

Act nodes represent what we can change, while event nodes represent what we can't change but can only predict. This is a point on which people are easily confused, so it's worth dwelling on. Act nodes relate to *alternative courses of action.* Events, whether they're caused by other people or by nature, so long as they're *out of the decision maker's control*, are represented by event nodes. The distinction between acts and events is the one made so nicely in the Prayer of St. Francis, which has been referred to before and is repeated here for convenience:

> *Lord, grant me the courage to change what can be changed, the serenity to accept what can not be changed, and the wisdom to know the difference.*

A difficult example may help sharpen the distinction between acts and events. Let's say that your planning includes a decision that you'll make in the distant future. Let's say that you're thirty, that you're formulating an investment plan, and that you need to take into account when you'll retire. The decision as to when to retire looks as though it ought to be represented as an act node. After all, it's an action, and it's your action. The problem is that you don't have enough information to make that decision now. The resolution of many uncertainties that are beyond your control—your health, your job status, your marital status, the economic and political state of the country—could incline that decision in different directions. It's not a decision you'd want to make now, but one you'd wisely prefer to put off until you have more information. The best way to treat that decision, even though it'll eventually be your own decision, may be as an event node.

Every path in a decision tree is a future scenario. Thus, in the tree above, there are four possible future scenarios. You could take the umbrella, and it could rain; you could take the umbrella, and it could not rain; and so forth. In the appendix on Thinking More Deeply About Uncertainty, we'll see how to place probabilities along the paths and how to place a value rating at the end of each path.

A few words are in order about the sequencing of act and event nodes in a decision tree. The fundamental rule is: *Act nodes and event nodes must be placed in chronological order* with respect to one another. It must be clear what uncertainties have and haven't been resolved when you make each choice. This rule is frequently violated in problems involving applying for schools or jobs. Do you see what the problem is with the following tree?

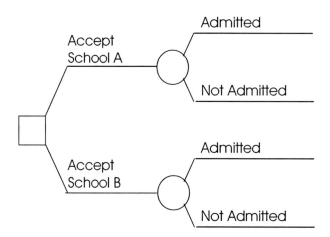

The problem with this tree is that the uncertainty as to whether the decision maker is or isn't admitted will be resolved *before* he or she can accept or reject the offer of admission. You can't accept an offer until it's been made. Because this uncertainty will be resolved by the time the decision has to be made, it doesn't have to be represented in the tree at all. All that the decision maker has to do is rank order the schools and then accept the highest ranked of those that make offers. (If the offers come in at different times, and you have to decide whether to accept or reject a definite offer while others are still uncertain, then event nodes are appropriate for those schools that haven't yet responded.)

If this decision weren't an Accept/Reject decision but an Apply/Not Apply decision, then it would have been appropriate to include the uncertainty regarding admission, since this uncertainty wouldn't be resolved until after application for admission had been made. Usually, the difficult decisions are Accept/Reject decisions, however, since little is at risk in the application process, while much rides on which school one attends. One can begin with a simple screening process for deciding which schools to apply to (applying when in doubt) and then move up the Decision Ladder when deciding among those that make you offers.

In the appendix on Thinking More Deeply About Uncertainty, we'll see how to put numbers in trees and evaluate them quantitatively. However, much of the value of decision trees has nothing to do with numbers, just as much of the value of decision tables has nothing to do with numbers. Decision trees can be helpful in thinking through possible sequences of acts and events. We've seen a simple example where the correct tree makes clear that the uncertainty surrounding acceptance to a graduate program is resolved before the decision to accept or reject an offer from that program. In the section on probability, we'll see how trees can help us think through complex probability relationships that we often badly oversimplify.

A personal anecdote illustrates nicely how decision trees can improve decision making without quantification and, in this case, without even being put on paper. My wife and I were at a mountain cabin with four major decision makers in the community and had just come off the trail from an afternoon of cross-country skiing, when we noticed that one of our party was missing! We decided to go back and look for her. All agreed that there were two general areas in which she might be found: the area up the mountain where we'd been skiing and the area down by the road that led back to the cabin. Everyone also agreed that she was more likely to be down by the road, and the initial inclination of the group was to look for her by the road.

A decision tree flashed into my mind's eye, and I saw that, while we'd considered the probabilities at the event node, we'd given no thought to the value ratings at the end points. I pointed out that, if she were down by the road and we didn't find her, the consequences wouldn't be serious. She'd likely follow the road back to the cabin, and, if she did need help, cars went by frequently enough. However, if she were up on the mountain and we didn't find her, the consequences could be serious: hypothermia and frostbite. I suggested that we look for her on the mountain. Now aware of an obviously important consideration that they'd overlooked, all agreed, and we went up the mountain to look for her *where we didn't expect to find her*. (As it turned out, our expectations were born out; she was down by the road and got back to the cabin before we did. All was well that ended well—and we'd made the right decision!)

In this case, the image of a decision tree had functioned as a visual checklist, calling to mind essential aspects of the decision problem that had been overlooked by five concerned people, including four of the most respected decision makers in the community. In other cases, an image or a drawing of a decision tree can improve thinking about complex sequences of choices and events. Examples are decisions that involve moves and countermoves between parties in a negotiation and decisions that involve deciding what, if any, further information to get before making the main decision.

When the decision is both risky and multiattribute, an appropriate representation is a tree/table diagram. An example is shown below for the umbrella problem:

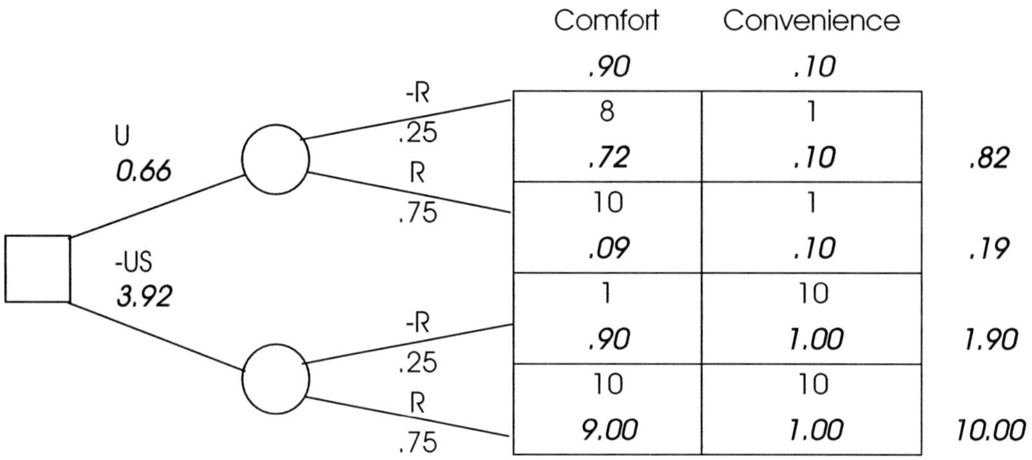

	Comfort	Convenience	
	.90	*.10*	
8	1	
.72	*.10*	*.82*
10	1	
.09	*.10*	*.19*
1	10	
.90	*1.00*	*1.90*
10	10	
9.00	*1.00*	*10.00*

U
0.66

-R
.25

R
.75

-US
3.92

-R
.25

R
.75

The calculations in the table part of the diagram should be familiar. Those in the tree part are explained in the appendix on Thinking More Deeply About Uncertainty.

Chapter 7. WHAT NOW?

A number of steps are suggested for increasing the chances that the knowledge acquired from reading the Three Secrets of Wise Decision Making *will be put to practical use.*

Few people know as much about decision making as you now know. What will you do next? It's easy to forget a book once you've gone on to the next one. Winston Churchill said that people "occasionally stumble on the truth, but most of them pick themselves up and hurry off as if nothing had happened." If you really want to remember what you've already learned from this book, if you want to continue to become more skilled in making decisions, if you want this book to be a beginning, rather than an end, there are several things you can do.

First, making use of our old friend external memory, find a permanent place for the book where you'll see it from time to time, so that its presence can remind you of your commitment to improved decision making. Also, make a copy of the Decision Checklist, on the inside front cover, and reduce it to a size that can be plasticized and conveniently carried in your wallet or purse. I have a copy on the back of my business card.

Second, commit yourself to being a "decision watcher". Just as a bird watcher becomes sensitive to the movement of a bird in the foliage or a the call of a bird amidst the din of life, you can learn to become more aware of the decisions that surround you. And, just as a bird watcher gets pleasure from recognizing various species of birds and takes pride in adding to a life list of species identified in the field, you can take pleasure in recognizing and "collecting" different kinds of decision problems: multiattribute, risky, risky multi-attribute, resource allocation, commons dilemma, single dominating alternative, uncertainty-proofed alternative, and so on.

Third, when you encounter an important decision problem, or even just an interesting one, think about how you'd handle it. If you're not sure, pick up the book, and review the relevant section. Even if the decision is not one you're currently facing, thinking about it can prepare you for future decisions.

Fourth, begin with what's easy, and look for small improvements. Start with the methods low on the Decision Ladder. If you approach the difficult methods gradually, they'll seem easier by the time you get there.

Fifth, save the analyses of your important decisions, both your fact and value tables and any notes. Review them later, when it's clear how the decision has turned out. There are two reasons for doing this. One is as a corrective for regret. This reason focuses on what you did *right*. If your decision doesn't turn out as well as you'd hoped, you may wish you had chosen some other alternative. A glance at your decision analysis can remind you that, given what you knew at the time you made the decision, the choice you're now wishing you'd made would have been an unwise one. You did the right thing.

The other reason for saving your decision analyses focuses on what you may have done *wrong* or, at least, what you could have done better. Reviewing past decisions can be an effective way to improve your decision making and to build up realistic confidence in your decision skills.

Sixth, remember to place your emphasis on process and to feel good about what you're doing. Think about how much more thoughtfully you're making decisions now than you ever imagined possible earlier.

Seventh, extend your experience in making decisions by taking an interest in the decision problems of others or of your community. Of course, it'd be very easy to do this in a way that would be intrusive. With proper attention to diplomacy, however, you can judge whether the other party would welcome suggestions or whether you'd best observe the decision process in silence.

Eighth, find someone whose judgment you respect and whom you enjoy being with to talk over your decisions with. You might lend them your copy of this book to get them interested. Such a friend can provide the distancing you need to keep you thinking rationally and the creative conversation you need to keep you thinking creatively and also provide a good check on the structure of your decision.

Ninth, look over the appendixes on Thinking More Deeply About Values, Thinking More Deeply About Alternatives, and Thinking More Deeply About Uncertainty now, and read them when you feel ready for them.

Tenth, read some of the following excellent books. Some have gone out of print, and others will be going out of print, but they can be found in many libraries or purchased through such sources as abebooks.com. Though books go out of print quickly these days, the wisdom in these books ages slowly.

- John S. Hammond, Ralph L. Keeney, & Howard Raiffa. (1999). *Smart Choices: A practical guide to making better decisions.* Boston, MA: Harvard Business School Press. A clear, informed, authoritative presentation of decision tools. Little psychological explanation of why we need the tools and how they work, however, and the featured "even swaps" method, which relies entirely on cross-attribute judgments, is more difficult and possibly more error-prone than the more widely used 1-to-10 method, which replaces many cross-attribute judgments with simpler single-attribute judgments.

- Reid Hastie & Robyn M. Dawes. (2001). *Rational Choice in an Uncertain World.* One of the best overall treatments of the psychology of decision making. Little in the way of decision tools.

- Max H. Bazerman. (1994). *Judgment in Managerial Decision Making.* NY: Wiley. The best introductory treatment of group decision making and negotiation that I know of. Little in the way of decision tools.

- J. E. Russo & P. J. H. Schoemaker. (1989). Decision Traps: The ten barriers to brilliant decision-making and how to overcome them. NY: Simon & Schuster. The best introductory treatment of framing effects.

- Scott Plous. (1993). *The Psychology of Judgment and Decision Making.* NY: McGraw-Hill. One of the best overall treatments of the psychology of decision making. Little in the way of decision tools.

- Robert T. Clemen. (1991). *Making Hard Decisions: An introduction to decision analysis.* Boston: PWS-Kent. A more difficult treatment of decision analysis that includes influence diagrams, time value of money, strategy regions, probability distributions, value of information, rules of rational choice, and complex multiattribute utility models.

- Ralph. L. Keeney. (1992). *Value-Focused Thinking.* Cambridge, MA: Harvard U. Press. The best book on problem structuring that I know of. Includes an insightful discussion about using failures of value independence to discover hidden values and a clear explanation of the relation between value trees and influence networks. Provides a good defense of the 1-to-10 method.

- Frank Yates (1992). *Judgment and Decision Making.* Englewood Cliffs, NJ: Prentice-Hall. The best introductory treatment of probability judgment that I know of.

- Detlof von Winterfeldt & Ward Edwards. (1986). *Decision Analysis and Behavioral Research.* Cambridge: Cambridge U. An exceptionally wise book, difficult in places but well worth living with and internalizing.

Appendix A. THINKING MORE DEEPLY ABOUT VALUES

This appendix introduces more advanced techniques for rating and weighting.

Value Curves

Whenever it's possible to obtain a *quantitative* objective measure of a value attribute (such as dollars, years, square feet, or miles), it's possible to plot a value curve. A value curve shows how the subjective 1-to-10 value ratings are related to the quantitative objective measure. Take income as an example, which can be easily measured in thousands of dollars per year. A typical value curve might look like this:

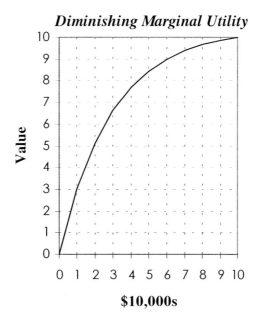

A value curve describes the quantitative relationship between a set of preference judgments and the underlying fact judgments. Income in dollars is the kind of information that is put in a fact table. It is, in principle, verifiable by others. Preference ratings are the kind of information that is put in a value table. This is information that can be ultimately verified only by the decision maker.

Value curves of this general shape (concave downward) show what's called "diminishing marginal utility". "Utility" is just another word for subjective value, or preference. "Marginal utility" is value at the margin, or edge. Marginal utility is *additional* value. Note that the utility of $0 is 0; the utility of $10,000 (a 1 on the horizontal axis) is about 3; and the utility of $20,000 (a 2 on the horizontal axis) is about 5. Thus, the *marginal* utility of the first $10,000 is 3 - 0 = 3, and the *marginal* utility of the second $10,000 is 5 - 3 = 2. Notice that the marginal utility of the second $10,000 is less than that of the first $10,000. In this case, marginal utility diminishes as objective value increases.

Diminishing marginal utility is common in value curves. When you think about it, it makes sense. (The shapes of all properly assessed value curves make sense when you think about them.) All that's needed to explain diminishing marginal utility for money is the assumption that we prioritize our expenditures: If we spend our early dollars on food, shelter, clothing, and medical care, those dollars will be worth a great deal, and, if we spend our later dollars on luxuries that we could do without, those dollars will be worth less.

Another reason for diminishing marginal utility could be satiety. The first cup of coffee in the morning may be worth a great deal to you, but the second cup is worth less, and the third cup is worth even less. You need only so much coffee.

The most common form of value curve is constant marginal utility, a straight line. In the graph at the top of the next page, the marginal utility of the first $10,000 is 1 - 0 = 1; that of the second $10,000 is 2 - 1 = 1; and so forth. Marginal utility is constant.

Undoubtedly, the most important reason so many value curves are straight lines is that the ranges of impact for most decisions are slight. Consider a choice among three jobs, with salaries of 80 hours, $45,000, and $50,000. If you locate these salaries on the first value curve, you'll see that they all fall in a very small region of the curve and that, over this region, the curve is, for all practical purposes, a straight line. All of these salaries are adequate to take care of basic food, housing, clothing, and medical care. The differences among them relate to niceties, all of which are nearly equal in value.

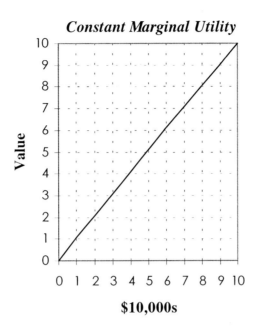

A curve you don't see very often at all is one with increasing marginal utility.

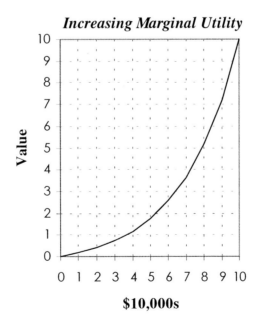

Increasing marginal utility makes sense in some situations. To illustrate with an example that fits the general, but not the precise, shape of this curve, let's say you're starting a small business, making widgets in your garage. If it costs $20,000 to get set up, investing less than that will be of no value to you at all. Let's say that this basic setup will enable you to make widgets for $4 apiece and sell them for $6 apiece, so that the marginal value of every additional $4 is an additional $2 profit. If you invest more than the $20,000, you'll be able to hire a manufacturing consultant who can tell you how to make widgets for $2 apiece, and the marginal value of every $4 will then rise to $8. If you invest even more money, you'll be able to afford an advertising consultant who'll enable you to raise the price to $8, and the marginal value of every $4 will then rise even further to $12.

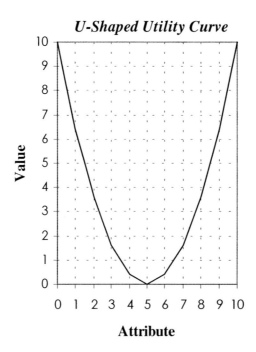

U-Shaped Utility Curve

What we have here are synergistic effects, literally "energies working together". The manufacturing consultant and the advertising consultant are not like additional employees who simply make more widgets alongside those who have already been making widgets. Merely doubling employees would double productivity, a linear effect. The effect of the consultants, instead, can be thought of as increasing the productivity of the employees who are already making widgets.

Another form value curves can take is U-shaped or inverted-U-shaped.

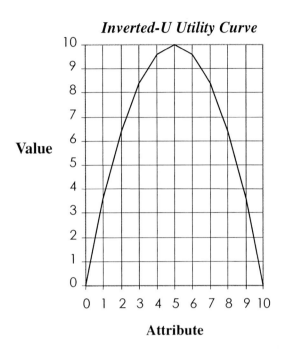

Inverted-U Utility Curve

Value

Attribute

Curves with decreasing, constant, or increasing marginal utility are called *monotonic*, because they go in one direction, always "uphill" or always "downhill". Curves of the kind we're now considering are called *non-monotonic*, because they don't go in one direction. Consider the earlier example of the value of the first, second, and third cups of coffee in the morning. How about a fourth, fifth, or sixth cup of coffee? At some point, this value curve will start going down. There's an optimal number of cups of coffee, where value is at its maximum, and both below and above this optimal number the value falls off from the maximum.

Curves of this sort are quite common where biological systems are involved. There's an optimum temperature, an optimum number of people in a family, an optimum size for a car, and so forth. Aristotle saw this as being true for a number of important values, suggesting that the conditions for happiness are a Golden Mean with respect to each value. We don't actually see curves of this sort very often, however, for the reason given above: The ranges of impact for most decisions are slight, and the small portion of the curve that's actually relevant to the decision usually approximates a straight line, or, at least, is just the part that goes up or the part that goes down. In the first reference to the number-of-cups-of-coffee example, we saw just the part of the curve that goes up. In the population problem facing the world today, we see just the part of the curve that goes down, where increasing population is associated with decreasing value. (Over the full range of possible world populations, one can imagine a population, or a broad range of populations, that would maximize average quality of life. A population below this wouldn't support an advanced culture; one above would strain the limits of our planet and perhaps also of our humanity. It's interesting to speculate on what level would be ideal for the world population.) Non-monotonic value curves do show up in decisions from time to time, and it's important to be on the lookout for them.

The right-side-up U is also possible. For example, a prototype computer printer was found to print well when the ink well was full and also when it was near empty. However, when it was partly full, it vibrated sympathetically with the print head and made the line of print wave.

Value and Probability Rulers

All we said earlier about weighting is that (a) attribute weights should be ordered in the same way as the magic wishes, and (b) attribute weights should reflect the relative importance of full-range changes on the various attributes. At that time we presented a simple method for putting numbers on attribute weights, point allocation. Here, we'll consider a superior method, based on *tradeoff judgments*.

Tradeoff judgments are based on choices among concrete outcomes, rather than abstract numbers. They avoid several judgmental errors that arise when numbers are used to express judgments directly (Poulton, 1989). They also show greater range sensitivity (Fischer, 1995; von Nitzsch, & Weber, 1993; Weber & Borcherding, 1993). There are two forms of the tradeoff method for measuring importance. One uses what we'll call a *value ruler*; the other uses what we'll call a *probability ruler*. In either case, we build on what we've learned from the "magic wishes".

A value ruler extends from the lowest to the highest value rating on the most important value attribute.

Amelia's used a value ruler. Her range table is repeated here for convenience.

Range Table (with Rankings)

	Contribu- tion to Society	Intellectual Challenge	Cultural Diversity	Compen- sation	Time for Family	Work Culture
		B	C	B	A	B
10		100%	70%	$60,000	40 hrs	100%
1		10%	10%	$25,000	80 hrs	0%

As the most important value, Time for Family became Amelia's value ruler. Amelia drew the sfollowing bar graph shown on the next page, to clarify her thinking.

Amelia's Time-for-Family ruler was 40 hours long, extending from an 80-hour work week at the bottom to a 40-hour work week at the top. This was the ruler she'd hold each of the other values up to determine how many hours each was equivalent to.

VALUE RULER for IMPORTANCE

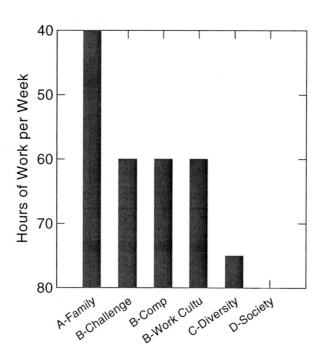

Having just finished the "magic wishes", all that Amelia knew about the heights of these bars was their order. The one marked "A" is more important than those marked "B"; they're more important than the one marked "C"; and it's more important than the one marked "D". She didn't know the exact heights. She thought of them as printed on a rubber page. Stretching the page in various ways wouldn't change the ordering of the tops of the bars, but it could change the distances among them. Her problem was to find out how to stretch the page properly, so it would represent differences in value ratings correctly. (The figure above shows the page "stretched" correctly.)

To do this, Amelia asked herself questions that, in effect, stood each of the other bars up against the Time-for-Family bar to see how high it came. She began by evaluating the importance of Cultural Diversity relative to that of Time for Family. As with the "magic wishes", she began by considering herself to be at the least favorable end of the range on both attributes. She began with the following two questions:

- Would I rather have Time for Family go from 80 work hours to 40 work hours or have Cultural Diversity go all the way from "10%" to "70%"? She already knew, from the "magic wishes", that the answer to this question would be for Time for Family to go from 80 work hours to 40 work hours.

- Would I rather have Time for Family go from 80 work hours to 79 work hours or have Cultural Diversity go all the way from "10%" to "70%"? She expected that the answer to this question would be for Cultural Diversity to go from "10%" to "70%", since the 1-hour change in Time for Family was intentionally trivial. (If she didn't answer this way, Cultural Diversity would probably not be important enough to include in the analysis.)

We always start with two extreme questions like these that clearly *bracket* the break-even point. Such questions make clear that there *must* be a break-even point. Since an decrease of 40 work hours is worth *more* than a full-range change on Cultural Diversity and an decrease of 1 work hour is worth *less*, there must be an increase somewhere between 1 hour and 40 hours that'll be exactly *equal in value* to a full-range change on Cultural Diversity. This is the *break-even point* that we're looking for.

The rest of Amelia's questions went as follows:

- Would I rather have a 20-hour increase in Time for Family or a full-range change on Cultural Diversity (from 10% to 70%)? Answer: The 20 hours.

- A 10-hour increase in Time for Family or a full-range change on Cultural Diversity? Answer: The 10 hours.

- A 5-hour increase in Time for Family or a full-range change on Cultural Diversity? Answer: Those are about equal. I don't think I'd care in that case.

So a 5-hour increase in Time for Family from an 80-hour work week to a 75-hour work week was about equal to a full-range change on Cultural Diversity from 10% to 70%. What did this tell Amelia about the relative weight for Cultural Diversity? To answer this question, she needed a value curve for her Time-for-Family ruler. (The use of a probability ruler, as we'll see, doesn't require a value curve.)

To get a value curve for Time for Family, she asked herself whether 60 hours would be halfway in value between 80 hours and 40 hours. She didn't think so. She felt that a change from 80 hours to 60 hours would make more of a difference than a change from 60 hours to 40 hours. In terms of units on her Time-for-Family ruler, she'd give a 0 to 80 hours, a .8 to 60 hours, and a 1.0 to 40 hours. Placing these three points on a graph and fairing a curve through them yielded the value curve below.

As a check, she asked herself whether a reduction from 80 hours to 70 hours (which comes about halfway up her scale to .50) would be about equal in preference to a reduction from 70 hours to 40 hours. She felt that that it would and, thus, didn't feel any need to correct her curve.

Note that this preference scale, unlike the 1-to-10 scale we've been using, extends from 0 to 1. There are reasons for this. The reason the scale begins at 0 is that, when measuring importance weights, it's essential to have a scale that begins with 0 to allow for zero importance. The reason the scale extends to 1, rather than 10, is, at this point, a historical connection with probability rulers that's beyond the scope of this book.

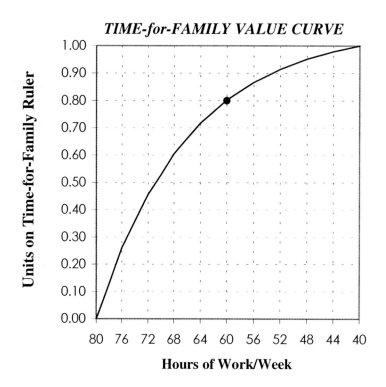

TIME-for-FAMILY VALUE CURVE

On Amelia's Time-for-Family value curve, it can be seen that the break-even improvement from 80 hours to 75 hours for Cultural Diversity moves us up from a value rating of 0 to one of about .25. This is .25 units out of the 1 unit along the whole scale, or 25% of the total. So Amelia's weight for Cultural Diversity was .25.

Similarly, the break-even improvement from 80 hours to 60 hours for the tied values Challenge, Compensation, and Work Culture moved Amelia up from a value rating of 0 to one of .8. (This value was judged directly by Amelia in arriving at the value curve.) So Amelia's weights for these values were .8, .8, and .8.

This gave Amelia weights for Society, Diversity, Work Culture, Compensation, Challenge, and Time for Family of, respectively, 0, .25, .8, .8, .8, and 1.0. These are *unnormalized weights*. They'll work just fine. However, *normalized weights*, which add up

198

to 1.00, are generally preferred. The table below displays Amelia's unnormalized weights and her normalized weights, along with the calculations required to get from one to the other.

Attribute	Unnormalized Weights	Normalized Weights
Time for Family	1.0	1/3.65 = .27
Challenge	.8	.8/3.65 = .22
Compensation	.8	.8/3.65 = .22
Work Culture	.8	.8/3.65 = .22
Diversity	.25	.25/3.65 = .07
Society	0.0	0/3.65 = .00
TOTAL	3.65	1.00

Normalized weights are derived from unnormalized weights by dividing each by their sum. This assures that, except for rounding errors, normalized weights will add up to 1.00.

Weights don't have to be normalized. Both unnormalized weights and normalized weights will lead to exactly the same decision in all cases. Many people prefer normalized weights, however; and there's good reason to do so: It's easier to make intuitive checks. For one thing, it's easier to check your arithmetic with normalized weights, since the weighted totals you obtain by multiplying down and adding across in your decision table should stay within the 1-10 range. For another, it's easier to use the point allocation and tradeoff methods as checks on one another, since they should yield the same weights, except for the location of the decimal point.

Although the full tradeoff method used by Amelia, in which every value attribute is measured, is the best way to obtain weights, there's a shortcut that requires measuring only the lowest and highest values (Stillwell, Seaver, & Edwards, 1981). This shortcut can be a welcome alternative when the decision is not terribly important, time is limited, the number of value attributes is large, many people are involved in the decision, or communication has to be by phone or mail. Although the shortcut weights are not theoretically as sound, they usually result in the same decisions, and, when they don't, the loss in value tends to be small (Stillwell, Seaver, & Edwards, 1981).

The shortcut is to judge weights only for the least and most important value attributes and then simply divide the difference between these extreme weights equally among the remaining attribute ranks. The figure shows how Amelia could have applied this method, if she'd wished to.

SHORTCUT IMPORTANCE WEIGHTS

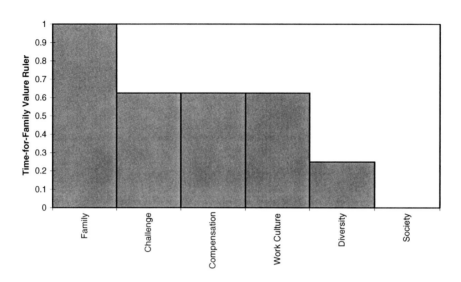

Ignoring Society, which Amelia still had been able to give no weight, due to lack of information, we begin with Diversity, with a weight of .25. We want to place the tied values, Challenge, Compensation, and Work Culture halfway between .25 and 1.00. That's a distance of .75, and half of .75 is .375. Thus, the weights for the tied values Challenge, Compensation, and Work Culture are all .25 + .375 = .625, and the weight for Family is .625 + .375 = 1.000. These shortcut weights thus move up in equal steps from .25 to 1.00. These are unnormalized weights, of course, and you might want to normalize them by dividing each by their sum.

Probability rulers, like value rulers, extend from the lowest to the highest preference on the most important value attribute, but there the similarity ends. The essential difference is that, while the value ruler makes use of various outcomes *between* the least and most preferred, such as various time amounts between 80 hours and 40 hours on Time for Family, the probability ruler makes use of no such intermediate outcomes. Instead, the scale on the probability ruler is made up of probabilities in an imaginary gamble. This gamble is called a *standard gamble* (von Neumann & Morgenstern, 1947), because "heads" always results in the most preferred level on the most important attribute and "tails" results in the lowest.

Standard Gamble for Importance Weights

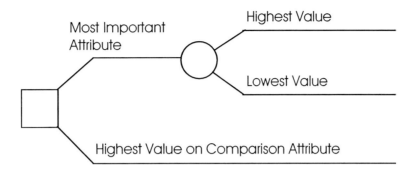

Applying the probability ruler, you always offer a choice between a *sure thing* (the highest preference on the comparison attribute) and the standard gamble. *The probability ruler, because it makes no use of intermediate outcomes, doesn't require a value curve.*

Let's see how the probability ruler can be applied to evaluating the importance of Cultural Diversity relative to that of Time for Family. We begin with the following two extreme questions:

- Would you rather have an increase from 10% to 70% on Cultural Diversity for sure OR a .99 chance at 40 hours versus a .01 chance at 80 hours on Time for Family? We can be fairly certain from the "magic wishes" that the decision maker will prefer the gamble, in this case. (If not, the importance weight for this attribute, too, can be set at .99 or 1.00.)

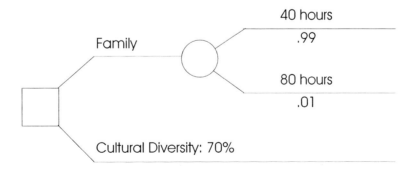

- Would you rather have 70% on Cultural Diversity for sure OR a .01 chance at 40 hours versus a .99 chance at 80 hours on Time for Family? In this case, we can be fairly certain that the decision maker will reject the gamble in favor of the certain option. (If not, the value attribute is probably not important enough to include in the analysis.)

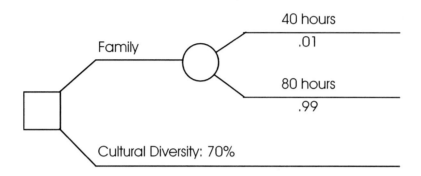

These two extreme questions make it clear that somewhere between a probability of .01, which is less desirable than the high level of Cultural Diversity, and .99, which is more desirable, there *must* be a break-even probability, where the gamble is equal to the high level of Cultural Diversity. This break-even probability, itself, will be the unnormalized importance weight for Cultural Diversity. Use of the probability ruler doesn't require any calculation at this point.

Let's say that the rest of the questions went as follows:

- Would you rather have an increase from 10% to 70% on Cultural Diversity for sure OR a .50 chance at 40 hours versus a .50 chance at 80 hours on Time for Family? Answer: The gamble.

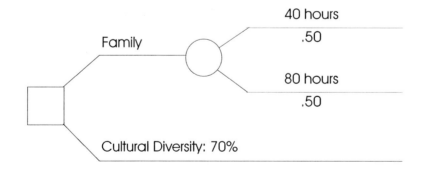

- Would you rather have 70% on Cultural Diversity for sure OR a .10 chance at 40 hours versus a .90 chance at 80 hours on Time for Family? Answer: Cultural Diversity.

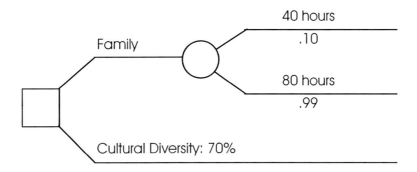

- Would you rather have 70% on Cultural Diversity for sure OR a .25 chance at 40 hours versus a .75 chance at 80 hours on Time for Family? Answer: That's about it. I wouldn't care.

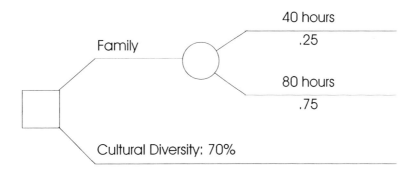

So the unnormalized weight for Cultural Diversity is .25. The unnormalized weight for Time for Family is 1.00 since 40 hours is equal, by definition, to a 1.00 chance at 40 hours versus a .00 chance at 80 hours on Time for Family. From this point on, you can either apply the standard gamble probability ruler to each of the other value attributes or take the shortcut and divide the difference between the highest and lowest weights evenly among the remaining attributes. Finally, you'll probably want to normalize the weights by dividing each by their sum.

So, what are the relative merits of the point allocation method, on the one hand, and the value ruler and probability ruler tradeoff methods, on the other? As noted, because the tradeoff methods involve choices among outcomes, rather than numbers, they avoid some biases that occur when using numbers to represent outcomes (Poulton, 1989). Also, the tradeoff methods seem to stimulate deeper thought. My own consistent experience, although I know of no research on this point, is that tradeoffs yield weights that are less nearly equal than those obtained from point allocation. Equal weights, as noted in discussing the effects of limited capacity on judgment, suggest inadequate thinking about differences among attributes.

Another advantage of probability rulers, as noted, is that they don't require value curves. Yet another is that they can be applied in cases where the most important attribute is not continuous, that is, has few or no intermediate outcomes. Let's say that the most important attribute in a decision is whether you get a certain job, house, or car. You can't think well about the preferences associated with various fractions of the job, or house, or car you hope to get. However, you could think well about the preferences associated with various probabilities of getting those things.

Another approach that's applicable to discontinuous attributes is use of a *time ruler.* This is one method used for measuring preferences of health states (Torrance, Thomas, & Sackett, 1972). The time ruler used to measure health states is the equivalent length of a healthy life. For example, if you wanted to measure the loss in preference associated with losing a leg, you might start with bracketing questions like:

- Would you rather live to 80 years with two good legs or to 80 years with one good leg? The expected answer: To 80 years with two good legs.

- Would you rather live one more day with two good legs or to 80 years with one good leg?" The expected answer: To 80 years with one good leg.

Somewhere between these extremes of one day to 80 years must be a length of healthy life that'll be judged equivalent in preference to 80 years with one good leg.

One problem with probability rulers is that the question asked is more complicated than that posed by either value rulers or time rulers. Another is that we don't think terribly well about extremely high or low probabilities. An approach that can help us to think better about extreme probabilities is thinking in terms of *reference events.* For example, instead of thinking about a probability of .01, think of drawing a blue ball from an urn with one blue ball and 99 yellow balls (Gigerenzer, 1991; Gigerenzer & Hoffrage, 1995; Gigerenzer, Hoffrage, & Kleinbolting, 1991; Kahneman & Tversky, 1996) Reference events are discussed in Thinking More Deeply About Uncertainty.

You could use a time ruler for discontinuous attributes, such as a job, house, or car, by thinking about the preferences associated with having these things for various lengths of time. *Before using a time ruler, however, you should satisfy yourself that the time intervals involved do not result in either habituation or sensitization of preferences.* Habituation is a reduction in either positive or negative preference as a function of time; we get used to some experiences with time and pay less attention to them. Sensitization is the opposite effect, an increase in either positive or negative preference as a function of time; with time, we come to "develop a taste for" some positive experiences, and, after a while, some negative experiences begin to "drive us crazy".

Of course, value rulers, probability rulers, and time rulers can be used to provide consistency checks on one another.

Appendix B. THINKING MORE DEEPLY ABOUT ALTERNATIVES

This appendix expands on our earlier discussion of the heuristic of analysis into sub-problems by considering independence among sub-problems. It also introduces analysis of alternatives as a way of thinking creatively about alternatives, using strategy tables.

More on Analysis into Sub-Problems

Not all attempts to reduce the number of alternatives by dividing the problem into sub-problems go as smoothly as the examples we considered earlier. For example, a cyclist was trying to decide whether to take a northern, middle, or southern route across the country and whether to go with Clancy, Pete, Roger, or Jim, all people with whom he'd biked at one time or another. Thus, he was faced with 3 x 4 = 12 alternatives in all: Take the northern route with Clancy, Take the middle route with Clancy, Take the southern route with Clancy, Take the northern route with Pete, etc. If he could treat these as two separate decision problems, he'd have to consider 3 alternatives in one sub-problem (the 3 routes) then 4 alternatives in the other (the 4 people), for a total of only 3 + 4 = 7 alternatives.

The difficulty was that Clancy, Pete, Roger, and Jim might well have preferences about which route to take. If our cyclist decided on a route first, he might eliminate as options in the second choice anyone who wouldn't want to take this route. On the other hand, if he decided on a companion first, he might eliminate as an option any route this person wouldn't want to take.

If the choice of route and the choice of companion were of about equal importance, he'd have to deal with this as a single decision problem with 12 alternatives. However, he felt that the choice of route was much more important. He felt that there were large differences among the routes, but, since he knew each of the possible companions well and got along with all, the differences among them were small. He could, therefore, choose a route first without fear that the preference for that choice would be much affected by a subsequent choice of companion. He couldn't have done it the other way around, however, for a prior choice of companion might have committed him to a substantially inferior route.

In general, there are three possible independence relationships among sub-problems A and B:

- *A and B are mutually independent.* (For example, what you're going to wear to dinner and what you're going to eat for dinner.) In such cases, solving A and B as separate problems reduces the number of alternatives from N_A x N_B to N_A + N_B. This is the heuristic of *analysis into sub-problems.*

- *B is independent of A, but A is not independent of B.* (For example, the choice of a cycling companion is relatively value independent of the choice of a cycling route; however, the choice of a cycling route is not at all value independent of the choice of a cycling companion.) In such cases, first analyze A as a separate problem, then analyze B as a separate problem. This is the *breadth-first, or planning, heuristic,* in which the more important decisions are made first and the less important ones are made later. The reduction in the number of alternatives is the same as for mutually independent sub-problems.

- *A and B are mutually dependent.* (For example, the people you invite to a small party are mutually dependent, since you want them to get along.) In such cases, the problem is best treated as a single problem.

Asymmetrical independence (the second case) can be a consequence of asymmetrical independence at the fact level, the causal impact in one direction being greater than that in the other direction. For example, mood might be dependent on the weather, but the weather is certainly not dependent on mood. Or, as in the cycling example, the asymmetry could be a consequence simply of difference in importance to the decision maker. In the example, the impact of route on companions is not as important as the impact of companions on route.

Earlier, we distinguished between decisions in which the problem is to choose the one best of a number of alternatives and decisions in which the problem is to choose as many of the best alternatives as a limited budget will permit. So far, we've been talking about the first kind of decision problem, but the independence problem can come up in the second kind, as well.

Consider a simple example. You have five dollars to spend on lunch. You look down the menu and mentally rank order the items in terms of the strength of your preference for each. Your top three items, from most preferred to least preferred, are: the key lime pie for $2.00, the carrot cake for $1.75, and the corned beef sandwich for $3.25. However, you wouldn't order key lime pie *and* carrot cake for lunch. The reason is that the value of the carrot cake is dependent on whether you're already having key lime pie or not. Once you've decided to order the key lime pie, the value of the corned beef sandwich moves into second place, and that of the carrot cake moves way down the list.

The ways of dealing with dependency among alternatives are the same as before. If the main course is more important than the dessert, choose it first, and then re-prioritize. If the main course and dessert are equally important, the appropriate unit of analysis is menus, rather than items on menus.

The classic case where resource allocation alternatives are not independent is investment portfolios. The value of any investment in an investment portfolio depends on the other investments. Adding a risky investment to a portfolio that's too conservative raises its value; whereas adding the same risky investment to a portfolio that's already too risky lowers its value. The term *portfolio effects* has come to be applied generally to refer to lack of independence among resource allocation alternatives.

Strategy Tables

Strategy tables are useful both for thinking creatively about alternatives and for getting an overview of a large number of alternatives. Below is a strategy table for planning a wedding.

In a strategy table, each act node is represented by a column, and the alternatives for that act node, by rows within the column. (See next page.) In this example, different act nodes have different numbers of alternatives. Any line drawn across the columns, such as one that would connect the shaded cells in the figure, represents a possible set of choices at each of the act nodes. This strategy table actually takes the place of a decision tree that would have 6 x 3 x 4 x 4 x 3 x 3 = 2592 end points—certainly a difficult tree to think about!

Location	Flowers	Food	Music	Gown	Honeymoon
Home $0	Level I $1000	Self $2400	None $0	Semiformal $0	Own Cabin $0
Outdoors $0		Caterer I $3000	Disk Jockey $350		
Church $800	Level II $2000			Dress I $500	SF $1100
Wedding House $1100		Caterer II $5000	Band $400		
Hotel $1200	Level III $3000	Caterer III $6000	Band, Singer $600	Dress II $1000	Kauai $3000
Vineyard $1300					

Prices in the table are for 200 guests and a wedding that would last five hours. Honeymoon prices are for round-trip fares plus one week's lodging. In addition, drinks for the wedding will run about $1000, and an honorarium for the minister will be $500. Photography will be handled within the family. The bride's parents hope to keep the price of the wedding and honeymoon down to around $10,000.

Thinking first about location, they didn't want to have the wedding at home, because their home isn't really big enough, and they didn't want to have it outdoors, because the weather isn't reliable enough. They didn't want to have it at a church, either. Because they preferred a wedding house to either a hotel or a vineyard and because it was cheaper than either, they tentatively decided on a wedding house for $1100.

Because there were such big differences in the prices for flowers, they thought this might be a good place to try to get creative and save money. They tentatively decided to see if they could make $1000 work.

Food is another place where there's a lot of money to be saved. Because they're good cooks, themselves, they could actually take care of the food. However, they'll have a lot of other things to do, and so they decided to see what they accomplish with $3000 by working with a caterer.

They decided to go with a small band or chamber group and a singer for $600. They place a great deal of importance on a singer, because they feel that it's primarily the minister, the singer, and those who give toasts who say the meaningful words that give depth to a wedding.

They decided tentatively on a $500 dress, and then toted up the bill to this point, to see how much (if anything!) was left over for the honeymoon. Adding $1000 for the liquor, a $500 honorarium for the minister, $1100 for the wedding house, $1000 for the flowers, $3000 for the food, $600 for the music, and $500 for the dress gave them a total of $7700. If they worked on getting a good travel package, they might even be able to afford the Kauai honeymoon!

Note that all that the bride's parents have decided on, at this point is a set of *classes* of alternatives. They've decided to have the wedding at a wedding house, but there are a great many wedding houses in the area. Choosing a wedding house and perhaps getting the wedding house to help with the food or the liquor is a sub-decision, in itself. Similarly, sub-decisions have to be made about a florist and flowers, a caterer and a menu, musicians and a program, and so forth. However, thinking in terms of classes of alternatives and, even more, thinking in terms of a strategy table has made it easy for them to rough out a plan to guide and give coherence to these sub-decisions.

Appendix C. THINKING MORE DEEPLY ABOUT UNCERTAINTY

This appendix discusses some powerful concepts for thinking quantitatively about uncertainty: probabilities, probability trees, attitude toward risk, and expected value.

Maximization of Expected Value

President Truman complained that what he needed was a "one-armed economist". Frequently, his economic advisers gave advice in the following format: On the one hand, such-and-such could occur, the economy would improve, and doing X would be best; on the other hand, this-and-that could occur, the economy would worsen, and doing Y would be best. Truman felt that this didn't do him much good. In order to make a decision, he needed one answer, not two. Calculating expected value is the best way to get a "one-armed economist" out of a "two-armed" one, a single answer in the face of uncertainty. (Decision analysts and economists prefer to use the more obscure word "utility" where we've been using "value".)

The principle of maximizing expected value should make clear the important, but often misunderstood, distinction between a *good decision* and a *good outcome*. A person bought a used car that the most reputable garage in town told him had at least 100,000 miles left on it before needing a major repair. It was clearly a good decision that maximized expected value for this decision maker. But two weeks later, the engine blew up! That was a bad outcome. The outcome was so unlikely, however, that it doesn't reflect in any way on the quality of the decision. In an clearly uncertain world, even the best decision can have a bad result. (See the earlier discussion of regret.)

A couple carried a zero-deductible on their homeowner's insurance. That was a bad decision, since the additional cost of the zero-deductible is not justified by the probable benefits. One winter evening, a live coal rolled out onto their carpet and damaged it, and they got a new carpet for free! That was a good outcome. The outcome was so unlikely, however, that it can't justify the decision to carry zero-deductible insurance. Similarly, all lottery winners are people who've made bad decisions!

Since we have control over our decisions but not the outcomes of those decisions, we should evaluate ourselves and others on the basis of the quality of our decision processes, not on the quality of the outcomes of our decisions. Though good decision processes can be expected to result in good outcomes in the long run, there can be no guarantee that they'll do so in any particular case. What's being recommended here is the emphasis on process that we've seen reduces defensive avoidance and characterizes creative thinkers. The basis for the recommendation this time is not that it enables one to deal more rationally with cognitive conflict but that it reflects a more realistic understanding of decision making in an uncertain world.

Obviously, if one alternative would be best in one future and another would be best in another, we haven't created an "uncertainty-proof" alternative. So we take that last step up the Decision Ladder, thinking about the *probabilities* of the various futures and weighting the value of each future by its probability. To provide a focus for this discussion, we'll introduce a new example, one in which uncertainty is a more salient aspect than in Amelia's problem.

> Hillevi has been studying for a career as a computer programmer. One day, she reads an article by a distinguished computer researcher and educator predicting that the market for programmers will be drying up. The article points out that many of the commonly used programs, such as word processing, spreadsheets, and financial programs now require only fine tuning and that many of the customizations that users need are becoming easy for them to create, themselves, using such user-friendly features as manipulation of objects and automatic recording of keystrokes.

> This leads her to the thought that maybe she should become a systems analyst. That way, she could either create software for solving clients' problems or use existing software to help them solve their problems. One downside to this alternative is the cost, in time and money, of the additional schooling in decision analysis, operations research, and finance. Another is that she doesn't think she'd enjoy this work as much.

To make a long story short, she comes up with the following 1-to-10 decision table:

	Costs of Schooling .10	Benefits of Career .90
Programmer	10	10
Analyst	1	1

The costs of schooling are fairly certain. At the end of this year, she'll be qualified to work as a programmer. To be able to work as a systems analyst would require an additional two years, at the minimum. What has just become uncertain as a consequence of reading the article is the career benefits. If she won't be able to build a lasting career in programming, then Programmer will no longer be a 10 on her scale, and Systems Analyst will be preferable. The following diagram represents this uncertainty.

Decision Tree/Table

	TOTAL VALUE	Costs of Schooling .10	Benefits of Career .90
Continues 10.0		10	10
Dries up 1.9		10	1
Analyst 5.5		1	6

This combination decision tree/table represents the uncertainty associated with the Programmer alternative by (a) including a row in the decision table for each future associated with that alternative and (b) connecting all the rows for that alternative to an *event node* at the end of the Programmer branch from the *act node*.

So far, this decision tree is no better than Truman's "two-armed economist": On the one hand, the market might continue, and Programmer will be worth 10.0; on the other hand, the market might dry up, and Programmer will be worth 1.9. How is she going to decide?

The answer is to choose the alternative with the highest *expected value (EV)*. Calculation of expected value at an event node involves estimating a probability for each of the futures at that node, weighting the total value of each future by its probability, and adding the products to get a sum for the node.

$$EV = p_1 V_1 + p_2 V_2 + ...$$

The reason for the "..." is that event nodes can have more than two branches, and the formula for expected value applies to any number of branches. The event node above

215

reflects only the possibilities that the market will let Hillevi continue as a programmer or not. Instead, she might want a node that allows for three possibilities: that the market dries up in 0-5 years, in 6-10, years, or in 11+ years. In this case, the equation for expected value would read:

$$EV = p_1V_1 + p_2V_2 + p_3V_3$$

In estimating probabilities, the rule is that you need a probability for each branch at an event node and that *the probabilities at any event node must add up to 1.00.* Before Hillevi had read the article, she'd been implicitly assuming a probability of 1.0 for the possibility that the market for programmers will continue as it has in the past and a probability of 0 for the possibility that it will dry up. (Since $1.00 + 0 = 1.00$, this satisfies the rule).

Now that the new possibility has been called to her attention, she realizes that she doesn't have any basis for saying whether the market is more likely to continue or dry up (or, for that matter, improve). The information in the article is about all she has to go on. Predictions by experts of this author's stature tend to be correct, but aren't always so. Putting all this together, she feels that the probability that this author is correct to be about .80. Thus, her probability that the market will dry up is .80, and her probability that it will continue must then be .20 (since .80 + the probability that it will continue must equal 1.00). She adds these probabilities to the diagram and computes expected value as:

$$EV \quad = .20(10.) + .80(1.9)$$

$$= 2.0 + 1.5$$

$$= 3.5$$

	TOTAL VALUE	Costs of Schooling .10	Benefits of Career .90
Programmer EV=3.5 — Continues .20	10.0	10	10
Dries up .80	1.9	10	1
Analyst EV=5.5	5.5	1	6

Notice that the EV of 3.5 is between the 10.0 and the 1.9. The EV can't be higher than the highest branch value nor lower than the lowest branch value. If it is, there's been a calculation error. Notice also that the EV of 3.5 is closer to 1.9 than to 10.0. This is because the 1.9 is weighted by the higher probability.

Notice also that the 5.5 for Analyst is between the 10.0 for Programmer/Continues and the 1.9 for Programmer/Dries Up. If the value for Analyst had been 1.5, say, then the decision maker should choose Programmer, since its worst possible outcome is better than the certain outcome for Analyst. If, on the other hand, the value for Analyst had been higher than either value for Programmer, the decision maker should choose Analyst. In either case, the uncertainty would be irrelevant to the decision; and, in either case, she should have realized at the sensitivity analysis stage that the decision wasn't sensitive to a change from 1.9 to 10.0 for Programmer and that there was no need[1] to consider probabilities or expected value.

Attitude Toward Risk

Let's say that you were offered a choice between $1 million for sure and a .50-.50 chance on $3 million. I've presented this imaginary choice to hundreds of people, and virtually all of them take the $1 million. *I* would.

However, the expected value of the gamble seems to be:

$$.50(\$0) + .50(\$3,000,000) = \$1,500,000.$$

This is greater than the $1 million for sure and suggests that all of us were wrong in preferring the $1 million for sure. What's going on?

The problem in this case is with the numbers we perform the calculations on. We performed the calculations on *objective* numbers, the kind that go in a fact table, not *subjective* values, the kind that go into a value table. Think about it. On a 1-10 value scale, where $0 is a 1 and $3 million is a 10, where would you place $1 million? One would expect that your first million dollars would add a lot more to your happiness than your second million. Let's say that $1 million is a 6 on this scale. (Most people give it a much higher rating, but this'll be enough to make the point.) What we have here is the decreasing marginal utility we encountered earlier.

---

1. I should say "little need", but that is a technical nicety that is beyond the scope of this book.

Now, let's compute the expected value of the gamble correctly, using 1-to-10 ratings:

$$.50(1) + .50(10) = 5.5.$$

This doesn't compare at all favorably with the 6.0 that we assigned to the $1 million for sure. The correct calculation is consistent with our intuition.

This example illustrates *risk aversion*. It's believed that people are risk averse most of the time (Arrow, 1971; Bernoulli, 1738; Pratt, 1964). For most of us, a bird in the hand is worth two in the bush—perhaps more. We're inclined to "take the cash and let the credit go". As Hamlet said, "We choose to bear the ills we suffer, rather than fly to others we know not of."

Risk proneness, on the other hand, is a preference for risk. While unusual, it isn't necessarily irrational. Here is a rather extreme example. Let's say that a military dictatorship has taken over a country, despite the resistance that you and others have put up. There's a one-time opportunity for you to get out quickly that'll cost $10,000. If you don't take the opportunity, you expect to be caught and executed. But you have only $9000. Would you exchange the $9000 for a .50-.50 chance at $10,000 in a game of chance?

If you do the calculations the wrong way, you'll focus on the *objective* dollars. The gamble will then be worth:

$$.50(\$0) + .50(\$10,000) = \$5,000.$$

Since this is less than the $9000 you have, you won't gamble; you won't get out quickly; and you'll probably die.

If you do the calculations correctly, you'll first ask yourself where, on a 1-10 value scale with $0 at 1 and $10,000 at 10 you'd rate $9000? Let's say you give it a 2. (I'd rate it lower.) This is the increasing marginal utility we encountered earlier.

Now, with the correct calculations, the gamble is worth:

$$.50(1) + .50(10) = 5.5.$$

This compares very favorably with the 2 we gave the sure thing. This choice at least gives you a 50% chance of living.

The point of this section is simple:

Expected value must be based on subjective values, for attitude toward risk to be taken into account.

In decision making, it's rational to be objective about fact judgments but not about value judgments.

Even if you do the calculations the correct way, you should treat expected value only as advisory. As always, we check analysis against intuition. If you don't actually want to take a gamble whose expected value is superior to a sure thing, you should reexamine both your analysis and your intuitive judgment.

Earlier, we considered value curves for diminishing, constant, and increasing marginal utility. All we have to add here is that these curves can be helpful in thinking about attitude toward risk. Diminishing marginal utility implies risk aversion, constant marginal utility implies risk neutrality, and increasing marginal utility implies risk proneness.

People can make things more complicated than this, however. Although it doesn't seem to be a good idea, we tend to be risk avoiding for gains and risk seeking for losses, as in the utility curve below (Kahneman & Tversky, 1979; Markowitz, 1952).

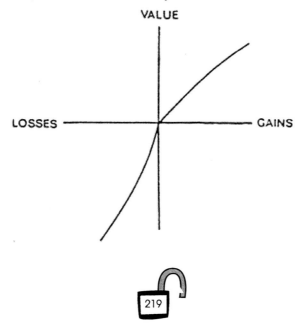

This curve breaks at the zero on our value scale, the status quo point that divides gains from losses. The value curve for gains shows diminishing marginal utility and risk aversion; that for losses shows increasing marginal utility and risk proneness. On the face of it, risk proneness for losses sounds unwise. When coupled with risk aversion for gains, it can actually lead to contradictions (Kahneman & Tversky, 1979).

For example, people whose values are described by the above curve can be induced to make contradictory decisions by changing the mere wording of the problem. If a person whose normal life expectancy would be 40 more years has to choose between *losing* 20 years of life for certain and a 50-50 chance on losing 0 years versus *losing* 40 years, that person would tend to take the chance on living to a normal life expectancy. On the other hand, if this same choice is framed as a choice between *gaining* 20 more years of life and a medical treatment that gives a 50-50 chance on gaining 0 more years of life versus gaining 40 more years of life, that person would tend to take the 20 years for certain, avoiding the risky option. Even medical doctors advising their patients show this inconsistent pattern of behavior (McNeil, Pauker, Sox, & Tversky, 1982).

Buyers tend to outperform sellers in negotiation studies (Bazerman & Neale, 1992). This is presumably because buyers stand to lose money and are willing to take greater risks in the situation that they have been placed in.

This complex utility curve tends to operate when we're thinking intuitively, and it can lead to unwise decisions. If we think hard about our values and, especially, if we zero our blessing counter, we can, hopefully, avoid the artificial distinction between gains and losses that leads us into this trap.

Probability Judgment

In daily life, we rarely talk about probabilities. We're more likely to use verbal phrases like "probable", "likely", and "an even chance". The trouble with verbal phrases like this, however, is that they're highly ambiguous. Even intelligence analysts understand "probable" to correspond to probabilities as low as .25 and as high as .90 (Barclay, Brown, Kelly, Peterson, Phillips, & Selvidge, 1977), and even judges understand "beyond a reasonable doubt" to correspond to probabilities as low as .50 and as high as 1.00 (Simon & Mahan, 1971). It depends on whom you're talking to. Obviously, such ambiguity can have serious consequences. The Joint Chiefs of Staff's report to President Kennedy on his analysis of the CIA's plan to invade Cuba said that the chances of success were "fair". "Fair" meant a probability of about .30 to those advising Kennedy (Wyden, 1979), but, apparently, President Kennedy attached a higher probability to this vague term. James Thurber spoke wisely when he quipped, "A pinch of probability is worth a pound of perhaps."

Probabilities measure strength of belief. Failure to understand this leads to some common misconceptions. The following statement expresses a misconception that's all too common and that even made it into a medical textbook:

> *Probabilities apply to populations of individuals, but not to particular individuals. To say that the probability of AIDS in a particular population is .005 is meaningful; 5 out of every 1000 individuals in that population can be expected to have AIDS. However, to say that the probability of a particular individual in that population having AIDS is .005 is meaningless. The person either has AIDS and the probability is 1.00, or doesn't have it and the probability is 0.*

While it's true that this person either has AIDS or doesn't have it, only God can assign a probability of 0 or 1.00 to an assertion that he or she does or doesn't have it. Any of us mortals who has to make a decision about this person will have to make it with less certainty.

Ron Howard, one of the founders of decision analysis and the person who coined the term "decision analysis", makes this point in a delightfully clear way (personal communication). He tosses a coin, immediately covers it with his hand, and observes that the probability that the coin came up heads is .50 for everyone present. (Notice that this is a meaningful statement, even though we're talking about an individual coin and not a population of coins.) Then he peeks at the coin and makes his point: *His* probability that the coin came up heads is no longer .50—it's either 0 or 1—though *no one else's* probability has changed and the objective state of the coin hasn't changed. Probabilities attach to personal beliefs about states of the world and not to the states of the world, themselves.

Ideally, our strength of belief would be based on relative frequencies in scientifically drawn random samples. Clinical trials are run on many medical treatments, and so it's often possible to make use of such data in important medical decisions. Similarly, data are collected on the relative safety of different occupations and of different modes of transportation, and these data can provide objective bases for probabilities.

Actually, a full-blown scientific study is not always needed in order to base strength of belief on sample data. A sample size of 2 or 3 can be adequate. Getting second opinions can be an efficient strategy when the expected consensus among the sources of information is high (Nisbett & Ross, 1980, p. 256-260). Since all of the new Oregon driver's licenses have the same format, you'd have to check only one to see whether they have color photos. Since most Londoners know the direction of the nearest underground, you have to ask only one. Since fewer would know what hours the British Museum is open, you might want to ask two—and, if they don't agree, then ask a third.

Often, however, we're unable to obtain data and must base our strength of belief entirely on judgment. Though we're all familiar with the concept of strength of belief, many, understandably, have difficulty in translating various strengths of belief into the less familiar world of probabilities. Even those who are accustomed to thinking in terms of probabilities can be helped to make probability judgments better and to obtain better probability judgments from others. To obtain the best probability judgments, attention should be given to motivation, problem structuring, and, finally, judgment elicitation, itself (Spetzler & Staël von Holstein, 1975).

We're about to spend some time considering ways to obtain first-class probability judgments. You could come away from this thinking, "If I had to do all that, I'd never make a decision!" I don't expect that you'd ever do *all* of what's described here or even that you'd often do *much* of it. My hopes are more modest. First, I hope that this discussion will give you a *general orientation* that will improve *all* your fact judgments about the present or the future and your thinking about the uncertainty of those judgments. Second, I hope that it will give you *specific tools* that you could use for those *few* fact judgments that a sensitivity analysis shows to be critical to an important decision.

Motivation

The person providing the probability judgments should be *motivated to provide accurate judgments* and not to make him or herself or someone else look good or to engage in wishful thinking or defensive pessimism.

- If it's you who's judging the probabilities, be clear about the fact that you'll make the best decisions with accurate probabilities, not biased ones. This should provide the courage needed to counteract tendencies toward irrationality. If someone else is judging the probabilities, try to communicate this fact to them. If someone else is judging the probabilities, you can sometimes eliminate motivational bias by not telling them how the probabilities will be used.

- If the person judging the probabilities, whether you or someone else, doesn't seem to be able to able to make unbiased judgments about this particular matter, try to find someone who can.

Problem Structuring

It's important to ask the probability question of a person who has the *relevant knowledge* and to ask the question in a way that conforms to the way that person normally thinks about that knowledge.

- Try to find someone with the relevant knowledge.

- Define each event node and its branches in a way that's natural and easy for that person to think about. This is a meaningfulness criterion.

- Specify a set of branches that cover all the possibilities and cover each possibility only once, so that the probabilities will add to 1. This a completeness and non-redundancy criterion.

- Define the branches on the event node in such a way that the distinctions among them are objective and, preferably, quantitative (e.g., inches of rainfall). This is a testability/measurability criterion.

- Avoid, so far as possible, labeling a branch "other". The probabilities of such vaguely specified categories are likely to be substantially underestimated (Fischhoff, Slovic, & Lichtenstein, 1978; Tversky & Koehler, 1994) Ideally, each branch at an event node will be specified at the same level of abstraction.

We're talking here about thinking critically about events, just as we talked earlier about thinking critically about values and alternatives. Clearly, many of the considerations are the same.

Understanding Biases

It's helpful to understand the kinds of biases that can distort our probability judgments, so we can guard against them. This is an area where a great deal of excellent research has been done.

Wishful thinking. People tend to estimate higher probabilities for events they'd like to happen (McGuire, 1960). This is especially likely to be the case when they're in a good mood (Isen, Means, Patrick, & Nowicki, 1982). Surprisingly, people who are depressed tend to judge probabilities the most accurately. A good caveat, then, would be judge probabilities only when in a sober mood. This is not the time to "think positively" or to "be optimistic". The time for such thinking is *after* you've made a good decision and are preparing to implement it.

A seemingly related bias is the *self-serving bias*, in which people estimate higher probabilities for situations in which they look good. Most people see themselves as above average, a statistical impossibility, and people are more likely to attribute their successes to ability and their failures to luck (see Taylor, 1989).

Illusion of control. People tend to think they have some control over "luck" and therefore tend to estimate higher probabilities for events to which they have made a behavioral commitment (Langer, 1975). For example, they're willing to gamble more on dice they've rolled than on dice someone else has rolled, and they demand a higher price for a lottery ticket they've selected than for one someone has selected for them.

The obvious corrective for these biases is distancing, asking yourself what probability you'd judge *for someone else.* How would you feel about how that stock is performing if someone else had purchased it?

Availability. We tend to judge probabilities on the basis of the ease with which instances come to mind. This seems reasonable, since high frequency instances come more readily to mind than low frequency instances. However, availability in memory is influenced not only by frequency but also by vividness, recency, and frequency of mention in the media. Thus, for example, we tend to think that dying in an automobile accident is more likely than dying of diabetes, even though they're about equally likely (Slovic, Fischhoff, & Lichtenstein, 1980). Deaths from automobile accidents are reported in the media far more frequently than deaths from diabetes, and this influences availability and our probability estimates.

The best way to correct for availability bias—and a good way to correct for all judgmental biases—is to start with objective frequencies. There's a strong tendency for people to neglect overall statistics and zero in on concrete information about the case at hand, often neglecting the more helpful information in favor of the less helpful (Kahneman & Tversky, 1973). If you're unable to obtain objective frequencies, thinking in detail about the information you should take into account in making an estimate helps in making an accurate best guess about the true value (MacGregor, Lichtenstein, & Slovic, 1988). For example, in trying to estimate the tons of fish caught by U. S. commercial fishermen last year, it helps to be aware that the following items of information could help you with your estimate: number of U. S. ports with commercial fishing boats, average number of fishing boats per port, tons of fish caught per trip per boat, and number of trips per year per boat.

It can be helpful to spend some time thinking about what could make things come out *differently* from the way you think they will (Lord, Lepper, & Preston, 1984). Because we tend to take the past as a predictor of the future, it's difficult to take seriously possibilities much different from what we've experienced. Though the past provides the best single guess about the future, the future holds many surprises and often turns out to be much better or much worse than we thought likely. Back in 1949, when computers took up entire buildings, *Popular Mechanics Magazine* confidently predicted, "Computers in the future may weight no more than 1.5 tons"! The prediction was in the right direction but too close to past experience.

The corrective for this bias, known as *overconfidence bias,* is to "stretch the range" of possibilities and to spend time thinking about factors that might lead to outcomes better than your most optimistic estimate and factors that might lead to outcomes worse than your most pessimistic estimate (Alpert & Raiffa, 1982). Thinking about extreme scenarios in vivid detail apparently increases their effectiveness (Schoemaker, 1993). In general, it's helpful to spend time thinking about reasons why you might be wrong (Hoch, 1985; Koriat, Lichtenstein, & Fischhoff, 1980). A related strategy for dealing with a different form of availability bias, hindsight bias, is seeking explanations for events that did *not* happen (Slovic & Fischhoff, 1977). While positive thinking is appropriate for maintaining hope in a rational process, for thinking creatively in structuring the decision problem, and for maintaining commitment in implementing the decision, this kind of negative thinking seems more helpful in getting fact judgments right and in getting the problem structured correctly.

It's important also to ask for complementary probabilities. For example, ask not only for the probability that it will rain but also for the probability that it won't rain. These probabilities should add to 1, but, in practice, they may not. The greater the number of branches at the event node, the more the sum of the judged probabilities is likely to exceed 1.00 (Wright & Whalley, 1983).

Representativeness. We tend to judge probabilities on the basis of *similarity* to a typical member of a category (Kahneman & Tversky, 1972). For example, when asked what bird is mentioned most frequently in written English, people think of robin, eagle,

225

and other birds that are typical. The correct answer is chicken, not a typical bird at all but one that appears on many menus. Similarly, in choosing among careers, we tend to think in terms of the typical, or stereotypic, doctor, movie star, etc. and thus overestimate our probability of success.

The correctives for representativeness bias are the same as those for availability bias: define the population and get representative data or, at least, ask yourself what a random sample would look like. For example, while the "typical" actor is thought of as busy acting, only some 5% of the members of the Screen Actors' Guild, an objectively defined population of actors, are actually employed in this capacity!

Probability Elicitation

It's important to ask about likelihood in ways that make it easy to translate strength of belief into probabilities. Think in terms of what are we referred to earlier as *reference events* with known probabilities. Is the event more likely than getting a head in the toss of a coin, than getting a one in the roll of a die, than drawing the ace of spades from a deck of 52 cards? A commonly used reference event is an imaginary urn with, say, 100 balls, some of which are red and some of which are white. Is the event more likely than drawing a red ball from an urn with 75 red balls and 25 white balls?

Sensitivity to Probabilities

Because Hillevi isn't at all confident about her probability estimates, she decides to do a sensitivity analysis on the probabilities. Although she isn't confident that .80 is the probability that she should judge for the author of the article being correct, she's confident that the probability isn't less than a .50-.50 chance and that it isn't near certainty. The range within which she's quite confident the probability should fall is .55 to .95. Thus, the appropriate range for the probability that things will continue as they are is .05 to .45. She then computes the expected values for Programmer and Analyst for various probabilities ranging from 0 to 1.00 and plots the graph on the next page.

Actually, all that it was necessary to do was compute the EVs for Programmer, since the EV for Analyst isn't affected by this probability but is constant at 5.5 (represented by the horizontal line). In computing the EVs for Programmer, only two calculations are needed, since all lines will be straight lines, and it takes only two points to define a straight line. The easiest points to calculate are those where the probability of the market continuing is 0 and 1.00, since these are simply the total values for the Dries Up and Continues rows, respectively. *Whenever the event node has only two branches, you can determine in your head the EVs for a sensitivity analysis on probabilities.* So the EVs for Programmer are on the dotted line that begins at 1.9, where the probability that the market will continue is set at 0, and ends at 10.0, where this probability is set at 1.

The first thing to notice in this graph is that, as the probability that the market will continue increases, the EV for Programmer also increases. This is as it should be and gives us some confidence that this part of the model has been set up correctly.

The second thing to notice is that the break-even probability is less than .45. Unfortunately, this is within her confidence interval of .05-.45. This range of uncertainty is important to her choice, since different regions within this range point to different alternatives. Ideally a confidence interval will fall entirely to one side or the other of the break-even point, so that, anywhere within her range of uncertainty, the same alternative will be preferred. In the present case, however, she should consider obtaining more information to narrow her confidence interval to the point where it excludes the break-even probability. At the same time, she should balance the increased confidence against the cost of obtaining the information. Since this is a career decision, increased confidence should be worth quite a bit.

SENSITIVITY to PROBABILITY of CONTINUING

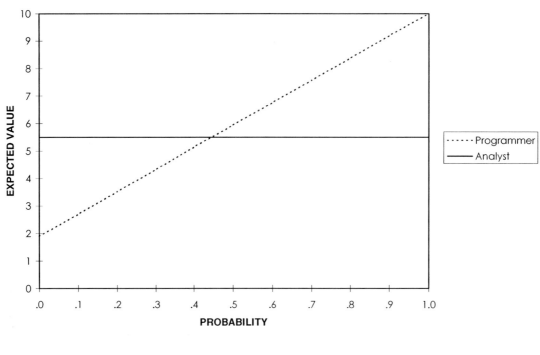

Probability Trees

Where more than one event node is involved, complexity can get out of hand rather quickly. Probability trees can make it much easier to handle this complexity (Schum & Martin, 1980, 1981). We'll consider three basic cases, conjunctions, disjunctions, and probability revision.

Conjunctions. You're applying to a very competitive graduate program. Your grades are good enough, but, to be admitted, you'll also have to have good Graduate Record Examination scores and a good letter of recommendation from your major professor. Both your GRE scores and the letter of recommendation are uncertain. Let's say that you feel there's an .80 chance that your GRE scores will be good enough and a .95 chance that your professor's letter of recommendation will be good enough. Then what's the probability that your application as a whole will be good enough—that your GRE scores will be good enough *and* (the conjunction) your letter of recommendation will be good enough?

We can represent these two uncertainties as event nodes in a probability tree. A probability tree differs from a decision tree in that it has only event nodes and no act nodes. A probability tree can be included as part of a decision tree or used, as here, for side calculations to improve the probability estimates that you enter in your decision tree. Thus, the additional event nodes needn't complicate your decision tree.

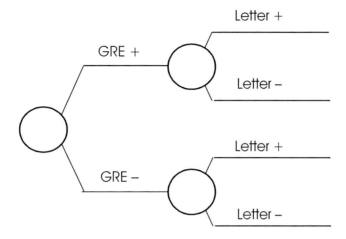

What this tree says is that there are four possible outcomes: (a) both the GRE and the letter could be good enough, (b) the GRE could be good enough but the letter not good enough, (c) the GRE could be not good enough but the letter good enough, and (d) both the GRE and the letter could be not good enough. Note that the same four possibilities could just as well have been represented by beginning with the Letter node and then branching to the GRE node. *While act nodes and events must be in chronological order with respect to one another, neighboring act nodes can be in any order with respect to one another, and neighboring event nodes can be in any order with respect to one another.*

The next tree adds the probabilities to these possibilities:

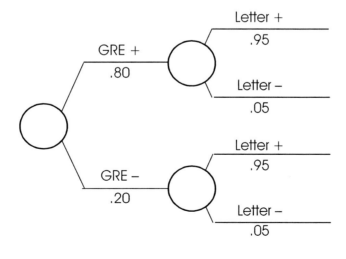

Once all this is laid out in a tree, we notice something that we hadn't noticed before. It *sounded* all right to say that there's an .80 chance that your GRE scores will be good enough and a .95 chance that your professor's letter of recommendation will be good enough, but the probability tree makes clear that there isn't just one probability that your professor's letter of recommendation will be good enough—there are two. These are called *conditional probabilities,* since each is conditional on what has preceded it in the tree. One of these is the conditional probability that the letter will be good enough *given that* your GRE is good enough, and the other is the conditional probability that the letter will be good enough *given that* your GRE is not good enough. (If you had drawn the tree in the other direction, then there'd be two conditional probabilities for your GRE being good enough.)

If these two conditional probabilities are the same, as indicated here, then the GRE and letter probabilities are said to be *independent.* According to these probabilities, finding out that your GRE score turned out well would give you no reason for optimism regarding the letter; the probability that it will be good enough is .95, no matter what your GRE score turns out to be. This is surely not true in general. People with very low GRE scores are quite unlikely to get good letters, and people with very high GRE scores are more likely to get good letters. It may be, however, that you know that your GRE scores won't vary over such a wide a range, and, in addition, you expect your professor's letter to be based more on your effectiveness in dealing with people than on the kind of ability the GRE measures. So, although independence may not be precisely right, we'll assume in this example that it's good enough as an approximation. However, all that will be said in the remainder of this discussion applies equally well to cases in which the conditional probabilities differ.

What does one do, then, with the probabilities in a probability tree? There are two rules for manipulating probabilities, the *addition rule* and the *multiplication rule*.

- *The Addition Rule:* To obtain the probability that either one *or* other of two mutually exclusive events will occur, ADD their individual probabilities.

- *The Multiplication Rule:* To obtain the probability that *both* of two independent events will occur, MULTIPLY their individual probabilities.

We've already encountered the addition rule in the requirement that the probabilities at any event node sum to 1.00. If there's a .50 chance that a coin will come up heads and a .50 chance that it will come up tails, then there's a .50 + .50 = 1.00 chance that it will come up *either* heads or tails. If there's a 1/6 chance that a die will come up snake eyes and a 5/6 chance that it won't, then there's a 1/6 + 5/6 = 1 chance that it will come up either snake eyes or not. The requirement that the branches at an event node be mutually exclusive means that the probability that we will go out one or the other of those branches is the sum of their separate probabilities, and the requirement that the branches at an event node be exhaustive means that this sum must equal 1.

Even though the multiplication rule is defined for independent probabilities, the calculations described below apply equally to both related and independent probabilities once they have been represented in a probability tree as probabilities and conditional probabilities. The following probability tree has been derived from the one above by applying the multiplication rule to obtain probabilities at the ends of the branches.

As long as you're working with probabilities in a properly structured tree, you don't have to worry about the requirements of mutual exclusivity or independence. Probabilities for different branches will always be mutually exclusive, and probabilities along the same branch will always be independent.

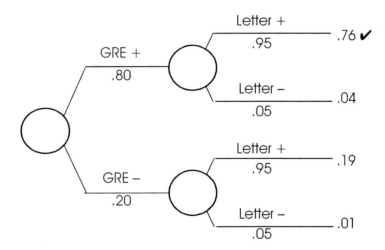

The probability that your GRE is acceptable *and* the letter is acceptable (.76) is the product of (a) the probability that your GRE is acceptable (.80) and (b) the conditional probability that the letter is acceptable given that your GRE is acceptable (.95). Any path in a probability tree is a *conjunction* of sub-paths. To get to the end of the path, you must go out the first sub-path *and* the second and so forth. Thus, the probability of getting to the end of any path is the product of the probabilities of going out each of its sub-paths.

Note that the probabilities at all the end points add up to 1.00. This entire probability tree can be thought of as a complex event node with four branches. The rule still applies: The probabilities at any event node must add up to 1.00. It may help to think of the first event node as cutting the "pie" of possibilities into two pieces, one 80% of the whole pie and the other 20% of the whole pie. Then the second layer of nodes further divides each of these pieces into two pieces. In the end, all of the four pieces have to fit back together to make up the whole pie.

Let's introduce a disjunction into the picture. You find a lovely apartment, but it costs more than you can afford alone, so you'll need a roommate to share expenses. There are two possibilities, Beth and Toni. You figure that there's a one-third chance that Beth will agree and a .50-.50 chance that Toni will agree. You'd prefer Beth, so you'll ask her first. Here is the probability tree, with the probabilities at the ends of the branches calculated. Note that probability trees don't have to be symmetrical.

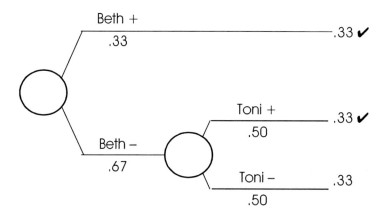

There are two ways you could wind up with a roommate. Either Beth could say yes (.33) OR Beth could say no and Toni could say yes (.67 x .50 = .33). Thus, the probability that either Beth or Toni will agree to share the apartment with you is .33 + .33 = .66. *We multiply probabilities on the same branch and add probabilities on different branches.*

Without the aid of a probability tree and probability calculations, we often think quite badly about the likelihoods of both conjunctions and disjunctions. Consider, for example, the following description (Kahneman & Tversky, 1982):

Linda is 31 years old, single, outspoken, and very bright. She majored in philosophy. As a student, she was deeply concerned with issues of discrimination and social justice, and also participated in anti-nuclear demonstrations.

Which of these statements about Linda is more likely to be true: (a) Linda is a bank teller; (b) Linda is a bank teller who's active in the feminist movement? Apparently because the stereotype of a bank teller who's active in the feminist movement fits the description better than the stereotype of a bank teller, most pick people pick (b). But consider the following probability tree:

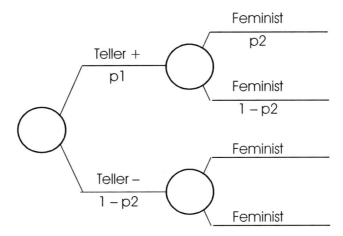

What this tree makes clear is that, *whatever* probability we set for a person who fits this description being a bank teller (call it p_1) and *whatever* conditional probability we set for a person who fits this description and is a bank teller also being a feminist (call it p_2), the probability that a person who fits this description is both a bank teller *and* a feminist is the product of these two probabilities, $p_1 \times p_2$. It's *impossible* for $p_1 \times p_2$ (the probability of being a bank teller and a feminist) to be larger than p_1 (the probability of being a bank teller). After all, every time we count a bank teller who's a feminist, we also add to the count of bank tellers!

A special case in which the multiplication rule can be quite helpful is in estimating very small probabilities. We have difficulty thinking about probabilities smaller than .01 (or probabilities greater than .99). Consider, for example, the probability of a U. S. driver being involved in a fatal automobile accident in a given year. This probability is estimated at .0003 (Scammon, 1980, p. 156), a difficult number to think about. In order to make it easier to think about, this probability can be decomposed into (a) the probability of a U. S. driver being involved in an automobile accident in a given year and (b) the conditional

233

probability that an automobile accident will involve a fatality. Comparable probabilities have been entered into the following tree:

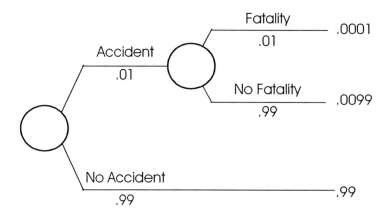

The probability of an accident and the conditional probability of a fatality given that there was an accident have each been arbitrarily set at .01 to show how this kind of decomposition, breaking compound events into component events, can bring very small probabilities within easy comprehension.

Probability revision. We suggested objective frequencies as the best corrective for errors in probability judgment, but a problem with statistics is that they apply to general categories and seldom fit our individual case perfectly. Perhaps for this reason and perhaps also because they're abstract, we often don't even think to use statistics to aid our judgment (Nisbett & Ross, 1980, p. 159). This is known as *base-rate neglect*. It occurs even when the base-rate information is not statistical but part of our own experience (Tversky & Kahneman, 1982).

A now-classic example of base-rate neglect is the common response to learning that someone has tested positive for AIDS. We tend to think that a person who has tested positive for AIDS *has* AIDS. If we know that the conditional probability that a person who has AIDS will test positive is close to .996, we're even more confident in this judgment. Nevertheless, because the prevalence of AIDS in the population (the base rate) is so low, .0076, a person who tests positive actually has no more than a .50-.50 chance of having AIDS! We'll provide the calculations shortly.

An opposite problem is basing our predictions too much on past experience and not being sufficiently sensitive to new information. This is known as *conservatism* (Edwards, 1968). It's presumably related to the undue importance of first impressions. Once we've formed an impression of someone or something, new information no longer has the same impact. The process of *Bayesian revision* can be used to deal with both base-rate neglect and conservatism.

Suppose that, at a wedding, someone next to you says, "The bride and groom seem to get along so wonderfully! I'm sure *this* marriage will last." Notice that this person says nothing about the divorce rate, though you know from the emphasis in her voice that she's fully aware of the high divorce rate. Personal experience tends to overwhelm statistics even when that experience is minimal and the statistics are extensive. The following probability tree represents the possibilities in this situation, using a plus to represent "got along wonderfully" and a minus to represent "did not get along wonderfully".

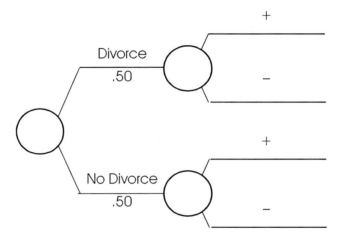

Notice that the event nodes are not in chronological order. Neighboring event nodes (that is, ones that are not separated by an act node), you'll recall, can be in any order with respect to one in another. Because it's usually easier to think about this way, a Bayesian tree typically begins with a node that represents what we're trying to predict, here, whether the couple will divorce or not divorce. These are often called *hypotheses*. The next layer represents the information on which we're basing our prediction, here, the fact that the couple "got along wonderfully".

The tree for testing hypotheses forces us to consider at least two hypotheses. This corrects a powerful human tendency to think of only one hypothesis at a time (Kuhn, 1962), which can lead to a number of errors in reasoning. A delightful example is provided by an experiment involving a light with one versus two switches. Children shown a board with *one* switch and a light and told, "When the switch is up, the light will be on," think erroneously that, if the light is on, the switch must be up. In contrast, children shown a board with *two* switches and a light and told, "When the switch on the left is up, the light will be on," are considerably less likely to think that, if the light is on, the switch on the left must be up (Wason, 1960). Taking seriously the possibility of other causes can stimulate greater care in thinking about causal connections.

The divorce rate has been assumed to be .50, and these probabilities have been entered into the tree, but surely they shouldn't be applied to this couple without some adjustment. How can we take into account the fact that they got along wonderfully? Let's assume that of couples who never divorce, 99% appear to get along wonderfully at their weddings and that, of couples who eventually get divorced, 90% appear to get along wonderfully at their weddings. After all, most people manage to do pretty well at their weddings. These probabilities have been entered into the next tree.

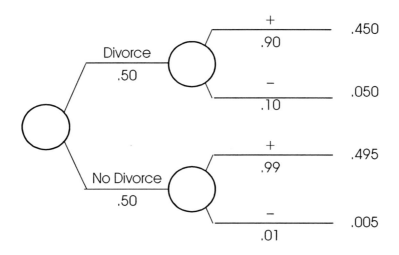

The Bayesian situation is different in an important way from conjunctions and disjunctions. In conjunctions and disjunctions, everything in the probability tree is uncertain. In Bayesian revision, not everything is uncertain. True, in the probability tree above, everything is represented as uncertain, but this might be thought of as the probability tree of our wedding guest *before* the wedding.

After the wedding, there's no longer any uncertainty at the second layer of nodes; the bride and groom, as a matter of fact, "got along wonderfully" at the wedding. In the tree below the possibilities that have been ruled out by our observation have been crossed out.

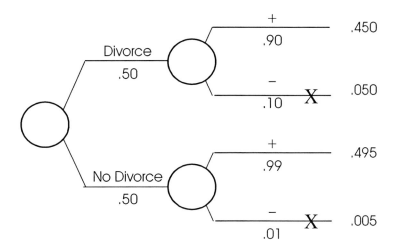

There are only two possibilities left: (a) "getting along wonderfully" and divorce, represented by a "probability" of .450; and (b) "getting along wonderfully" and no divorce, represented by a "probability" of .495. The two "probabilities" that remain carry information about the relative likelihood of the only remaining uncertainty, Divorce versus No Divorce. Since these are the only possibilities left, their probabilities should add to 1.00. This we can make them do by renormalizing the .450 and .495 in the same way that we renormalize importance weights, dividing each by their sum.

$$.450/(.450 + .495) = .476$$

$$.495/(.450 + .495) = .524$$

These revised probabilities are rounded to two places and entered into the following tree, which has been simplified by omitting the part that's no longer uncertain.

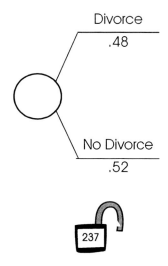

Note that the revised probabilities differ very little from the initial probabilities. That's because knowing that a couple "got along wonderfully" at their wedding is not very informative, or *diagnostic*, with regard to whether the marriage will last. We can tell that the observation that a couple "got along wonderfully" at their wedding is not very informative in this respect from the fact that the conditional probabilities (.90 and .99) are not that different from one another.

The following example, which I came up with in trying to explain Bayesian reasoning to a couple of students after class, presents the reasoning as simply as I know how. We were sitting around a table with chairs in a room with 10 tables, 9 of which had chairs and 1 of which was in the front of the class for the lecturer and had no chairs.

To get a prior probability, I asked the students to assume that a $20 bill had been randomly placed under one of the 10 tables and then asked what the probability would be that it was under the table we were sitting at. Both answered without hesitation, "One out of ten, or .10." To get a revised probability, I then asked them to assume that the bill had been placed under one of the tables with chairs and asked what, then, would be the probability that it was under the table we were sitting at. Both answered, again without hesitation, "One out of nine", which we calculated to be .11.

The calculations required to solve the AIDS problem introduced earlier are similar. They're shown in the probability tree below. To the information presented earlier, we've added the probability that a person who *does not* have AIDS will test positive, .008 This is 1 minus the specificity of the test, the conditional probability of a correct negative result.

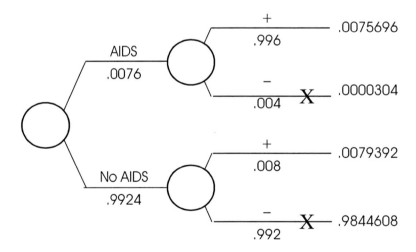

The revised probability that such a person actually has AIDS is:

$$.0075696/(.0075696 + .0079392) @ .49$$

Both the person thinking about a positive test for AIDS and our wedding guest made two mistakes. First, they ignored the statistics for the general case. This is base-rate neglect. Second, in evaluating the information they did use, they thought only about the connection between the data and the hypothesis that it brought to mind. "Getting along wonderfully" suggests not divorcing, and the conditional probability that those who do not divorce got along wonderfully at their weddings is high. A positive test for AIDS suggests having AIDS, and the conditional probability that those who have AIDS will test positive is high Neither gave much, if any, thought to the connection between the data and any alternative hypothesis. Considering only one conditional probability when evaluating the informativeness, or diagnosticity, of information is called *pseudodiagnosticity* (Beyth-Marom & Fischhoff, 1983; Doherty, Mynatt, Tweney, & Schiavo, 1979) and is thought to be related to *confirmation bias,* a preference for confirming over disconfirming information (Hovland & Weiss, 1953; Wason, 1960; Einhorn & Hogarth, 1978, 1986; Montgomery, 1983). Probability trees can protect us from both kinds of errors.

REFERENCES

Adams, J. L. (1986). *Conceptual Blockbusting.* Reading, MA: Addison-Wesley.

Adorno, T. W., Frenkel-Brunswik, E., Levinson, D. J., & Sanford, R. N. (1950). *The Authoritarian Personality.* NY: Harper.

Alpert, M., & Raiffa, H. (1982). A progress report on the training of probability assessors. In D. Kahneman, P. Slovic, & A. Tversky (Eds.), *Judgment Under Uncertainty: Heuristics and biases.* Cambridge: Cambridge U. Press.

Altemeyer, B. (1988). *Enemies of Freedom: Understanding right-wing authoritarianism.* SF: Jossey-Bass.

Anderson, B. F. (1971). *The Psychology Experiment: An introduction to the scientific method* (2nd ed). Monterey, CA: Brooks/Cole.

Anderson, B. F. (1975). *Cognitive Psychology: The study of knowing, learning, and thinking.* NY: Academic Press.

Anderson, B. F. (1980). *The Complete Thinker: A handbook of techniques for creative and critical problem solving.* Englewood Cliffs, NJ: Prentice-Hall.

Anderson, B. F., Deane, D. H., Hammond, K. R., McClelland, G. H., & Shanteau, J. C. (1981). *Concepts in Judgment and Decision Research: Definitions, sources, interrelations, comments.* NY: Praeger.

Anderson, B. F., & Johnson, W. (1966). Two methods of presenting information and their effects on problem solving. *Perceptual & Motor Skills,* **23**, 851-856.

Arendt, H. (1963). *Eichmann in Jerusalem: A report on the banality of evil.* NY: Viking Press.

Arrow, K. J. (1971). *Essays on the Theory of Risk-Bearing.* Chicago: Markham.

Arrow, K. J. (1992). I know a hawk from a handsaw. In M. Szenberg (Ed), *Eminent Economists: Their lives and philosophies.* Cambridge: Cambridge U. Press.

Bacon, F. (1620/1955). *Novum Organum.* Chicago: Encyclopaedia Britannica.

Baltes, P. B., & Smith, J. (1990). Toward a psychology of wisdom and its ontogenesis. In R. J. Sternberg (Ed.), *Wisdom: Its nature, origins, and development.* NY: Cambridge U. Pp. 87-120.

Barber, B., & Fox, R. C. (1958). The case of the floppy-eared rabbits: An instance of serendipity gained and serendipity lost. *American Journal of Society,* **64,** 128-136.

Barclay, S., Brown, R. V., Kelly, C. W., III, Peterson, C. R., Phillips, L. D., & Selvidge, J. (1977). *Handbook for Decision Analysis.* McLean, VA: Decisions & Designs, Inc.

Bazerman, M. H., & Neale, M. A. (1992). *Negotiating Rationally.* NY: Free Press.

Beach, L. R., & Mitchell, T. R. (1978). A contingency model for the selection of decision strategies. *Academy of Management Review,* **3,** 439-449.

Beauchamp, T. L., & Childress, J. F. (1989). *Principles of Biomedical Ethics, 3$_{rd}$ ed.* Oxford: Oxford U.

Beauchamp, T. L., & Walters, L. (1994). *Issues in Bioethics, 4th ed.* Belmont, CA: Wadsworth.

Bell, D. E. (1982). Regret in decision making under uncertainty. *Operations Research,* **30,** 961-981.

Bernoulli, D. (1738). Specimen theoriae novae de mensura sortis. *Comentarii Academiae Scientarium Imperiales Petropolitanae,* **5,** 175-192.

Beyth-Marom, R., & Fischhoff, B. (1983). Diagnosticity and pseudodiagnosticity. *Journal of Personality & Social Psychology,* **45,** 1185-1195.

Broadbent, D. E., The magic number seven, after fifteen years. In Alan Kennedy & Alan Wilkes (Eds.). *Studies in Long Term Memory* : New York, Wiley, 3-18.

Brown, C. A. (1981). The effect of factor range on weight and scale values in a linear averaging model. Doctoral Dissertation. Boulder, CO: University of Colorado.

Brown, C. A. (1986). The Central Arizona Water Control Study: A case for multiobjective planning and public involvement. In H. R. Arkes & K. P. Hammond (Eds.), *Judgment and Decision Making: An interdisciplinary reader.* Cambridge: Cambridge U.. Pp. 144-158.

Brown, J. S. (1948). Gradients of approach and avoidance responses as a function of stimulus intensity and strength of motivation. *Journal of Comparative & Physiological Psychology,* **33**, 209-228.

Butler, A. B., & Scherer, L. L. (1998). The effects of elicitation aids, knowledge, and problem content on option quantity and quality. *Organizational Behavior & Human Decision Processes,* **72**, 184-202.

Chambers, D., & Reisberg, D. (1985). Can mental images be ambiguous? *Journal of Experimental Psychology: Human perception & performance,* **11**, 317-328.

Chapman, L. J. (1967). Illusory correlation in observation report. *Journal of Verbal Learning & Verbal Behavior,* **6**, 151-155.

Chapman, L. J., & Chapman, J. P. (1967). Genesis of popular but erroneous psychodiagnostic observation. *Journal of Abnormal Psychology,* **72**, 193-204.

Chase, W. G., & Simon, H. A. (1973). The mind's eye in chess. In W. G. Chase (Ed.), *Visual Information Processing.* NY: Academic Press.

Chihuly, D. (1997). *River of Glass.* Video tape. Seattle, WA: Portland Press.

Christie, R., & Jahoda, M., (Eds.) (1954). *Studies in the Scope and Method of "The Authoritarian Personality".* NY: The Free Press.

Collins, J. C., & Porras, J. I. (1994). *Built to Last: Successful habits of visionary companies.* NY: Harper Business.

Covey, S. (1989). *The Seven Habits of Highly Effective People.* NY: Simon & Schuster.

Crawford, R. P. (1964). *Direct Creativity with Attribute Listing.* Burlington, VT: Fraser.

cummings, e. e. (1959). *Voices to Voices, Lip to Lip: 100 selected poems.* NY: Grove Press (Evergreen Edition).

Dawes, R. M. (1979). The robust beauty of improper linear models. *American Psychologist,* **34**, 571-582.

Dawes, R. M., Faust, D., & Meehl, P. E. (1989). Clinical vs. actuarial judgment. *Science*, March, 1668-1674.

Dawes, R. M., Van de Kragt, A. J. C., & Orbell, J. M. (1989). Not me or thee but we: The importance of group identity in eliciting cooperation in the dilemma situations: Experimental manipulations. In B. Rohrmann, L. R. Beech, C. Vlek, & S. R. Watson (Eds.), *Advances in Decision Research.* Amsterdam: North-Holland. Pp. 83-98.

De Soto, C. B. (1961). Learning a social structure. *Journal of Abnormal & Social Psychology,* **60,** 417-421.

De Soto, C. B., & Albrecht, F. (1968). Cognition and social orderings. In R. P. Abelson, E. Aronson, W. J. McGuire, T. M. Newcomb, M. J. Rosenberg, & P. H. Tannenbaum (Eds.), *Theories of Cognitive Consistency.* Chicago: Rand McNally.

Doherty, M. E., Mynatt, C. R., Tweney, R. D., & Schiavo, M. D. (1979). Pseudodiagnosticity. *Acta Psychologica,* **43**, 111-121.

Drucker, P. F. *Management: Tasks, responsibilities, practices.* NY: Harper & Row, 1974.

Edwards, W., & Barron, F. H. (1994). SMARTS and SMARTER: Improved simple methods for multiattribute utility measurement. *Organizational Behavior & Human Decision Processes*, **60**, 306-325.

Einhorn, H. J., & Hogarth, R. M. (1978). Confidence in judgment: Persistence in the illusion of validity. *Psychological Review,* **85**, 395-416.

Einhorn, H. J., & Hogarth, R. M. (1986). Judging probable cause. *Psychological Bulletin,* **99**, 3-19.

Etzioni, A. (1988). *The Moral Dimension: Toward a new economics.* NY: Free Press.

Festinger, L., Riecken, H. W., & Schachter, S. (1956). *When Prophecy Fails.* Minneapolis: U. of Minnesota.

Feynman, R. P. (1985). *"Surely You're Joking, Mr. Feynman!"* N. Y. W. W. Norton.

Fischer, G. W. (1995). Range sensitivity of attribute weights in multiattribute value models. *Organizational Behavior & Human Decision Processes*, **62**, 252-66.

Fischhoff, B. (1975). Hindsight ≠ foresight: The effect of outcome knowledge on judgment under uncertainty. *Journal of Experimental Psychology: Human perception & performance,* **1,** 288-299.

Fischhoff, B., Slovic, P., & Lichtenstein, S. (1978). Fault trees: Sensitivity of estimating failure probabilities to problem representation. *Journal of Experimental Psychology: Human perception & performance*, **4**, 330-334.

Fisher, R., & Ury, W. (1981). *Getting to Yes: Negotiating agreement without giving in.* Boston: Houghton Mifflin.

Fromm, E. (1941). *Escape From Freedom.* NY: Holt, Rinehart, & Winston.

Gabrielli, W., & Von Winterfeldt, D. (1978). Are importance weights sensitive to the range of alternatives in multiattribute utility measurement? Social Science Research Institute Report No. 78-6. Los Angeles: University of Southern California.

Gardiner, P.C., & Edwards, W.. Public values: Multiattribute utility measurement in social decision making. In M. Kaplan & S. Schwartz (Eds.) *Human Judgment and Decision Processes.* New York: Academic Press, 1975, 1-37.

Getzels, J. W., & Csikszentmihalyi, M. (1976). *The Creative Vision: A longitudinal study of problem finding in art.* N. Y.: Wiley.

Ghiselin, B., *The Creative Process.* Berkeley, Calif.: University of California Press, 1952.

Gigerenzer, G. (1991). How to make cognitive illusions disappear: Beyond "heuristics and biases." In W. Stroebe & M. Hewstone (Eds.), *European Review of Social Psychology, Vol. 2.* Pp. 83-115.

245

Gigerenzer, G., & Hoffrage, U. (1995). How to improve Bayesian reasoning without instruction: Frequency formats. *Psychological Review,* **102**, 684-704.

Gigerenzer, G., Hoffrage, U., & Kleinbolting, H. (1991). Probabilistic mental models: A Brunswikian theory of confidence. *Psychological Review,* **98**, 506-528.

Simon, H. A., & Gilmartin, K. (1973). A simulation of memory for chess positions. *Cognitive Psychology,* **5**, 29-46.

Goldberg, L. R. Simple models or simple processes? *American Psychologist,* 1968, **23,** 483-496.

Hammond. K. R. (1966). *Human Judgment and Social Policy.* NY: Oxford U. Press.

Hammond, K. R., & Adelman, L. (1976). Science, values, and human judgment. *Science,* **194**, 389-396.

Hammond, K. R., Hamm, R. M., Grassia, J., & Pearson, T. (1987). Direct comparison of the efficacy of intuitive and analytic cognition in expert judgment. *IEEE Transactions on Systems, Man, & Cybernetics,* **SMC-17**, No. 5, 753-770.

Hardin, G. (1968). The tragedy of the commons. *Science,* **162,** 1243-1248.

Hardin, G. (1993). *Living Within Limits: Ecology, economics, and population taboos.* NY: Oxford U. Press.

Herek, G. M., Janis, I. L., & Huth, P. (1987). Decision making during international crises. *Journal of Conflict Resolution,* **31,** 203-226.

Heron House. (1980). *The Odds on Virtually Everything.* NY: Putnam.

Hoch, S. J. (1985). Counterfactual reasoning and accuracy in predicting personal events. *Journal of Experimental Psychology: Learning, memory, & cognition,* **11,** 719-731.

Hovland, C. I., & Weiss, W. (1953). Transmission of information concerning concepts through positive and negative instances. *Journal of Experimental Psychology,* **45,** 175-182.

Hume, D. (1988). *A Treatise of Human Nature*. Ed. L. A. Selby-Bigge. Oxford. Book I, Part III.

Hume, D. (1946). *Inquiries Concerning the Human Understanding*. Oxford: Selby-Bigge.

Isen, A. M. (1997). Postive affect and decision making. In W. M. Goldstein & R. M. Hogarth (Eds.), *Research on Judgment and Decision Making*. Cambridge: Cambridge U. Pp. 509-536.

Isen, A. M., Daubman, K., & Nowicki, G. P. (1987). Positive affect facilitates creative problem solving. *Journal of Personality & Social Psychology*, **52**, 1122-1131.

Isen, A., Means, B., Patrick, R., & Nowicki, G. (1982). Some factors influencing decision-making strategy and risk taking. In M. S. Clark & S. T. Fiske (Eds.), *Affect and Cognition*. Hillsdale, NJ: Erlbaum.

Janis, I. L. (1972). *Victims of Groupthink*. Boston: Houghton Mifflin.

Janis, I. L., & Mann, L. (1977). *Decision Making: A psychological analysis of conflict*. NY: Free Press.

Janis, I. L., & Mann, L. (1982). A theoretical framework for decision counseling. In I. L. Janis (Ed.), *Counseling on Personal Decisions: Theory and research on short-term helping relationships*. New Haven: Yale U. Pp. 47-72.

Jones, S. K., Frish, D., Yurak, T. J., & Kim, E. (1998). Choices and opportunities: Another effect of framing on decisions. *Journal of Behavioral Decision Making*, **11**, 211-226.

Jones, S. K., Yurak, T. J., & Frisch, D. (1997). The effect of outcome information on the evaluation and recall of individual's own decisions. *Organizational Behavior & Human Decision Processes*, **71**, 95-120.

Jungermann, H., von Ulardt, I., & Hausmann, L. (1983). The role of the goal for generating actions. In P. Humphres, O. Svenson, & A. Vari (Eds.), *Analyzing and Aiding Decision Processes*. Amsterdam: North-Holland.

Kahneman, D., & Tversky, A. (1972). Subjective probability: A judgment of representativeness. *Cognitive Psychology*, **3**, 430-454.

Kahneman, D., & Tversky, A. (1973). On the psychology of prediction. *Psychological Review,* **80,** 237-251.

Kahneman, D., & Tversky, A. (1979). Prospect Theory: An analysis of decision under risk. *Econometrica*, **4,** 263-291.

Kahneman, D., & Tversky, A. (1982). On the study of statistical intuitions. *Cognition,* **11,** 123-141.

Kahneman, D., & Tversky, A. (1982). Evidential impact of base rates. In D. Kahneman, P. Slovic, & A. Tversky (Eds.), *Judgment Under Uncertainty: Heuristics and biases.* Cambridge: Cambridge U. Press. Pp. 153-162.

Kahneman, D., & Tversky, A. (1996). On the reality of cognitive illusions. *Psychological Review,* **??**, 582-591.

Katz, D. (1960). The functional approach to the study of attitudes. *Public Opinion Quarterly,* Summer, 163-204.

Keeney, R. L. (1992). *Value-Focused Thinking: A path to creative decisionmaking.* Cambridge, MA: Harvard U.

Keller, L. R. (1988). Decision problem structuring: Generating states of nature. Technical Report. Irvine, CA: Graduate School of Management, UC Irvine.

Keller, L. R., & Ho, J. L. (1988). Decision problem structuring: Generating options. *IEEE Transactions on Systems, Man, & Cybernetics,* **18,** 715-728.

Keller, L. R., & Ho, J. L. (1990). Decision problem structuring. In A. P. Sage (Ed.), *Concise Encyclopedia of Information Processing in Systems & Organizations.* NY: Pergamon. Pp. 103-110.

Kepner, C. H., & Tregoe, B. B. (1965). *The Rational Manager: A systematic approach to problem solving and decision making.* NY: McGraw-Hill.

Kolmogorov, A. N. (1933). *Grundbegriffe Der Wahrscheinlichkeits- rechnung.* Berlin: Springer. Translated edited by N. Morrison (1950) as *Foundations of the Theory of Probability.* NY: Chelsea.

Koriat, A. S., Lichtenstein, S., & Fischhoff, B. (1980). Reasons for confidence. *Journal of Experimental Psychology: Human learning & memory*, **6**, 107-118.

Kuhn, T. S. (1962). *The Structure of Scientific Revolutions.* Chicago: U. of Chicago.

Langer, E. (1975). The illusion of control. *Journal of Personality & Social Psychology*, **32**, 311-328.

Langer, E. (1989). *Mindfulness.* Reading, MA: Addison-Wesley.

Larrick, R., Morgan, J., & Nisbett, R. (1990). Teaching the use of cost-benefit reasoning in everyday life. *Psychological Science,* **1,** 362-370.

Larrick, R., Nisbett, R., & Morgan, J. (1993). Who uses the normative rules of choice? In R. Nisbett (Ed.), *Rules for Reasoning.* Hillsdale, NJ: Lawrence Erlbaum. Pp. 277-296.

Leeper, R. A. (1951). Cognitive processes. In S. S. Stevens (Ed.), *Handbook of Experimental Psychology.* N. Y.: Wiley.

Lichtenstein, S., Fischhoff, B., & Phillips, L. D. (1977). Calibration of probabilities: The state of the art to 1980. In H. Jungermann & G. deZeeuw (Eds.), *Decision Making and Change in Human Affairs.* Dordrecht, Holland: D. Reidel.

Linville, P. W. (1987). Self-complexity as a cognitive buffer against stress-related illness and depression. *Journal of Personality & Social Psychology,* **52,** 663-676.

Lipshitz, R., Klein, G., Orasanu, J., & Salas, E. (2001). Focus article: Taking stock of Natural Decision Making. *Journal of Behavioral Decision Making*, **14**, 331-352.

Lord, C. G., Lepper, M. R., & Preston, E. (1984). Considering the opposite: A corrective strategy for social judgment. *Journal of Personality & Social Psychology,* **47,** 1231-47.

MacKinnon, D. W., "The Nature and Nurture of Creative Talent," American Psychologist, (17), 1962, 484-495.

MacCrimmon, K. R., & Taylor, R. N. (1976). Decision making and problem solving. In M. D. Dunnette (Ed.), *Handbook of Organizational Psychology.* Chicago: Rand McNalley.

Maier, N. R. F. Reasoning in humans. II. The solution of a problem and its appearance in consciousness. *Journal of Comparative Psychology,* 1931, **12**, 181-194.

Maier, N. R. F. (1931). Reasoning in humans. II. The solution of a problem and its appearance in consciousness. *Journal of Comparative Psychology,* **12,** 181-194.

Malthus, T. R. (1826). *An Essay on the Principle of Population, 6ᵗʰ ed.* London.

March, J. G. (1972). Model bias in social action. *Review of Educational Research,* **42,** 413-429.

Markowitz, H. (1952). The utility of wealth. *Journal of Political Economy,* **60,** 151-158.

Maslow, A. H. (1970). *Motivation and Personality* (2ⁿᵈ ed.) NY: Harper & Row.

MacKenzie, R. A. (1972). *The Time Trap.* NY: AMACOM.

McGarvey, R. (1989). Getting your goals. *US Air Magazine,* July, 26-30.

McGeoch, J. A., & Irion, A. L. (1952). *The Psychology of Human Learning.* N. Y.: Longmans, Green.

McGuire, W. J. (1960). A syllogistic analysis of cognitive relationships. In M. J. Rosenberg, *et al.* (Eds.), *Attitude Organization and Change.* New Haven: Yale U. Press.

Meehl, P. E. (1986). Causes and effects of my disturbing little book. *Journal of Personality Assessment,* **50,** 370-375.

Metfessel, M. (1949). A proposal for quantitative reporting of comparative judgments. *Journal of Psychology,* **24,** 229-235.

Milgram, S. (1963). Behavioral study of obedience. *Journal of Abnormal & Social Psychology,* **67,** 371-378.

Milgram, S. (1974). *Behavioral Study of Obedience to Authority: An experimental view.* NY: Harper & Row.

Mill, J. S. (1861/1957). *Utilitarianism.* O. Piest (Ed.) Indianapolis: Bobbs-Merrill.

Miller, G. A., "The Magical Number Seven, Plus or Minus Two: Some Limits on our Capacity for Processing Information," *Psychological Review*, 63, 1956, 81-97.

Morrison, H., & Slovic, P. (1962). Preliminary results: Effect of context on relative judgments of area. Paper read at Eastern Psychological Association Meeting. Atlantic City.

Myers, D. G. (1992). *The Pursuit of Happiness: Discovering the pathway to fulfillment, well-being, and enduring personal joy.* N. Y.: Avon Books.

National Commission for the Protection of Human Subjects of Biomedical and Behavioral Research. (1978). *The Belmont Report.* Washington, D. C.: DHEW Publication No. 0578-0012.

Newell, A., & Simon, H. A. (1972). *Human Problem Solving.* Englewood Cliffs, NJ: Prentice Hall.

Nisbett, R., & Ross, L. (1980). *Human Inference: Strategies and shortcomings of human judgment.* Englewood Cliffs, NJ: Prentice-Hall.

Oakley, K., & Bolton, W. (1985). A social-cognitive theory of depression in reaction to life events. *Psychological Review,* **92,** 372-388.

Parducci, A. (1965). Category judgment: A range-frequency model. *Psychological Review,* **72,** 407-418.

Parducci, A. (1968). The relativism of absolute judgments. *Scientific American,* **219,** 84-93.

Parducci, A. (1984). Value Judgments: Toward a *relational* theory of happiness. In J. R. Eiser (Ed.), *Attitudinal Judgment.* NY: Springer-Verlag.

Payne, J. W. (1982). Contingent decision behavior. *Psychological Bulletin,* **92,** 382-402.

Payne, J. W., Bettman, J. R., & Johnson, E. J. (1993). *The Adaptive Decision Maker.* Cambridge: Cambridge U. Press.

Pettigrew, T. F. (1959). Regional differences in anti-Negro prejudice. *Journal of Abnormal & Social Psychology,* **59,** 28-36.

Polya, G. (1957). *How To Solve It.* Garden City, NY: Doubleday Anchor.

Posner, M. I. (1978). *Chronometric Explorations of Mind.* Hillsdale, NJ: Lawrence Erlbaum.

Potter, R. E., & Beach, L. R. (1994). Decision making when the acceptable options become unavailable. *Organizational Behavior & Human Decision Processes,* **57,** 468-483.

Poulton, E. C. (1989). *Biases in Quantifying Judgments.* Hillsdale, NJ: Erlbaum.

Prelec, D., & Herrnstein, R. J. (1991). Preferences or principles: Alternative guidelines for choice. In R. J. Zeckhauser (Ed.), *Strategy and Choice.* Cambridge, MA: MIT Press. Pp. 319-340.

Reisberg, D. (1996). The non-ambiguity of mental images. In C. Cornold, R. Logie, M. Brandimonte, G. Kaufman, & D. Reisberg (Eds.), *Stretching the Imagination: Representation and transformation in mental imagery.* NY: Oxford U. Press.

Rico, G. L. (1977). Metaphor, cognition, and clustering. In S. L. Carmean & B. L. Grover, (Eds.), *The Eighth Western Symposium on Learning: Creative thinking.* Bellingham, WA. Pp. 75-91.

Redelmeier, D. A. & Shafir, E. (1995). Medical decision making in situations that offer multiple alternatives. *Journal of the American Medical Association,* **273,** 302-305.

Redelmeier, D. A. & Tversky, A. ((1990). Discrepancy between medical decisions for individual patients and for groups. *New England Journal of Medicine,* **322,** 1162-1164.

Rogers, C. (1954). Towards a theory of creativity. *ETC: A review of general semantics,* **11,** 249-260.

Ross, L. (1977). The intuitive psychologist and his shortcomings: Distortions in the attribution process. In L. Berkowitz (Ed.), *Advances in Experimental Social Psychology, Vol. 10.* NY: Academic Press.

Rotter, J. (1966). Generalized expectancies for internal versus external control of reinforcement. *Psychological Monographs,* (Whole No. 609), **80,** No. 1, 1-28.

Russo, J. E., & Schoemaker, P. J. H. (1989). *Decision Traps: Ten barriers to brilliant decision making and how to oversome them.* NY: Simon & Schuster.

Savage, L. J. (1954). *The Foundations of Statistics.* NY: Wiley.

Schlesinger, A. M., Jr. (1965). *A Thousand Days: John F. Kennedy in the White House.* Boston: Houghton Mifflin.

Schoemaker, P. J. H. (1993). Multiple scenario development: Its conceptual and behavioral foundation. *Strategic Management Journal*, **14**, 193-213.

Schoemaker, P. J. H., & Russo, J. E. (1991). Strategies for making decisions: A pyramid of choice procedures. (Technical Report). Chicago: Graduate School of Business, U. of Chicago.

Schum, D. A., & Martin, A. W. (1980). *Empirical Studies of Cascaded Inference in Jurisprudence: Methodological considerations.* (Technical Report No. 80-01.) Houston, TX: Rice U.

Schum, D. A., & Martin, A. W. (1981). *Assessing the Probative Value of Evidence in Various Inference Structures.* (Technical Report No. 80-02.) Houston, TX: Rice U.

Schwenk, C. (1990). Effects of Devil's advocacy and dialectical inquiry on decision making: A meta-analysis. *Organizational Behavior & Human Decision Processes*, **47**, 161-176.

Schwenk, C., & Cosier, R. (1980). Effects of the expert Devil's advocate and analytical inquiry methods on prediction performance. *Organizational Behavior & Human Decision Processes*, **26**, 409-424.

Seligman, M. E. P. (1988). Why is there so much depression today? In I. S. Cohen (Ed.), *G. Stanley Hall Lectures, Vol. 9.* Washington, DC: American Psychological Association.

Sen, A. (1977). Rational fools: A critique of the behavioral foundations of economic theory. *Philosophy & Public Affairs*, **6**, 317-344.

Shafir, E. B., Osherson, D. N., & Smith, E. E. (1993). The advantage model: A comparative thoery of evaluation and choice under risk. *Organizational Behavior & Human Decision Processes*, **55**, 325-378.

Shanteau, J. (1988). Psychological characteristics and strategies of expert decision makers. *Acta Psychologica*, **68**, 203-215.

Shepard, R. N. (1964). On subjectively optimum selection among multiattribute alternatives. In M. W. Shelly, II, & G. L. Bryan (Eds.), *Human Judgments and Optimality.* NY: Wiley. Pp. 257-281.

Shiffrin, R. M. (1988). Attention. In R. C. Atkinson, R. J. Herrnstein, G. Lindzey, & R. D. Luce (Eds.), *Stevens' Handbook of Experimental Psychology, 2_d ed. Vol. 2: Learning & cognition.* N. Y.: Wiley. Pp. 739-812.

Shiffrin, R., & Schneider, W. (1977). Controlled and automatic human information processing: II. Perceptual learning, automatic attending and a general theory. *Psychological Review, 84*, 127-190.

Shoemaker, P. J. H., & Waid, C. C. (1982). An experimental comparison of different approaches to determining weights in additive utility models. *Management Science*, **28**, 182-196.

Shubik, M. (1971). The dollar auction game: A paradox in noncooperative behavior and escalation. *Journal of Conflict Resolution*, **15**, 109-111.

Siegel, J. J. (1994). *Stocks for the Long Run.* NY: Irwin.

Silviera, J. "Incubation: The Effect of Interruption Timing and Length on Problem Solution and Quality of Problem Processing." (unpublished doctoral dissertation, University of Oregon, 1971).

Simon, H.A., (1955). A behavioral model of rational choice. *Quarterly J. of Economics,* 69, 99-118.

Simon, R. J., & Mahan, L. (1971). Quantifying burdens of proof: A view from the bench, the jury, and the classroom. *Law & Society Review*, **5** (No. 3), 319-331.

Simonson, I. (1989). Choice based on reasons: The case of atraction and compromise effects. *Journal of Consumer Research,* **16**, 158-174.

Slovic, P., & Fischhoff, B. (1977). On the psychology of experimental surprises. *Journal of Experimental Psychology: Human perception & performance*, **3**, 344-551.

Slovic, P., Fischhoff, B., & Lichtenstein, S. (1980). Facts vs. fears: Understanding perceived risk. In R. Schwing & W. A. Albers, Jr. (Eds.), *Societal Risk Assessment: How safe is safe enough?* NY: Plenum

Slovic, P., & Lichtenstein, S. (1973). Comparison of Bayesian and regression approaches to the study of information processing in judgment. In L. Rappoport & D. A. Summers (Eds.), *Human Judgment and Social Interaction*. N. Y.: Holt, Rinehart and Winston. P. 49.

Solomon, R. L. (1980). The opponent theory of acquired motivation: The costs of pleasure and the benefits of pain. *American Psychologist,* **35,** 691-712.

Spetzler, C. S., & Staël von Holstein, C.-A. S. (1975). Probability encoding in decision analysis. *Management Science,* **22**, 340-358.

Spetzler, C. S., & Zamora, R. M. (1974). Decision analysis of a facilities investment and expansion problem. In R. A. Howard & J. E. Matheson (Eds.), *Readings on the Principles and Applications of Decision Analysis. Vol. I: General Collection.* Menlo Park, CA: Strategic Decisions Group. Pp. 227-258.

Staw, B. M. (1976). Knee-deep in the Big Muddy: A study of escalating commitment to a chosen course of action. *Organizational Behavior & Human Performance,* **16**, 27-44.

Stein, M. I., *Stimulating Creativity: Vol 1, Individual Procedures.* New York: Academic Press, 1974.

Stein, M. I., *Stimulating Creativity: Vol 2, Group Procedures.* New York: Academic Press, 1975.

Sternberg, R. J. (1990). *Wisdom: Its nature, origins, and development.* Cambridge: Cambridge U. Press.

Stevenson, B. (Ed.) (1949). *The Home Book of Quotations: Classical and modern.* NY: Dodd, Mead.

Stillwell, W. G., Seaver, D. A., & Edwards, W. (1981). A comparison of weight approximation techniques in multiattribute utility decision making. *Organizational Behavior & Human Performance,* **28,** 62-77.

Szekely, L. (1945). Zur Psychlolgie des Geistigen Schaffens. *Schweitzer- ische Zeitschrift für Psychologie und ihre Anwendungen, 4,* 110-124.

Szekely, L. (1950). Productive processes in learning and thinking. *Acta Psychologica, 7,* 388-407.

Taylor, S. E. (1989). *Positive Illusions.* NY: Basic Books.

Taylor, S. E., & Gollwitzer, P. M. (1995). The effects of mindset on positive illusions. *Journal of Personality & Social Psychology, 69,* 312-226.

Thaler, R. (1980). Toward a positive theory of consumer choice. *Journal of Economic Behavior & Organization, 1,* 50.

Torrance, G. W., Thomas, W. H., & Sackett, D. L. (1972). A utility maximization model for evaluation of health care programs. *Health Services Research, 7,* 118-133.

Tversky, A., & Kahneman, D. (1972). Availability: A heuristic for judging frequency and probability. *Cognitive Psychology, 4,* 207-232.

Tversky, A., & Kahneman, D. (1974). Judgment under uncertainty: Heuristics and biases. *Science, 185,* 1124-1131.

Tversky, A., & Koehler, D. J. (1994). Support Theory: A nonextensional representation of subjective probability. *Psychological Review, 101,* 547-567.

Tversky, A., & Shafir, E. (1992). The disjunction effect in choice under uncertainty. *Psychological Science, 3,* 305-309.

Tversky, A., & Simonson, I. (1993). Context-dependent preferences. *Management Science, 39,* 1179-89.

Tyler, L. (1969). *The Work of the Counselor, 3rd ed.* NY: Appleton-Century-Crofts.

Van Zee, E. H. (1989). Use of Infomation in Decision Deliberation. Unpublished doctoral dissertation. Seattle, WA: U. of Washington.

Van Zee, E. H., Paluchowski, T. F., & Beach, L. R. (1992). The effects of screening and task partitioning upon evaluations of decision options. *Journal of Behavioral Decision Making, 5*, 1-23.

Varey, C., & Kahneman, D. (1992). Experiences extended across time: Evaluation of moments and episodes. *Journal of Behavioral Decision Making, 5*, 169-85.

von Neumann, J., & Morgenstern, O. (1947). *Theory of Games and Economic Behavior.* Princeton, NJ: Princeton U.

von Winterfeldt, D., & Edwards, W. (1986). *Decision Analysis and Behavioral Research.* Cambridge: Cambridge U. Press.

von Nitszch, R., & Weber, M. (1993). The effect of attribute ranges on weights in multiattribute utility measurements. *Management Science, 39*, 937-43.

Wason, P. C. (1960). On the failure to eliminate hypotheses in a conceptual task. *Quarterly Journal of Experimental Psychology, 12*, 129-140.

Wason, P. C., & Johnson-Laird, P. N. (1972). *The Psychology of Reasoning: Structure and content.* Cambridge, MA: Harvard U.

Watzlawick, P., Weakland, J. H., & Fisch, R. (1974). *Change: Principles of problem formation and problem resolution.* NY: W. W. Norton & Co.

Weber, M., & Borcherding, K. (1993). Behavioral influences in weight judgments in multiattribute decision making. *European Journal of Opinion Research, 67*, 1-12.

Weintraub, S. (19??). *The Last Great Victory.* NY: Dutton

Whitman, W. (1892/1963). *Prose Works 1892. Vol. 1. Specimen days.* F. Stovall (Ed.) NY: New York U. Press.

Wicklegren, W. (1974). *How to Solve Problems.* SF: W. H. Freeman.

Wright, G., & Whalley, P. (1983). The supra-additivity of subjective probability. In B. P. Stigum & F. Wenstop (Eds.), *Foundations of Utility and Risk Theory with Appli cations.* Dordrecht, Holland: Reidel. Pp. 233-244.

Wright, P. L. (1974). The harassed decision maker: Time pressures, distractions, and the use of evidence. *Journal of Applied Psychology*, **59**, 555-561.

Wright, P. L. & Weitz, B. (1977). Time horizon effects on product evaluation strategies. *Journal of Marketing Research*, **14**, 429-443.

Wyden, P. (1979). *Bay of Pigs*. NY: Simon & Schuster. Pp. 89-90.

Yerkes, R. M., & Dodson, J. D. (1908). The relationship of strength of stimulus to rapidity of habit formation. *Journal of Comparative & Neurological Psychology*, **18**, 459-482.

Zander, A., & Armstrong, W. (1972). Working for group pride in a slipper factory. *Journal of Applied Social Psychology*, **36**, 498-510.

Zukav, Gary. (1979). *The Dancing Wu Li Masters: An overview of the new physics*. NY: Morrow

INDEX